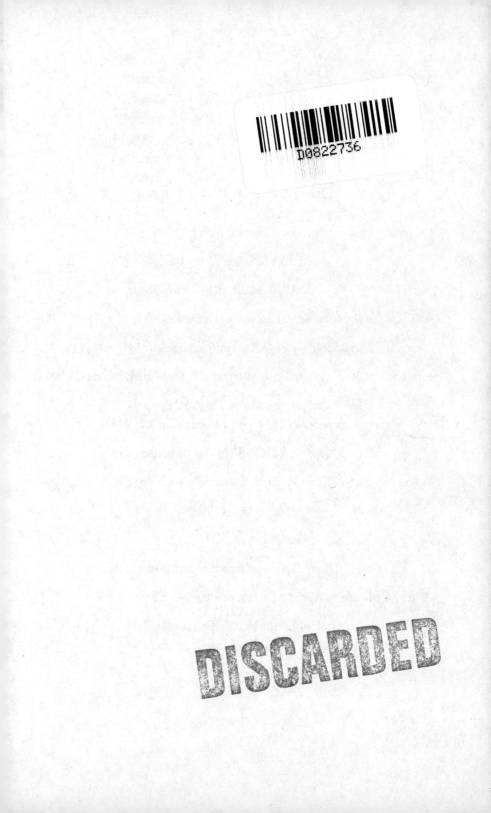

Other Books by Paul Hellyer

Agenda: A Plan for Action (1971)

Exit Inflation (1981)

Jobs for All: Capitalism on Trial (1984)

Canada at the Crossroads: A Liberal Agenda for the 90's and Beyond (1990)

Damn the Torpedoes: My Fight to Unify Canada's Armed Forces (1990)

Funny Money: A Common Sense Alternative to Mainline Economics (1994)

Surviving the Global Financial Crisis:
The Economics of Hope for Generation X (1996)

Arundel Lodge: A Little Bit of Old Muskoka (1996)

The Evil Empire: Globalization's Darker Side (1997)

Stop:Think (1999)

Goodbye Canada (2001)

One Big Party: To Keep Canada Independent (2003)

A Miracle in Waiting: Economics that Make Sense (2010)

Light at the End of the Tunnel:
A Survival Plan for the Human Species (2010)

THE
MONEY MAFIA

A World in Crisis

Paul T. Hellyer

THE MONEY MAFIA: A WORLD IN CRISIS
COPYRIGHT © 2014, 2016 PAUL T. HELLYER

Published by:
Trine Day LLC
PO Box 577
Walterville, OR 97489
1-800-556-2012
www.TrineDay.com
publisher@TrineDay.net

Library of Congress Control Number: 2014945681

Hellyer, Paul T.
–1st ed.
p. cm.

Epud (ISBN-13) 978-1-63424-007-9
Mobi (ISBN-13) 978-1-63424-008-6
Print (ISBN-13) 978-1-63424-006-2
1. International finance. 2. Finance -- Government Policy. 3. Monetary
policy -- United States -- History. 4. Global environmental change. 5.
Unidentified flying objects -- Sightings and encounters 6. Human-alien
encounters. I. Hellyer, Paul T. II. Title

FIRST EDITION
10 9 8 7 6 5

Printed in the USA
Distribution to the Trade by:
Independent Publishers Group (IPG)
814 North Franklin Street
Chicago, Illinois 60610
312.337.0747
www.ipgbook.com

For

All God's Children on Earth and in the Universe

ACKNOWLEDGMENTS

The fact that this book is in print so soon after the manuscript was finished is something of a modern miracle. The following are just some of the people that deserve praise for their contributions.

I am indebted to Dr. Jerry Ackerman, Ann Emmett, Kent Hotaling, Ruth MacKechnie, and Margaret Rao, in addition to one other who wishes to remain anonymous, for making numerous suggestions as to how the manuscript might be improved. Jerry Ackerman and Ann Emmett, long-time stalwarts of the Committee on Monetary and Economic Reform (COMER), of which Ann Emmett is the President, were particularly helpful on the monetary side. All the participants did a line-by-line review of the issues and identified the inevitable errors and omissions. At the end of the day responsibility for those that slipped through the net, and for the positions taken, rest with me alone.

My Executive Assistant, Nina Moskaliuk, contributed many hours of research that proved to be most helpful. Nina also typed the manuscript and painstakingly prepared the extensive footnotes.

It is difficult to express in words my appreciation to my friend, editor and publisher Kris Millegan. He had the vision of what needed to be done and the expertise to make the miracle happen.

Last, but certainly not least, I would like to thank my wife Sandra for her patience and understanding of the challenge I faced, and for putting up with me these many long months when I have been pre-occupied with "the book" at the expense of a more normal existence.

TABLE OF CONTENTS

Abraham Lincoln, 1865.

INTRODUCTION

"I see in the near future a crisis approaching that unnerves me and causes me to tremble for the safety of my country … corporations have been enthroned and an era of corruption in high places will follow, and the money power of the country will endeavor to prolong its reign by working upon the prejudices of the people until all wealth is aggregated in a few hands and the Republic is destroyed."[1]

– President Abraham Lincoln

I had not intended to write this book. In 2010, when *Light at the End of the Tunnel: A Survival Plan for the Human Species*, was published I believed that I had said just about everything that I wanted to say. As the months passed, however, I was overwhelmed by a deluge of new information so fundamental and so frightening that I felt it simply must be in the public domain so that we can talk about it and take such action as is required. Abraham Lincoln's premonition of 1864 has risen from the ashes of time, and is about to overwhelm us.

A small group of very powerful people have been using the cover of globalization to undermine the powers of nation states with the ultimate goal of creating an unelected World government under their control.

The inevitable result, already evident from worrisome statistics, will be a two-class society where a very small minority possess immense wealth while the majority will be condemned to relative poverty. Even worse, the poor and the powerless, who are increasingly being denied the benefit of hard-won rights going back to the Habeas Corpus Act of 1679,[2] augmented by the evolution of a system of rule by law, will be denied the legal protections for which their ancestors fought and died.

1

The small group primarily responsible for these changes I have labeled "the Cabal" for ease of identification. In the book I say who they are, and expand on my understanding of what they have already achieved. It is so far-reaching that it has changed the face of America and most of the Western world. There are millions of unemployed young people who are being told that they should not expect the good life enjoyed by their parents and grandparents. This is pure propaganda, but it has been so effective that the lie is seldom challenged. In fact, we do have the capability of providing "the good life" for all humankind.

First, however, we will have to establish the kind of democracy we dream of and deserve – government of, by and for the people – all of the people, and not just the rich elite.

For example, it is certainly in the interests of the vast majority of people to arrest global warming before the consequences reach the disaster levels predicted by the Intergovernmental Panel on Climate Change in its latest report published on March 31, 2014. The *New York Times* noted that "ice caps are melting, sea ice in the Arctic is collapsing, water supplies are coming under stress, heat waves and heavy rains are intensifying, coral reefs are dying, and fish and many other creatures are migrating toward the poles or in some cases going extinct."[3]

Needless to say the oceans are rising at a pace that threatens coastal communities and the worst is yet to come. Food supplies will be affected and, as always, it's the world's poorest people who are likely to be most adversely affected. It is my firm belief, that is discussed in the book, that the Cabal, which includes the oil cartel, already owns patents for clean energy that are essential to replace carbon-based fuels quickly. For decades, however, they have kept the technology secret. In a real democracy this would not be allowed to happen!

In reality, the richest, most powerful 1% of the population have been waging war against the 99% poor and middle class. In an article entitled "How Wall Street Occupied America" Bill Moyers, the well-known iconoclast investigative journalist, attributes the opening shot to an August 23, 1971 memorandum written by Lewis Powell – a board member of the death-dealing tobacco giant

Philip Morris and a future jurist of the U.S. Supreme Court, for his friends at the Chamber of Commerce.[4] The war may have begun even sooner but the memo acted as a call to arms for the rich elite.

Thousands of young casualties, recognizing the hopelessness of the status quo, organized to Occupy Wall Street. Their efforts were heroic in support of what should be recognized as a noble cause. The distribution of income and influence is out of bounds and must be rebalanced. Proof of that came when the New York police favored the robbers rather than the victims. In a just society they would have protected the protesters and arrested some of the top dogs on Wall Street.

A strategic weakness in the Occupy Wall Street attack was that the protestors began their battle well aware of what they didn't want, but were unable to articulate what they did want. This book will provide much information to support the worthiness of their cause. Even more important it will provide an integrated blueprint for action that, if implemented as a package, would revolutionize the world. It is a plan to replace war with peace, injustice with justice, immoral inequality with improved equality of opportunity and, topping the list, an end to the wanton destruction of our beautiful planet with an immediate mobilization to preserve it for the benefit of generations yet unborn. These are indeed the challenges that young people everywhere are yearning for, and on which they can unite to move forward.

Those very few of you who are familiar with my work will recognize that I have borrowed significant material from previous books, especially *Light at the End of the Tunnel: A Survival Plan for the Human Species*, my most recent one. I shall refer to this book as *"Light."* The material is as relevant today as it was when first written. So there was no point in re-inventing the wheel.

One other point. Some of the most important material in the book has been difficult to verify because the subject matter is so highly classified. I have used the best references available in the public domain, backed up by sources who have to remain anonymous. I am confident that the information provided is accurate enough to support the conclusions reached and the action plan that I have recommended.

Chapter One

THE NEW WORLD ORDER

"Dictatorship naturally arises out of democracy, and the most aggra-vated form of tyranny and slavery out of the most extreme liberty."

– Plato

Whuen U.S. President George H. W. Bush proudly pro-claimed a New World Order, quite a few hearts beat a little faster as the words seemed to echo their hopes for a new, fairer, more wonderful world of universal peace and prosper-ity. It sounded almost like a trumpet blast heralding the imminent arrival of the Kingdom of God on Earth.

Now we can see a new world coming into view. A world in which there is the very real prospect of a new world order.

What a wonderful world that would be where every child of every race, color, and creed on Earth could expect a shirt on his or her back, clean potable water to drink, nourishing food to eat, med-ical care as required, and sufficient free education to prepare for a useful and fulfilling life. We Earthlings have more than adequate resources to convert this dream into reality, including millions of young people looking for such a wonderful challenge.

All that we have to do to create the miracle is to change our priorities after a genuine change of heart. We must curb our war-like nature and divert some of the money from developing new and more efficient killing machines to the pro-active pursuit of peace on Earth. The transition should be easier for idealistic young peo-ple than it will be for jaundiced, old battle-scarred adults. Surely

5

that is the direction of evolution as we work our way out of our cocoons and emerge as truly beautiful spiritual beings.

We may never know exactly what image President Bush had in mind when he read those words. To give him the benefit of the doubt, we should assume that he had no inkling of the New World Order that some of his most influential backers had in mind. In fact there was nothing new about it. The New World Order is, in reality, the reincarnation of a Third Reich of the 1930s and '40s. It is the same plan for world domination that the Nazis wrote but on an even grander scale.

Worse, it is further advanced and far more likely to succeed. The approach is much more subtle and seductive. It is being sold as a world of international rules and cooperation. Individual countries are being coached to transfer their sovereignty to international organizations controlled by their ultimate enemies. Even the G20 has been sucked in and, to date, has been little more than a rubber stamp to this Machiavellian plan.

Every "Free Trade" treaty is a step down the path to serfdom. Even the use of the words "Free Trade" has been deliberately misleading, the same as words like the "New World Order" are without putting them in context. The purpose of the treaties is to transfer power from poor people to rich people, from poor and small countries to bigger, richer countries, and, most significant of all, to abandon rule by elected representatives and hand it over to the New World Order gang.

This time around, they are being a lot smarter because their weapons are international agreements and money power, propaganda, and mind control. All of this is going on under the eyes of World War II veterans who fought to rid the world of oppression, but who haven't caught on to the subterfuge of those who, although defeated in battle, learned from their mistakes.

Those of us who have "got the picture" and are pledged to hold high the torch of freedom in honor of those who died, are fighting a rearguard action. We can only hope and pray that it isn't too late. To lose this war by simply sitting on our couches and doing nothing would be an unparalleled betrayal of all that is good and right.

The seeds of the Fourth Reich were sewn before the smoke and dust of battle had settled following Victory in Europe, May 8, 1945. They were sewn in the U.S. by "Operation Paperclip" which, no doubt, was well-intentioned on the part of its instigators. Unfortunately, they were unable to estimate the long-term consequences – a classic case of not being able to see the forest for the trees. At this point, in case there are any skeptics who think that I have abandoned years of writing non-fiction in favor of a shot at science fiction, I am going to quote the first three paragraphs on "Operation Paperclip" as they appear in Wikipedia, the free encyclopedia, which is available to everyone through Google.

Operation Paperclip

"Operation Paperclip was the Office of Strategic Services (OSS) program used to recruit scientists of Nazi Germany for employment by the United States in the aftermath of World War II (1939-45). It was conducted by the Joint Intelligence Objectives Agency (JIOA), and in the context of the burgeoning Cold War (1945-91), one purpose of Operation Paperclip was to deny German scientific expertise and knowledge to the U.S.S.R.,[1] the U.K.,[2] and the newly-divided East and West Germanies themselves.

"Although the JIOA's recruitment of German scientists began after the Allied victory in Europe on 8 May 1945, U.S. President Harry Truman did not formally order the execution of Operation Paperclip until August of that year. Truman's order expressly excluded anyone found 'to have been a member of the Nazi Party, and more than a nominal participant in its activities, or an active supporter of Nazi militarism.' However, those restrictions would have rendered ineligible most of the leading scientists the JIOA had identified for recruitment, among them rocket scientist Wernher von Braun, Kurt H. Debus and Arthur Rudolph, and the physician, Hubertus Strughold, each earlier classified as a 'menace to the security of Allied Forces.'

"To circumvent President Truman's anti-Nazi order and the Allied Potsdam and Yalta agreements, the JIOA worked independently to create false employment and political biographies for the scientists. The JIOA also expunged from the public record the scientists' Nazi Party memberships and regime affiliations. Once 'bleached' of their Nazism, the scientists were granted security clearances by the U.S. government to work in the United States. Paperclip, the project's operational name, derived from the paperclips used to attach the scientist's new political personae to their 'U.S. Government Scientist' JIOA personnel files."[3]

A little background is useful in setting the context. Having failed to conquer the Soviet Union, Nazi Germany found itself at a logistical disadvantage. Its resources were depleted and its military-industrial complex was unprepared to defend the Greater German Reich against the Red Army's westward counterattack. So by early 1943, the German government began recalling a number of scientists, engineers and technicians from combat duty in order to prepare for a protracted war with the U.S.S.R.

First, however, they had to be identified and then checked for their political and ideological reliability. Werner Osenberg, the engineer-scientist heading the German Military Research Association recorded the names of the politically-cleared men to the Osenberg List, thus reinstating them to scientific work.[4]

In March 1945, at Bonn University, a Polish laboratory technician found pieces of the Osenberg List stuffed in a toilet; the list subsequently reached MI6, who transmitted it to U.S. Intelligence.[5,6] Then U.S. Army Major Robert B. Staver, Chief of the Jet Propulsion Section of the Research and Intelligence Branch of the U.S. Army Ordnance Corps., used the Osenberg List to compile his list of German scientists to be captured and interrogated; Wernher von Braun, Nazi Germany's premier rocket scientist, headed Major Staver's list.[7]

In Operation Overcast, Major Staver's original intent was only to interview the scientists, but what he learned changed the operation's purpose. On 22 May, 1945, he transmitted to U.S. Pentagon headquarters Colonel Joel Holmes' telegram urging the evacuation of German scientists and their families, as most "important for [the] Pacific war" effort.[8] Allied Intelligence described nuclear physicist Werner Heisenberg, the German nuclear energy project principal, as "worth more to us than ten divisions of Germans." In addition to rocketeers and nuclear physicists, the Allies also sought chemists, physicians, and naval weaponeers.[9] Throughout its operations to 1990, *Operation Paperclip* imported 1,600 men as part of the intellectual reparations owed to the U.S. and the U.K., some $10 billion in patents and industrial processes.[10,11]

The technological advantages gained from the expertise of the German scientists are undeniable. They were ahead of the curve in rocket science and in the development of flying saucers. Have the Nazis ever give up their totalitarian philosophy? Did they ever accept defeat at the hands of the allies and the part the U.S. played in the later stages of the war?

These are not just rhetorical questions, they have to be seriously addressed. What are the connections between the U.S. Nazis, or neo-tots as I sometimes call them, the Bavarian Illuminati and the Germans who may have shifted their military headquarters to a distant and secret location? Are they working as a team to destroy the U.S. and Western civilization in an absolute determination to emerge the masters of all they survey? There has been little if any public discussion of the influence of the important Nazis in the civil and military echelons of power. There has been no public discussion of possible collaboration between the Bavarian Thule Society and the Bavarian Illuminati and like-minded Americans all dedicated to the same end – a "one world" government dominated by themselves.

Similarly, there is very little public debate about the three organizations that, collectively, run the United States through their near total domination of the political process. They are sometimes called the Three Sisters; but their proper names are the Bilderbergers, the Council on Foreign Relations and the Trilateral Commission.

The most powerful people in these organizations have made no secret of the "End Game." A couple of quotations leave no doubt of what has been planned for us. The essential steps have been implemented one by one for decades, and we are rapidly nearing the end of the game.

James Warburg, son of the Council on Foreign Relations' founder, Paul Warburg, and a member of Franklin D. Roosevelt's "brain trust," which was made up of individuals from outside government, including professors, lawyers, and others who came to Washington to advise him on economic affairs, delivered blunt testimony before the Senate Foreign Relations Committee on February 17, 1950: "We shall have world government whether or not you like it – by conquest or consent."[12]

And most tellingly, in an address to the Bilderberg Group at Evian, France, May 21, 1992 – and transcribed from a tape recording made by a Swiss delegate, Michael Ringier, Publisher and CEO of Ringier Inc. – Henry Kissinger said, "Today, Americans would be outraged if UN troops entered Los Angeles to restore order; tomorrow, they will be grateful. This is especially true if they were told there was an outside threat from beyond, whether real or promulgated, that threatened our very existence. It is then that all people of the world will plead with world leaders to deliver them from this evil. The one thing that every man fears is the unknown. When presented with this scenario, individual rights will be willingly relinquished for the guarantee of their well-being granted to them by their world government."[13]

This final threat is a veiled reference to a possible attack, real or simulated, by extraterrestrials. It is a subject to which I shall return in the chapter on the Military-Industrial Complex.

Chapter Two

THE THREE SISTERS

*Those who analyze and study the structures of power in the world
today are in no doubt about the dominance of the mighty American Empire with its weapons of mass destruction, its armies spread
around the globe (745 bases in 120 countries), its attempts at con-
trolling and dominating every country in the world, its arrogant effort
to impose its will upon the whole human world and, through its space
programs,on the entire universe. In the final analysis, the globalization we are up against is the globalization of the American Empire.*

– Albert Nolan[1]

The whole plan for a New World Order might have with-
ered on the vine had it not been for the powerful pro-active support of the Three Sisters – The Council on Foreign
Relations, the Bilderbergers and The Trilateral Commission. Their
collective influence is so all pervasive that it has achieved the status
of "shadow government" in the U.S. In reality, the shadow government is the real government of the U.S. and elected politicians are
the puppets dancing to the strings to which they are attached.

No doubt there are many members of one or more of the Three
Sisters who may not be fully aware of the "End Game." They might
actually disapprove if they were adequately briefed. Still, they are
unwitting accessories to the implementation of a plan that many
of us consider totally diabolical – the end of self-government and
its replacement by a pompous oligarchy imposing its amoral standards on much of an unsuspecting world.

The implementation to date has been so slick and smooth as to
appear like a natural and inevitable evolution when, in fact, it has
been neither. It has been a coldly calculated and ruthlessly imple-

mented business plan to concentrate power, control and wealth in the hands of a corporal's guard of rich men and women – mostly men, as you won't see many women enter the secret conclaves of the Bilderbergers' annual meetings.

The result, of course, is that the rich are getting richer and the poor are getting poorer, at least relatively and, of late, in many cases absolutely. Millions of people are dying from starvation and ill health because the distribution systems controlled by, and the priorities established by the rich and powerful are not geared to meet the needs of the world's impoverished. The elite make a lot more money by launching cold and hot wars.

Although I have been aware of the power and "End Game" of the Three Sisters and have written about it in earlier books, including *"Light,"* I was really shocked when I read *The True Story of the Bilderberg Group* by Daniel Estulin,[2] the Russian émigré to Canada. Estulin literally risked his life "to rip the mask off the New World Order and show it for what it is," as he says at the end of his chapter, "Bilderberg Unmasked." If you are not a member of the Bilderberg Group and would like to have some knowledge as to how the world is really run, get a copy of Estulin's book and read the truth exposed.

The Council on Foreign Relations

The Council on Foreign Relations (CFR or Council) is the oldest of the three organizations. Although it was active in the 1920s, it only came into a position of great influence with the outbreak of World War II. As early as October 1940, years before Germany surrendered to the Allied armies to vaporize Hitler's vision of Empire, the Council's Economic and Financial Group drafted a memorandum outlining a comprehensive policy, "to set forth the political, military, territorial and economic requirements of the United States in its potential leadership of the non-German world area including the United Kingdom itself as well as the Western hemisphere and Far East."[3]

The "Grand Area," as the non-German block was called in 1941, was insufficiently grand. The preferred ideal was all-inclusive, one world economy dominated by the United States.[4] It was at this stage that there was a virtual merger of the Council and the U.S.

State Department which, in late 1941, created a special committee to consider positive planning, the Advisory Committee on Positive Foreign Policy, on which Council members played important roles, and set the stage for key decisions that would affect the post-war world.

The Council influenced plans for international economic institutions including the International Monetary Fund (IMF) and the International Bank for Reconstruction and Development (World Bank), no doubt with the noblest intentions. It was also deeply involved in the creation of the United Nations where the motive appeared to be more self-serving. At a meeting in May 1942, one of the Council members, Isaiah Bowman, argued that the United States had to exercise the strength to assure "security," and at the same time, "avoid conventional forms of imperialism."[5] The way to do this, he suggested, was to make the exercise of that power international in character through a United Nations body.[6]

The Council made no attempt to disguise the fact that the purpose of the Grand Area and later world hegemony was to support an expanding U.S. economy – to provide it with raw materials, and markets for its products. This was labeled the "national interest." It was equally clear that the "national interest" was the interest of the ruling elite whose members comprised the Council. The real interests of the majority of rank-and-file Americans was never a factor in the equation.

The pervasive power of the Council can be better visualized when you know, as Estulin points out:

"Of CIA directors, only James R. Schlesinger, who briefly headed it in 1973, was not a CFR member. He was, however, a protégé of CFR member Daniel Ellsberg, famous for the release of the Vietnam era 'Pentagon Papers,' and his appointment was approved by Henry Kissinger, a key Bilderberg, CFR and TC leader.

"Of U.S. presidents, we have seen a string of CFR members winning the elections every four years. In 1952 and 1956, CFR Adlai Stevenson challenged CFR Dwight Eisenhower. In 1969, it was CFR Nixon vs. CFR Kennedy. In 1964, the conservative wing of the Republican Party 'stunned the Establishment' by nominating its candidate, Barry Goldwater over Nelson Rockefeller. Rockefeller and the CFR wing portrayed Barry Goldwater as 'a dangerous radical who would abolish Social Security, drop atom bombs on Hanoi, and in general be a reincarnation of the Fascist dictator Mussolini.[7] Goldwater was humiliated, and Johnson won in a landslide.

"In fact, from 1928 to 1972, a CFR member has won every presidential election (except Lyndon Johnson who more than compensated the Establishment by filling most of the top positions in Government with CFR members.)"[8]

It is easy to understand why ambitious politicians line up to become members of the Establishment. It is far better and safer to be "anointed" as an insider than to be "vilified" as an outsider.

In 1978, Sir Winston Lord, President of the Council on Foreign Relations, said: "The Trilateral Commission doesn't secretly run the world. The Council on Foreign Relations does that."[9] One can understand his bravado. But, if I were writing something along those lines, I would say: "The Bilderbergers, the Council on Foreign Relations and the Trilateral Commission, in close collaboration with their underground allies, run the world."

The Bilderbergers

Bilderberg was the brainchild of Dr. Joseph Retinger, a top aide to General Wladyslaw Sikorski, head of the Polish government in exile in London. Even during World War II, he suggested regular meetings of the foreign ministers of continental countries, and established close relationships with men who were to become post-war leaders.

After the war, Retinger explained his concern for European unification in a meeting at Chatham House, home of the Royal Society on International Affairs, the British equivalent of the Council on Foreign Relations. His recipe for a divided Europe, which had rejected both Hitler's New World and communism, was to move towards a federal union of neighboring European countries in which the states would "relinquish part of their sovereignty."[10]

The idea was not new, of course, but Retinger gave it currency at a critical time in the post-war development of Europe. He was also a catalyst in establishing closer ties between Europe and America at a time when there was a lot of anti-Americanism on the continent. It was as a result of this process that the group which became known as the Bilderbergers evolved.

The name comes from the group's first meeting place, the Hotel de Bilderberg of Oosterbeek, Holland, in May 1954. The meeting was chaired by Prince Bernhard of Holland who, along with Paul Rykens of Unilever, drew up the original list of participants; two from each country, with representatives from business, banking, politics and academia. The list included a fair balance of conservative and liberal views that were not too far left – as perceived by the Prince and the steering committee chosen by him. The group was pragmatic enough to ensure that their views would carry weight regardless of who formed the government of the day.

One should not discount the positive influence the group has had on inter-governmental relations and on the resolution of international problems. It has contributed to just about every major debate the West has faced. Membership, which is not officially acknowledged, reads like a Who's Who of power and influence. President John F. Kennedy virtually staffed the State Department with Bilderberg alumni, including Secretary of State Dean Rusk and Under-Secretary of State George W. Ball.

It didn't take long, however, before the methods and motives of the Bilderberg Group became subjects of concern. The idea of a united Europe to prevent the outbreak of another world war, which was so progressive and wonderful in theory, has now produced a continent in crisis. Germany is the dominant power and controls the destiny of the group in a way and to an extent not too different from what it hoped to achieve with World War II; but this time, without a single shot being fired. It has all been achieved through diplomacy and money power.

Bilderbergers are very clever as they extend their empire of influence. Each year they hold their annual meeting in a different country. Well, guess what? Invariably the invitation list will include the top political leaders, the most powerful industrialists and bank presidents, and the operating heads of the most popular media outlets. So the meeting will conclude with the international Bilderberg octopus having acquired additional sucker-bearing arms. As Estulin concludes:

> With time the several objectives of this extraordinarily secret organization became clear. They include **One International Identity; Centralized Control of the People** – by means of mind control they plan to direct all humanity to obey their wishes; **A Zero-Growth Society** – to destroy vestiges of general prosperity; **A State of Perpetual Imbalance; Centralized Control of All Education; Centralized Control of All Foreign and Domestic Policies; Expansion of NATO** (which was intended to be a mutual defence pact and not an intervention force); **One Socialist Welfare State** – the Bilderbergers envision a socialist welfare state, where obedient slaves will be rewarded and non-conformists targeted for extinction.[11]

So, if you are interested in human rights, regardless of race, color, religion or sexual orientation, in freedom of expression and freedom of religion, or in just about any worthwhile aspect of life on Earth, then get off your couch and do something. The quality of life you save may be your own.

P.S. The Bilderberg Group had managed to keep its meetings secret for decades until the one planned for Toronto May 30 – June 2, 1996. In this case Daniel Estulin author of the most informative book *The True Story of the Bilderberg Group* got wind from an inside source that one of the subjects under discussion would be the break-up of Canada, Estulin's adopted country. This is not too surprising for anyone familiar with the history of the Three Sisters, because the Council on Foreign Relations, with offices in New York and Washington, had long coveted Canada's rich, vast territory and dreamed of a continental union. The fact that top members of the Council on Foreign Relations were also Bilderbergers made that secret organization the ideal place for discussion.

Estulin was incensed that the Toronto conference, hosted by Conrad Black at the posh CIBC Leadership Centre north-west of Toronto, would be spawning ground for the imminent break up of

Canada to be secured through a unilateral declaration of independence by Québec to be launched the following year.

At the time Canadians were unaware of just how close we came to splitting when the referendum was held. We only became aware in May 1997 when a book written by former Québec Premier Jacques Parizeau, *Pour un Québec souverain,* confirmed that had the "yes" camp triumphed in Québec's October 1995 referendum that he would have made a unilateral declaration of independence within days. "Mr. Parizeau says he was secretly engaged in a 'great game' to engineer the fastest possible rupture of Québec from the Canadian federation. He said it was conceived on the advice of the former French president, Valery Giscard d'Estaing, whom he visited, in France, at the start of 1995. Giscard d'Estaing allegedly encouraged Mr. Parizeau to believe that a unilateral declaration of independence by Québec would be rewarded quickly by recognition of the new nation from Paris. He reasoned that the nod from Paris would then be followed by a similar act of recognition from Washington. But it is not clear, however, whether Mr. Parizeau received any official encouragement from the French government itself.[12] In any event it would be interesting to know if there was collusion between members of the Three Sisters and the Québec government.

Had Québec separated from Canada there is little doubt that would have been the beginning of the end for both. First, either the Eastern provinces or the Western provinces would have decided that North-South trade would suit them best. Ultimately Ontario would have been isolated and the big guns would have capitulated. Finally, Québec, a French-speaking island surrounded by an English-speaking American sea, would have begun to erode and eventually wound up as another Louisiana.

The best guarantee that Québec and Canada will both survive is to be on the same team as they were in 1776 and 1812-14.

The Trilateral Commission

The youngest of the three major groups pushing globalization and a New World Order is the Trilateral Commission, which was officially founded in July 1973. Its roots can be traced to Zbigniew Brzezinski, then a professor at Columbia University. He wrote a series of papers acknowledging Japan's increasing power and influence on the world stage, and then organized the Tripartite Studies under the auspices of the Brookings Institution, known in Washington as the think tank for Democratic administrations.

These studies helped convince David Rockefeller that trilateralism could be a useful instrument in building a community of interest among North America, Western Europe and Japan at a time when relations among the three were deteriorating. When he and Brzezinski presented the idea of a trilateral arrangement to the Bilderberg annual meeting in 1972, it received an enthusiastic response – the endorsement Rockefeller needed to follow up and make the dream a reality.

This organization is the most open with regard to aims and objectives. It is elitist and anti-democratic. A 1975 report entitled "The Crisis of Democracy: Report on the Governability of Democracies to the Trilateral Commission," states: "The vulnerability of democratic government in the United States comes not primarily from external threats, though such threats are real, not from internal subversion from the left or right, although both possibilities could exist, but rather from internal dynamics of democracy itself in a highly educated, mobilized and participant society."[13] Wow, the principal danger to democratic government is democracy! That is a concept that you have to dig deep to come up with. What about the danger to democracy of actions taken by governments "elected" by the people, but only after being chosen and installed in positions of leadership by these elite groups?

The political power of the Trilats, a convenient abbreviation that I will use to cover the joint and several influences of the Trilateral Commission, the Council on Foreign Relations and the Bilderbergers is ominous! When they became concerned about the protectionist measures of the Nixon administration, they began to look around for someone to replace him. The name Jimmy Carter appeared on a short list of three, and he was the one who ultimately got the nod. It was the Trilat connections in the media that helped an obscure agronomist achieve national prominence and become a leading contender for the Democratic Party nomination for president. The operation succeeded as planned; and when Carter became president, he named seventeen Trilats to important positions in his administration.[14] When, after four years, the Trilats became somewhat disillusioned with Carter, who may have been a bit too independent for their liking, they decided to replace him with another of their own, George Bush.[15] A small problem arose when Bush ran for the Republican nomination. Opponents in five states ran full-page ads saying: "The same people who gave you Jimmy Carter are giving you George Bush." In the face of this setback, the Trilats had to settle for a Reagan-Bush ticket, and George Bush had to bide his time while Reagan, who had been looked upon with some skepticism, really came through for them with the Canada-U.S. Free Trade Agreement.

Later, after George Bush finally had his turn, the Trilats picked another one of their own, Bill Clinton, to be their standard bearer. Clinton attended the Bilderberger meeting in 1991 where the desirability of a North American Free Trade Agreement was mentioned to him.[16] He returned as the "anointed" one and although his personal life made the road to stardom a somewhat rocky one, with the help of his powerful allies he prevailed.

Clinton's pay-off to his benefactors was profound and continuing. Most dramatic was his successful negotiation of the North American Free Trade Agreement (NAFTA) in order to provide the U.S. Round Table on Business (and Canadian business, too, including U.S.-owned businesses in Canada that were generous contributors to the propaganda campaign) unrestricted access to an unlimited supply of cheap Mexican labor. This process was ably recorded in *The Selling of "Free Trade": NAFTA, Washington and the Subversion of U.S. Democracy*, by John R. MacArthur, publisher of *Harper's* magazine.[17] It is a case history of the manipulation of the Congress which anyone interested in politics should read.

Of even greater long-term significance, Clinton transformed the Democratic Party from one that sometimes listened to and cared about the concerns of traditional allies including trade unionists, environmentalists, the poor and social activists, into just another party, only marginally but not too significantly different from the Republican Party. His robust promotion of "Free Trade," including the proposed Free Trade Area of the Americas (FTAA), robbed U.S. nationalists, and other thoughtful Americans concerned about the serious loss of sovereignty, of any effective voice in determining their future. The Clinton rightward shift was an answer to the Trilats' prayers. He also denied American voters the kind of ideological choice that they had traditionally enjoyed, and so desperately need.

Chapter Three

GLOBALIZATION
(The Big Lie Cover Story for the New World Order)

"The New World without borders will be like a zoo without cages.
Only the most powerful of the species will survive."

–Paul Hellyer

The reasons for globalization were always obscure, but they can be summarized as follows: the elimination of the middle class by allowing multinational corporations to move production jobs offshore to foreign producers; a reversal of hard-won trade union gains since World War II; and, <u>above all, the transfer of power to unelected, unaccountable, international bureaucrats under the control of the New World Order clique.</u>

It is important to point out at the outset that "globalization" is not just one big ball of wax. An analogy that I find useful is to compare it to cholesterol. There is good cholesterol and bad cholesterol. The good cholesterol is life-enhancing, whereas the bad cholesterol can kill you.

Similarly, there is good globalization and bad globalization. The good globalization is technologically driven. The internet, for example, apart from its addictive qualities, or the temptation to wander off in search of pornography or gambling, is a marvelous benefit of technology. It opens a whole new world of knowledge and information on a scale hitherto undreamed of. Its benefits are widely dispersed, and extensive; it can, for example, save writers weeks or months in checking facts and sources. Satellite phones and global positioning systems (GPS) are other useful marvels.

These widely-enjoyed benefits are in sharp contrast to bad globalization, which is agenda driven. The agenda is the coldly cal-

21

culated business plan of the richest, most powerful people in the world to re-engineer the global economy and governance in a way that will increase both their power and their already overly generous slice of the economic pie.

The New World Order is a world without economic borders. It is a kind of *laissez-faire* economic Darwinism, where capital is King of the jungle. It has been labeled neo-classical economics, a revised but unrepentant version of the ideas of Milton Friedman and his colleagues from the University of Chicago, and sometimes known as the Washington Consensus, the rules by which the world must be run. Whatever the tag, the transformation that has been under way is so far-reaching as to be almost beyond belief.

If it is allowed to run its course, no country will be able to protect its industries even long enough for them to mature to the point where they could compete in a global market. Neither could any nation state set higher environmental standards than the market would tolerate, nor protect its labor from exploitation without paying a high price in jobs lost to countries where nineteenth century standards remain in effect.

No country would be able to prevent the sale of an industry to a foreign player wishing to include it in its empire, or shut it down to eliminate the competition, or move it to another country where lower wages and environmental standards would permit higher profits. Under the new rules, foreigners can buy your natural resources and export them without any value added in the country of origin.

It doesn't require much imagination to understand what the New World Order will be like for most people; it will be a life of total powerlessness. In the case of small and medium powers, like Canada, for example, there will be the added frustration of seeing the level of excellence already achieved slowly ebbing away, and with it, its significance as a nation state. As companies are bought by foreigners, and head offices move, the good jobs disappear. The tax base is also eroded because foreign-owned companies pay lower taxes than domestically-owned companies.

At the same time, one country after another is losing its right to use its own central bank to help finance essential services when the tax revenue from other sources is being eroded. Nor is it by accident that countries are being encouraged to adopt either the U.S. dollar or the euro as a replacement for their own currency. It is all part of a scheme to rob people of one of their most valuable assets, so the rich can usurp them – a scam to which I shall return later.

Brainwashing

You may well wonder how such a grand deception, on a global scale, could be sold to an unsuspecting public. So too, apparently, did its sponsors.

Greg Palast, author of *The Best Democracy Money Can Buy*, and whistleblower extraordinaire, has unearthed some fascinating information about secret meetings between European and American captains of industry and finance. He even managed to get minutes of some of their meetings. In an interview with *Acres USA*, Palast had this to say:

"One of the most amazing things in one of these meetings is when they talk about how to sell globalization to the public. They can't figure out how to sell this thing to the public because they can't figure out what the benefits of globalization really are to the average person. They actually sat there and said: 'Why don't we pay some professors a bunch of money, and get them to come up with a study that globalization is good for people?'

"Then the officer for Reuters, the big news service that's in every big paper on the planet, said: 'You come up with the material and we'll help you out, we'll place the stories in the papers.' It really freaked me out to find this propaganda system to sell people on the means of their own economic destruction."[1]

It freaked me out too to see that Reuters, with its reputation as a totally responsible and reliable news agency, would be willing to collaborate in disseminating ideas that are propaganda at best and subversive at worst. Then I found the name of the Reuters CEO on the list of Bilderberg attendees, and I understood.

The neo-cons, who are mostly a bunch of very rich old cons, have been peddling their propaganda for decades. And, they have provided a real "bunch of money" to hire dozens of accommodating professors to write myriad papers proving beyond reasonable doubt that black is white.

As far back as 1943, a group of anti-New Deal businessmen established the American Enterprise Institute. It provided intellectual public relations in the 1950s and 1960s and worked directly with members of Congress, the federal bureaucracy and the media.[2]

The Heritage Foundation is another one of the best-known U.S. think tanks as a result of its close association with Ronald Reagan, and its powerful influence on his policies. Its success inspired the creation of 37 mini-Heritages across the U.S. providing synergy, an illusion of diversity, and the impression that the experts quoted actually represented a broad spectrum of views. Other smaller U.S. think tanks include the venerable Hoover Institution on War, Revolution and Peace; the Cato Institute; and the Manhattan Institute for Policy Research.[3]

The United Kingdom has its own network including the Centre for Policy Studies, the anti-statist Institute of Economic Affairs, and the Adam Smith Institute. Even Canada is not immune from propaganda factories. We have the very influential Fraser Institute in British Columbia, the C.D. Howe Institute in Toronto, and a number of new regional institutes based on the same model.

These institutions have much in common. They are financed by foundations and large corporations which are anti-populist in philosophy. In general, they believe that the least government is the best government; that nation states have outlived their usefulness; that markets are infallible regulators of economic activity; and that the rich have no obligation to share their wealth with the poor on whom they depend for labor and as customers for their goods and services.

This, then, is the philosophy of the captains of industry and finance that Greg Palast said had been meeting secretly to promote their globalization agenda. These same people, who are re-engineering the world for their own benefit, have no compunction about using both governments and international institutions as batboys. They use them to promote international treaties that diminish the power of nation states to act on behalf of their citizens; to jaw-bone poor countries into selling their assets at firesale prices; and to help enforce contracts, even when those contracts were not negotiated in good faith, and were much more favorable to one side than the other. As Joseph E. Stiglitz, former chief economist of the World Bank said: "There is, in fact, a long history of 'unfair' contracts, which Western governments have used their muscle to enforce."[4]

The Free Trade Panacea

I must admit that I am a free trader at heart, and always have been. One of my first speeches in the Canadian House of Commons more than half a century ago was on that subject. At that time I proposed a two percent annual reduction in tariffs that would see them eliminated in fifty years. It was a rate of reduction that would allow a gradual change that could easily be absorbed without any drastic upheaval in living standards in the more industrialized countries.

Perhaps the same goal could have been achieved in twenty-five years without unacceptable disruption; but there was no way we could foresee the "Shock and Awe" approach that the big guns were eventually able to implement with its gut-wrenching consequences for manufacturing industries in the more advanced countries. Unfortunately few of us had any notion of what was really going on in the world, as I can attest to from the reaction to some of my earlier writings on the subject.

A principal aim of the One World advocates was to gain access to cheap labor so they could reduce costs without any corresponding reduction in the prices of their products, thereby increasing profit margins significantly. In the process, they succeeded in reversing decades of social progress on every front. They could, at a stroke, undo the wage gains unions had won in the post-World War II years through hard-fought negotiations. As a result of moving production to cheap-labor countries, they were able to employ child labor, in a manner reminiscent of Dickensian England. The cheap labor, adult or child, would lack the protection of workplace safety standards and would toil without the negotiated health and welfare benefits enjoyed by the workers being displaced. And, of course, the industrialists could pollute to their hearts' content in places where concern for clean air, water and soil were not yet on the public radar.

The undeniable benefits to the manufacturers could only be realized in a world where their products could not be denied entry into traditional markets simply because they were made under circumstances that would be quite unacceptable in the importing country. This meant changing the whole woof and warp of international law in a way that would remove from politicians the right to legislate in the real interests of their electors because they were rendered powerless under the terms of new international treaties.

The Trilats faced two problems: where to start and what to call the treaties. An early agreement with Israel was routine and barely noticed. But where better to start the first big test than with Canada. We are a naïve lot, who play by Boy Scout rules.

A former colleague in the Trudeau government, Hon. Donald Macdonald, himself a Bilderberger, was handpicked to head a commission on the subject of free trade. Macdonald recommended in favor, calling it "A Leap of Faith."[5] This report influenced the Prime Minister, Brian Mulroney, who had been almost violently opposed to such a move, and who had suggested that no one in his right mind would pursue it. A couple of other insiders, at least one of whom was a Bilderberger, added their private powerful pleas. The prime minister was convinced, and the play began.

The choice of words was critical. Free trade has a nice ring to it, whereas if the treaty had been called "Unrestricted Investment," or something that would have been closer to the truth, it is almost certain that public opinion would have killed the deal before it got off the ground. So "Free Trade" got the nod.

The Canada-U.S. Free Trade Agreement (FTA)

> *"The Canadians don't understand what they have signed.*
> *In 20 years they will be sucked into the U.S. economy."*
>
> – Clayton Yeutter[6]

Yeutter denies having said this, but an eye and ear witness disagrees, and the prophecy proved to be well-founded. The Canada-U.S. agreement, of which Yeutter was a senior negotiator, was one of the first of its kind – a template for the evolution of the New

World Order that the people who really run the U.S. envisaged. Like the vast majority of my fellow Canadians, I was naïve enough to believe that the FTA was a trade agreement because that is what I heard on television and radio, *ad nauseam*, and what I read in the newspapers. It was also what the Canadian and U.S. governments were telling us, and it was the message that big business was hammering home in its full-page ads.

Most Canadians still believe that "free trade" means free trade. But it doesn't! It is much more complicated than that. Anyone who has actually read the FTA or its successor, the North American Free Trade Agreement (NAFTA), as I eventually did, will know that these treaties are primarily about investment and corporate rights.

Of course, the FTA eliminated tariffs between the two countries over a ten-year period; but these were already coming off under the General Agreement on Tariffs and Trade (GATT). So, by the time the FTA was signed, the vast majority of items were already duty free; and for those items where tariffs still applied, Canada had an advantage because our tariffs were higher than those in the U.S. – an advantage we gave up without getting anything in return.

From the outset, the two countries had very different objectives. These were stated during an initial meeting of Prime Minister Brian Mulroney's Chief of Staff, Derek Burney, and Senior Deputy United States Trade Representative, Michael B. Smith, on July 31, 1985. Canadians wanted just two things: "Exemption from U.S. Dumping and Anti-Subsidy Laws, and a gradual phase in, indeed a back-end loading of tariff eliminations." The U.S. had two demands: "Immediate abolition of the infamous Foreign Investment Review Board (FIRB), and a faster implementation of tariff reductions, given the fact that Canadian tariffs were already higher than U.S. tariffs."[7]

In the end, the Americans achieved both of their demands; and Canada struck out on both of its two bottom line objectives. We did not get an exemption from U.S. anti-dumping and countervailing duty laws which can and have been applied almost capriciously whenever the American political situation demands as anyone in the softwood lumber or several other contentious industries can attest. So, Canada did not get the "guaranteed access" to U.S. markets that PM Mulroney had promised. But, the Americans did get their "license to buy Canada" which was what the treaty was all about.

In effect, it was the Trilats first "shot across the bow" to show free countries, in a free world, that they were no longer free to run their affairs in the best interests of their citizens but must bow the knee to "King Capital," who would henceforth be able to determine their destinies. In the first fifteen years after the signing of the treaty, about 13,000 Canadian companies were sold to foreigners – the majority to our cousins south of the border. And the pace never slackened as the global monopoly game got under way in earnest.

Of course, the European members of the "Club" got in on the act which is now worldwide. The aim of the game is, as always, to eliminate competition to the point where market forces are replaced by market power, at the consumers' expense. In effect, the business elite wanted to achieve in nickel, aluminum, food and other industries what they had already achieved in oil – an expensive result that is all too obvious at the gas pump.

In recent years, some of Canada's few remaining global companies like the International Nickel Company and Alcan Manufacturing have been bought out and all of our steel manufacturers are now foreign-owned. The most prominent, Stelco of Hamilton, Ontario, was sold to U.S. Steel and shut down to eliminate the competition despite promises to maintain production.

In the course of the 2008 U.S. presidential race, more than one candidate hinted that if elected, they would abrogate NAFTA and seek a better treaty. Instead of being alarmed at the prospect, I was one of the few Canadians who relished the thought that the U.S. might do what spineless Canadian leaders have refused to do – give the six months notice for abrogation, and start at once to negotiate a "Fair Trade" agreement that would facilitate easy access to each others markets while allowing us to regain some control over the destiny of our own industries and resources.

This idea is anathema to most of our bureaucrats and editorialists who have been thoroughly brainwashed by the ideology of seamless borders. Canadians point to the benefits of free trade without analyzing the bottom line. They have been mesmerized by the numbers. The cross-border volume has sky-rocketed, so these figures are cited as proof positive that the FTA and NAFTA have been big contributors to Canada's prosperity. But, figures lie; or at least, they don't tell the whole truth.

Canada's biggest gains in exports to the U.S. since the FTA was signed have been in automobiles and energy. In both cases the connection to the FTA, if any, has been minimal. In the case of automobiles, the increase was largely attributable to the Auto Pact with the U.S. which represented Canadian "protectionism" at its best and most successful – an advantage that no longer exists under the New World Order, so we see more of our hugely successful auto industry disappearing. At the time of writing, the following article appeared in the Toronto *Globe and Mail* newspaper.

"Vehicle production in Canada is poised to slump by as much as 25 per cent by 2020, as global auto makers invest heavily in rival auto centres such as Mexico, the United States and other growing markets.

"Car makers built 2.454 million vehicles in Canada last year, but that number is forecast to slide by more than 600,000 – to 1.823 million by the end of the decade, Joe McCabe, president of auto consulting company AutomotiveCompass LLC, said Wednesday ...

"It's the latest indication that Canada is on the road to becoming a second-tier player in an industry that provides tens of thousands of high-paying jobs, makes a huge contribution to exports, and represents about 2.5 per cent of Ontario's gross domestic product."[8]

The most dramatic increase in exports, by far, was electricity, natural gas and crude oil. This was due to the nearly insatiable demand for energy south of the border. The agricultural sector, too, initially appeared to prosper. Canadian farmers did everything right; they expanded exports three times, but their net income remained static. That has been the bottom line. Despite all of the increased activity, average Canadians are little, if any, better off *vis-à-vis* average Americans than they were in 1989 when the Free Trade Agreement came into effect. Inevitably some people have benefited considerably from the agreements; but for the rest of us, it has just been treading water.

That is bad enough without the burden of knowing that we pioneered a new system where power was transferred from our elected representatives to foreign corporations. When one of our municipalities or provinces adopts a policy intended to protect our interests, and some foreign company claims that its operations and profits, or even its planned or hoped-for profits are affected, it can sue the Canadian government for millions of dollars: and quite a few have done just that, with claims approaching $2 billion to date.

Meanwhile, the loss of manufacturing jobs continues relentlessly. In my home province of Ontario, the H.J. Heinz Co. is about to close its Leamington tomato-processing plant after 100 years, at the cost of 750 full-time jobs. This plant is not only the town's major industry, but it has long provided a market for area tomato growers. Other Ontario manufacturers have quietly closed their doors without much national attention.

"Thus Delhi and Dunnville lost their Bick's pickle plants in 2011. The American owner, J.M. Smucker, had decided to consolidate production in the U.S.

"That followed a decision by Kraft Foods to shut canning plants in the Niagara and London areas, in order to move production to China.

"And that in turn followed Hershey's 2007 decision to shutter its Smith Falls chocolate plant in eastern Ontario. That production went to Mexico and the U.S."[9]

"For Ontario, all of this is part of a wrenching change that began 24 years ago. Until Canada entered into its 1989 free trade deal with the U.S., tariff-protected manufacturers had thrived in big cities and small towns alike.

"But free trade changed all of that. Entire sectors collapsed, as U.S.-owned companies shifted production south of the border.

That trend accelerated, first when the North American Free Trade Agreement brought low-wage Mexico into the mix and, finally, when worldwide trade liberalization shifted manufacturing to China."[10]

Many small towns and cities in the U.S. have suffered similarly as manufacturing has been transferred offshore to one low wage country after another. Some has returned but the high level of unemployment and the significant number of "ghost towns" is evidence enough that the massive disruption of the new "era of globalization" has weighed heavily on the lives and prospects of many Americans. They, too, must share that feeling of silent hopelessness as their world collapses around them and they find themselves powerless to stop the carnage.

Time marches on and the next round of power grabbing by the One-World Gang is much more ominous. Canada has been negotiating a treaty with the European Union. Bargaining took place in secret – a measure of the contempt in which electors are held by their federal government – so we the public don't know the parameters of the talks. A tentative agreement was signed by Prime Minister Stephen Harper on October 18, 2013. Since the election of 2015 Prime Minister Justin Trudeau indicated that he would follow in Harper's footsteps, based on the same faulty advice from the same public officials. Should he succeed it will be "game over" for Canada

Treason, First; High Treason Next

In retrospect, signing the Canada-U.S. Free Trade Agreement and then the North American Free Trade Agreement was treason, even though participants were probably unaware of it at the time. Giving foreign corporations greater rights than those enjoyed by the citizens of the host country is so foreign to all principles of justice and fair play that it has to be a "violation of allegiance to one's country" the first definition in the Webster's Dictionary. It reminded me of David Korten's prescient book *When Corporations Rule the World.*[11] Corporations are not supposed to run the world; people and their elected governments are.

Canadian politicians are still bragging that we led the world down the path of multiple trade agreements when we signed the original Canada-U.S. Trade Agreement, and then NAFTA. As the larger truth unfolds, we will feel remorse that we have been a key player in aiding and abetting the biggest betrayal since the Garden of Eden.

We can start making amends by refusing to close the Canada-Europe Trade Agreement (CETA). This would be a signal to the U.S. that it, too, should abandon any move in that direction. It isn't just trade with a large market of 500 million that is at stake, although it is difficult to see how a tiny country of 35 million can hope to go toe-to-toe with such a large giant and avoid getting smothered in the contest. It is the fine print that is so offensive and worrisome. As Prime Minister Stephen Harper said, the treaty also includes investments, public markets, services, and labor mobility which is why *The Economist* magazine called the pact a new world model for future commercial accords.[12] Regrettably, *The Economist* appears to have sided with the Bilderbergers at the expense of the people.

The provision that I would label as "high treason" is the inclusion of financial services, including banking. There is only one possible way to end the economic malaise and massive worldwide unemployment, and that is an equally massive infusion of government-created, debt-free money – as I will explain in the next chapter. CETA would prevent Canada from using its constitutional power over money and banking to end austerity and create prosperity as it did from 1939-1974. To compromise the ability to use that power by giving European banks the right to sue for loss of potential profits, would be high treason of the first degree.

The Trans-Pacific Partnership

The Trans-Pacific Partnership (TPP), until recently being pushed by the United States is even worse than CETA, which hardly seems possible. With it, we will not only lose control of our financial system but our health, environment, and, most important, control over the quality and safety of our food supply.

A fabulous article entitled "Monsanto, the TPP, and Global Food Dominance" was written by Ellen Brown, one of the world's foremost experts on banks and banking, and posted on www.Max-Keiser.com on November 27, 2013. The author of *The Web of Debt*,[13] a must read if you really want to understand banking, Ellen has given me permission to use several paragraphs from the following article.

Profits Before Populations

"According to an Acres USA interview of plant pathologist Don Huber, Professor Emeritus of Purdue University, two modified trends account for practically all of the genetically modified crops grown in the world today. One involves insect resistance. The other, more disturbing modification involves insensitivity to glyphosate-based herbicides (plant-killing chemicals). Often known as Roundup after the best-selling Monsanto product of that name, glyphosate poisons everything in its path except plants genetically modified to resist it.

"Glyphosate-based herbicides are now the most commonly used herbicides in the world. Glyphosate is an essential partner to the GMOs (genetically modified organisms) that are the principal business of the burgeoning biotech industry. Glyphosate is a 'broad-spectrum' herbicide that destroys indiscriminately, not by killing unwanted plants directly but by tying up access to critical nutrients.

"Because of the insidious way in which it works, it has been sold as a relatively benign replacement for the devastating earlier dioxin-based herbicides. But a barrage of experimental data has now shown glyphosate and the GMO foods incorporating it to pose serious dangers to health. Compounding the risk is the toxicity of 'inert' ingredients used to make glyphosate more potent. Researchers have found, for example, that the surfactant POEA can kill human cells, particularly embryonic, placental and umbilical cord cells. But these risks have been conveniently ignored.

"The widespread use of GMO foods and glyphosate herbicides helps explain the anomaly that the U.S. spends over twice as much per capita on healthcare as the average developed country, yet it is rated far down the scale of the world's healthiest populations. The World Health Organization has ranked the U.S. LAST out of 17 developed nations for overall health.

"Sixty to seventy percent of the foods in U.S. supermarkets are now genetically modified. By contrast, in at least 26 other countries – including Switzerland, Australia, Austria, China, India, France, Germany, Hungary, Luxembourg, Greece, Bulgaria, Poland, Italy, Mexico and Russia – GMOs are totally or partially banned; and significant restrictions on GMOs exist in about sixty other countries.

"A ban on GMO and glyphosate use might go far toward improving the health of Americans. But the Trans-Pacific Partnership, a global trade agreement for which the Obama Administration has sought Fast Track status, would block that sort of cause-focused approach to the healthcare crisis.

Roundup's Insidious Effects

"Roundup-resistant crops escape being killed by glyphosate, but they do not avoid absorbing it into their tissues. Herbicide-tolerant crops have substantially higher levels of herbicide residues than other crops. In fact, many countries have had to increase their legally allowable levels – by up to 50 times – in order to accommodate the introduction of GM crops. In the European Union, residues in food are set to rise 100-150 times if a new proposal by Monsanto is approved. Meanwhile, herbicide-tolerant 'super-weeds' have adapted to the chemical, requiring even more toxic doses and new toxic chemicals to kill the plant.

"Human enzymes are affected by glyphosate just as plant enzymes are: the chemical blocks the uptake of manganese and other essential minerals. Without those minerals, we cannot properly metabolize our food. That helps explain the rampant epidemic of obesity in the United States. People eat and eat in an attempt to acquire the nutrients that are simply not available in their food.

According to researchers Samsell and Seneff in "Biosemiotic Entrophy: Disorder, Disease, and Mortality" (April 2013):

Glyphosate's inhibition of cytochrome P450 (CYP) enzymes is an overlooked component of its toxicity to mammals. CYP enzymes play crucial roles in biology ….

Negative impact on the body is insidious and manifests slowly over time as inflammation damages cellular systems throughout the body. Consequences are most of the diseases and conditions associated with a Western diet, which include gastrointestinal disorders, obesity, diabetes, heart disease, depression, autism, infertility, cancer and Alzheimer's disease."

"More than 40 diseases have been linked to glyphosate use, and more keep appearing. In September 2013, the National University of Rio Cuarto, Argentina, published research finding that glyphosate enhances the growth of fungi that produce aflatoxin B1, one of the most carcinogenic of substances. A doctor from Chaco, Argentina, told Associated Press, 'We've gone from a pretty healthy population to one with a high rate of cancer, birth defects and illnesses seldom seen before.' Fungi growth have increased significantly in U.S. corn crops.

"Glyphosate has also done serious damage to the environment. According to an October 2012 report by the Institute of Science in Society:

"Agribusiness claims that glyphosate and glyphosate-tolerant crops will improve crop yields, increase farmers' profits and benefit the environment by reducing pesticide use. Exactly the opposite is the case .... [T]he evidence indicates that glyphosate herbicides and glyphosate-tolerant crops have had wide-ranging detrimental effects, including glyphosate resistant super weeds, virulent plant (and new livestock) pathogens, reduced crop health and yield, harm to off-target species from insects to amphibians and livestock, as well as reduced soil fertility."

Politics Trumps Science

"In light of these adverse findings, why have Washington and the European Commission continued to endorse glyphosate as safe? Critics point to lax regulations, heavy influence from corporate lobbyists, and a political agenda that has more to do with power and control than protecting the health of the people.

"In the ground-breaking 2007 book *Seeds of Destruction: The Hidden Agenda of Genetic Manipulation,* William Engdahl states that global food control and depopulation became U.S. strategic policy under Rockefeller protégé Henry Kissinger. Along with oil geopolitics, they were to be the new 'solution' to the threats to U.S. global power and continued U.S. access to cheap raw materials from the developing world. In line with that agenda, the government has shown extreme partisanship in favor of the biotech agribusiness industry, opting for a system in which the industry 'voluntarily' polices itself. Bio-engineered foods are treated as 'natural food additives,' not needing any special testing.

"Jeffrey M. Smith, Executive Director of the Institute for Responsible Technology, confirms that U.S. Food and Drug Administration policy allows biotech companies to determine if their own foods are safe. Submission of data is completely voluntary. He concludes:

"In the critical arena of food safety research, the biotech industry is without accountability, standards, or peer-review. They've got bad science down to a science."

"Whether or not depopulation is an intentional part of the agenda, widespread use of GMO and glyphosate is having that result. The endocrine-disrupting properties of glyphosate have been linked to infertility, miscarriage, birth defects and arrested sexual development. In Russian experiments, animals fed GM soy were sterile by the third generation. Vast amounts of farmland soil are also being systematically ruined by the killing of beneficial microorganisms that allow plant roots to uptake soil nutrients.

"In Gary Null's eye-opening documentary 'Seeds of Death: Unveiling the Lies of GMOs,' Dr. Bruce Lipton warns, 'We are leading the world into the sixth mass extinction of life on this planet…. Human behavior is undermining the web of life.'

The TPP and International Corporate Control

"As the devastating conclusions of these and other researchers awaken people globally to the dangers of Roundup and GMO foods, transnational corporations are working feverishly with the Obama administration to fast-track the Trans-Pacific Partnership, a trade agreement that would strip governments of the power to regulate transnational corporate activities. Negotiations have been kept secret from Congress but not from corporate advisors, 600 of whom have been consulted and know the details. According to Barbara Checherio in *Nation of Change*:

"The Trans-Pacific Partnership (TPP) has the potential to become the biggest regional Free Trade Agreement in history….

"The chief agricultural negotiator for the U.S. is the former

Monsanto lobbyist, Islam Siddique. If ratified the TPP would impose punishing regulations that give multinational corporations unprecedented right to demand taxpayer compensation for policies that corporations deem a barrier to their profits.

"... They are carefully crafting the TPP to insure that citizens of the involved countries have no control over food safety, what they will be eating, where it is grown, the conditions under which food is grown and the use of herbicides and pesticides."

"Food safety is only one of many rights and protections liable to fall to this super-weapon of international corporate control. In an April 2013 interview on The Real News Network, Kevin Zeese called the TPP 'NAFTA on steroids' and 'a global corporate coup.' He warned:

"No matter what issue you care about – whether its wages, jobs, protecting the environment... this issue is going to adversely affect it.... If a country takes a step to try to regulate the financial industry or set up a public bank to represent the public interest, it can be sued...."[14]

What you have just read appears to be a recipe for mass genocide on a scale beyond anything recorded in our histories of the world and almost beyond comprehension by the most flexible of minds.

If This Isn't High Treason, What Is?

The Bank of England.

Chapter Four

THE MONEY MAFIA

"Give a man a gun and he can rob a bank:
give a man a bank and he can rob the world."

– Rip Bob Diamond

For more than half-a-century I have kept a file on the Mafia so that I would know what they were doing, and how I, first as a young man, and then as a more mature politician, could avoid being compromised, even in some small way. The Sicilian branch that I refer to, has been deeply entrenched in some Canadian cities, especially the very cosmopolitan Montréal where it had a choke hold on the construction industry. A recent official inquiry suggests that they were taking about 2%-2$^{1/3}$% off the top of every municipal contract.

I have been following the Money Mafia even longer – since the Great Depression of the 1930s. I have seen it increase its share of the take, at every opportunity, until it reached about 95%, which is approximately the new international standard. The rate is set by the cartel's own secret governing body, the Bank for International Settlements (BIS) which, incredibly, enjoys sufficient power and influence to persuade leaders of the G20 group of nations to rubber stamp its regulations. These are known as the Basel Accords, first Basel I, then Basel II and now Basel III.

The Basel III Accord says that your bank has to have about five cents capital invested for every dollar it lends to you. That should catch your attention right away! How in Heaven's name can your bank lend you a dollar if it has only five cents capital for every dollar it lends? The answer is that it isn't actually lending you money, because it doesn't have that much money. It is lending you its credit that it converts into a bank deposit, which has become a universally accepted substitute for legal tender money.

When you repay the loan, however, you have to give the bank a dollar worth 100 cents, plus interest. If this sounds like some kind of a racket, a giant Ponzi scheme bigger and more lucrative than any other in history, that would be right. It is a con job unlike any other.

Consider the basic unfairness. A student has to borrow, say, a $50,000 bank credit to pay for a college education. It may take all of his or her spare cash for years to repay the $50,000 plus interest. Yet, the bank's original investment was only $2,500. Doesn't that sound like a stacked deck?

It is, and it affects both the lifestyle and career plans of many students. Some postpone marriage until their debt level is under control. Most put off large capital expenditures such as cars and houses. This has a negative effect on business and, consequently, reduces the number of job opportunities that would be otherwise available. So, when young people today say their prospects are not as good as their parents enjoyed they are right. What they may not realize is that the most significant difference over the intervening years is the level of personal and national debt.

Canadian household debt climbed to a new all-time high at the end of 2015, when Canadians owed $1.65 for every dollar they earned.[1] The trend toward higher levels of debt has become widespread. In just 4 years between 2006 and 2010, debt escalated by more than 75% in Britain and Greece. In the U.S., the Congress spends a great deal of time and emotional energy raising its legal debt limit in order to avoid default. One may wonder why they don't invest equal time and energy in examining what is wrong with a system where debt levels continue to rise.

But, while public servants may wonder whether austerity cuts will eliminate their positions, and the unemployed wonder when they will be able to get jobs, the rich keep getting richer. As Susan George explains in the September 2013 edition of the *Canadian Centre for Policy Alternatives Monitor*:

"One can look at this self-created disaster (austerity) in two ways. Eminent prize-winning economists like Paul Krugman and Joseph Stiglitz believe that the European leadership is brain-dead, ignorant of economics, and needlessly committing economic suicide. Others note that the cuts conform exactly to the desires of such entities as the European Roundtable of Industrialists or BusinessEurope: cut wages and benefits, weaken unions, privatize everything in sight, and so on. As inequalities have soared, those at the top have done nicely. There are now more 'High Net Worth Individuals,' with a much greater collective fortune, than in 2008 at the height of the crisis. Five years ago, there were 8.6 million HNWIs worldwide with a pile of liquid assets of $39 trillion. Today, they are 11 million strong with assets of $42 trillion. Small businesses are failing in droves, but the largest companies are sitting on huge piles of cash and taking full advantage of tax havens."[2]

If the U.S. Congress and all G20 politicians would really look at the International Banking and Financial System critically and objectively, they would inevitably conclude that it is legalized grand larceny on a scale almost beyond belief. The system has permitted the accumulation of personal and family fortunes so vast, resulting in power so pervasive, that they can buy almost anything, and anyone they wish to control. Meanwhile honest politicians will soon conclude that the system is unstable, unsustainable and so fundamentally flawed that only massive reforms, that will change the balance of power worldwide, will be acceptable to the masses once they understand the extent to which they have been misled.

To achieve that level of understanding, however, will require a much more universal knowledge of what money is, and where it comes from.

What is Money?

History records that there have been many kinds of money. Gold, silver, copper and iron coins were the long-time favorites, but there have been many substitutes to meet individual circumstances. The long list includes items as varied as sea shells, wampum (beads), cattle and even playing cards.

When the French Intendant in New France (now Québec, Canada) was short of coins because the King of France had failed to send enough to pay the troops, he cut ordinary playing cards in four and used them as currency. The system worked well until he cut too many of them and their value fell. This was an early lesson of the inflationary risk of increasing the money supply faster than the increase in goods and services available to make them valuable.

Sometimes these forms of money became inadequate to facilitate the rate of growth in commerce. So paper money became a deviation from the time-honored dual system of metallic coins and barter. This appears to have occurred in China where they invented *fei-ch'ien* (flying money) which they used in a way similar to our bank drafts to send money from one place to another during the T'ang dynasty (A.D. 618-907). Later, when iron coins were the main currency in Szechwan province, the heavy weight led people to deposit them in some proto-banks and use the receipts for financial transactions. Many historians believe that the use of these receipts as a money substitute was the origin of paper money.[3]

Paper money was used quite extensively when I was a young man. During World War II, for example, Canadian soldiers, sailors and airmen were paid in cash. Similarly, much retail business was conducted in cash because there were no credit cards, let alone debit cards. Even then, however, the majority of the money supply consisted of bank deposits created by the banks when they made loans.

The system works this way. Suppose that you want to borrow $35,000 to buy a new car. You visit your friendly banker and ask for a loan. He or she will ask you for collateral – some stocks, bonds, a second mortgage on your house or cottage or, if you are unable to supply any of these, the co-signature of a well-to-do friend or relative. When the collateral requirement is satisfied, you will be asked to sign a note for the principal amount with an agreed rate of interest.

When the paperwork is complete, and the note signed, your banker will make an entry on the bank's computer; and, presto, a $35,000 credit will appear in your account that you can use to buy your car. The important point is that seconds earlier that money did not exist. It was created out of thin air – so to speak.

This makes a lie of the biggest myth in banking, i.e. that the money you borrow today is money that someone else deposited yesterday, or a few days ago. That is technically possible, but the probability is so minute that it can be dismissed. It is most profitable for banks to be fully lent, so the odds are that the "money" credited to your account is created especially for you. It is, in fact, only virtual money – nothing but a computer entry.

A very dramatic example of the banks raking in most of the chips can be seen in the house-building business in which I was involved in the 1950s and early 1960s. Most builders have to borrow from their banks when starting a new house. The physical process involves miners going underground to obtain the metals for the hardware and plumbing; brick-makers tending the ovens to provide a nice variety of color and textures for the exterior walls, foresters cutting the trees to make the lumber, and carpenters building the shell, and so on. These tradesmen provide the long hours and accept the personal risk of making the miracle happen. At the other end of the scale, what do the banks contribute? A computer entry. But, who owns the house? The bank, of course.

If the builder can find a buyer willing to pay the amount of the bank loan with a little left over, he will have made a modest profit. If not, and a loss occurs, he has to cough up the difference at his own expense. In either case, the odds are that the buyers will need a mortgage for the major part of the purchase price, so the bank will have a new debtor from whom to collect principal and interest.

The bankers' system of money creation is one of double-entry bookkeeping. Your note becomes an asset on the bank's books, and the new money that is deposited to your account, a liability. The profit for the bank comes from the difference between the low rate of interest, if any, you would be paid on your deposit if you didn't spend the borrowed money immediately, and the much higher rate you would be obliged to pay on your note – the technical term is "the spread." When you repay the loan, either voluntarily, or in the event the bank demands repayment, the "money" is extinguished and disappears into the ether from whence it came.

Graham Towers, the first and arguably the brightest Governor of the Bank of Canada said: "Money is just a bookkeeping entry; that is all it is." If he were alive today, he would say: "Money is just a computer entry; that's all it is." So we have millions and millions of unemployed men and women all around the world just for the lack of a few well-placed computer entries. That fact, as I wrote in *Light at the End of the Tunnel*, is a crime against humanity in the literal sense of these words.

The Banking Scam

Banking was conceived in iniquity and was born in sin. The Bankers own the earth. Take it away from them, but leave them the power to create money, and with the flick of the pen they will create enough money to buy it back again. However, take that power away from them and all the great fortunes like mine will disappear, and they ought to disappear, for this would be a happier and better world to live in. But if you wish to remain the slaves of Bankers, and pay the cost of your own slavery, let them continue to create money.
–Sir Josiah (later Baron) Stamp, Director, Bank of England 1928-1941

Those words of Baron Stamp are profoundly wise and worthwhile, yet we have ignored them as if they were never uttered. It is as if our brains become paralyzed when we think of money and banking even though the result of that paralysis is permanent slavery to the bankers and the dubious pleasure of paying the cost of our own bondage.

One has to wonder how we wound up bound hand and foot by debt. To understand requires some knowledge of the origin and evolution of the banking system from its modest beginnings to its now near-total control of the international financial system. The top bankers' business plan has been one of the most clever and persistent in recorded history. Its success was far from accidental.

The history of banking goes back millennia and requires a whole thick book to tell the story. Even the history of European banking can be traced back to Roman times. It is what has happened in the last three centuries or so that is most relevant to our current crisis. So my launching point will be the introduction of paper money to England which appears to have begun late in the 17th century.

The Goldsmiths' Scam

Before 1640, it was the custom for wealthy merchants to deposit their excess cash – gold and silver – in the Mint of the Tower of London for safekeeping. In 1640, Charles I seized the privately owned money and destroyed the Mint's reputation as a safe place. This action forced merchants and traders to seek alternatives and, subsequently, to store their excess money with the goldsmiths of Lombard Street, who had already built strong fireproof boxes for the storage of their own valuables.[4]

The goldsmiths accepted gold deposits for which they issued receipts which were redeemable on demand. These receipts were passed from hand to hand and were known as goldsmiths' notes, the predecessors of banknotes. The goldsmiths paid interest of 5% on their customers' deposits and then lent the money to their more needy clients at exorbitant rates becoming, in fact, pawnbrokers who advanced money against the collateral of valuable property.[5] They also learned that it was possible to make loans in excess of the gold actually held in their vaults, because only a small fraction of their depositors attempted to convert their receipts into gold at any one time. Thus began the fractional reserve system, the practice of lending "money" that doesn't really exist. It was to become the most profitable scam in the history of mankind. It was also the quicksand on which the Bank of England was subsequently founded in 1694 – more than 300 years ago.

The Bank of England's Scam

England's crushing defeat by France in the 1690 Battle of Beachy Head became the catalyst for England's rebuilding itself as a global power. England had no choice but to build a powerful navy. No public funds were available, and the credit of William III's government was so low in London that it was impossible for it to borrow the £1,200,000 (at 8%) that was needed.

In order to induce subscription to the loan, the subscribers were to be incorporated by the name of the Governor and Company of the Bank of England. The bank was given exclusive possession of the government's balances, and was the only limited-liability corporation allowed to issue bank notes.[6] The lenders would give the government cash (bullion) and issue notes against the government bonds. In other words the bank was allowed to lend the same money twice – once to the government and again to its preferred customers – and collect interest from each. This was not the first case of paper money issued by private banks in the modern era but it was the first of great and lasting significance in the English-speaking world.[7]

This arrangement was similar in principle to the system developed by the goldsmiths. By lending the same money twice the bank could double the interest received on is capital. Nice work if you can get it, and you can get it with a bank charter. It is not too surprising, then, that discussions of this advantage encouraged some members of parliament to become shareholders in the bank. Money lenders learned early, and have never forgotten, that it pays to have friends in parliament.[8]

Bankers are by nature a greedy lot. So they were not content with being able to lend the same money to two people, they began lobbying for an even sweeter deal. In the early years of the 20th century, federally chartered U.S. banks were required to maintain gold reserves equal to 25% of deposits. That allowed them to lend the same money four times. In Canada, when I was young, banks were required to maintain 8% cash reserves; so, they could lend the same money 12½ times.

In recent times, with the advent of the monetarist revolution inspired by Milton Friedman and his colleagues at the University of Chicago, and the elimination of cash reserves in favor of a new system labelled "capital adequacy," the leverage (the number of times banks can lend the same money) soared. Bank leverage in the U.S. rose from about 12½ in 1974 to 25 or 30 in the 1980s. This incredible abuse occurred because even ridiculously low capital requirements set by the Bank for International Settlements were never properly enforced.

Greed Knows No Bounds

One would think that their licenses "to create" $20,000 in accounts receivable for every $1,000 capital invested would be so embarrassingly lucrative that the banksters would just keep silent and enjoy their vast fortunes. But that is not so. More than enough is never enough! They are constantly looking for new corners to cut in their persistent efforts to rob the public.

Looking back at some old files I re-read about bank collusion in commercial fraud cases like Enron and then WorldCom. These major scandals stoked cocktail conversation for months. But in a way these stellar cases were only the tip of a much more ominous iceberg – widespread cheating by many of the most prestigious firms on Wall Street.

The list read like a Who's Who of world finance; Merrill; Credit Suisse Group's CSFB; Morgan Stanley; Goldman Sachs; Bear Stearns; J.P. Morgan Chase; Lehman Brothers; U.S. Bancorp. At firm after firm, according to prosecutors, analysts wittingly duped investors to curry favor with corporate clients. Investment houses received secret payments from companies they gave strong recommendations to buy. And for top executives whose companies were clients, stock underwriters offered special access to hot initial public offerings, according to the *New York Times*.[9]

Brian Miller, writing in the Toronto *Globe and Mail*, said:

> There's little repentance on Wall Street these days. Even after 10 major securities firms agreed to pay a combined $1.4 billion in penalties and costs to put the scandal behind them – a tiny fraction of their profits during that era – not one had admitted any wrongdoing and probably never will.[10]

Fast forward to more recent times I found a clipping entitled "Settlement talks heat up at JP Morgan. Bank head Jamie Dimon meets with U.S. Attorney-General Eric Holder in attempt to broker $11-billion deal to end federal scrutiny," an article by David Henry and David Ingram that appeared in the Toronto *Globe and Mail* on September 27, 2013.

> JP Morgan Chase & Co. chief executive Jamie Dimon met Thursday morning with U.S. Attorney-General Eric Holder as

the nation's biggest bank attempts to end investigations into its sales of shoddy mortgage securities leading up to the financial crisis.

The bank and federal and state authorities are trying to resolve the probes with a potential $11-billion (U.S.) settlement, according to sources familiar with the matter.

After the meeting the U.S. Justice Department, which lasted about an hour, Mr. Holder told reporters that he had met with representatives of JP Morgan but did not mention Mr. Dimon by name. He declined to give details of the talks.

Speaking at a press conference on an unrelated topic, the Attorney-General also said that the Justice Department plans to make announcements in the coming weeks and months."[11]

A couple of months later a deal was reached with JP Morgan that involved a $13 billion settlement. A headline in a report by TheRealNews.com "Documents in JP Morgan settlement reveal how every large bank in U.S. has committed mortgage fraud." A conversation between Jaisal Noor, TRNN Producer and Bill Black, an associate professor of economics and law at the University of Missouri-Kansas City, and author of *The Best Way to Rob a Bank Is to Own One*, begins as follows:

> **Black:** So, this'll be the first installment in what we can learn from the statement of facts that constitutes JP Morgan's admissions. This in the settlement that the Department of Justice is billing as the $13 billion settlement. As I've explained in the past, it's not that big, but it's still quite large in dollar terms. And we owe a debt of gratitude to Judge Rakoff, who's been giving the Securities and Exchange Commission a hard time about settling cases and getting absolutely no useful admissions from the people that perpetrated the frauds.
>
> And so the Justice Department was embarrassed into getting this statement of fact, which was obviously closely negotiated with JP Morgan to try to not establish its criminal liability, but still is a remarkable document in terms of what it tells us about the fraud second epidemics, not just at JP Morgan, but also criminality at Washington Mutual and at Bear Stearns. And it tells us about the whole secondary market frauds. And

it tells us a great deal about why the Justice Department is batting .000 against the elite frauds.[12]

– . –

Tax evasion is another piece of the financial puzzle. "Swiss bankers helped hide billions from U.S. taxes, senators say."

The first three paragraphs of this article by Tanya Talaga, Global economics reporter, that appeared in the *Toronto Star* on February 27, 2014, read as follows:

> Like a scene out of a spy novel, U.S. senators claim Swiss bankers slipped into America on tourist visas, held meetings with potential clients in secret elevators and even passed a bank statement inside a sports magazine to a customer at a swank Manhattan restaurant.
>
> The clandestine moves were done in an attempt to help U.S. Swiss bank account holders from paying taxes to Uncle Sam, a Senate subcommittee probe charges.
>
> As of 2006, 22,000 Americans had assets worth nearly $12 billion hidden away at Credit Suisse, the vast majority of that money undeclared, according to the senator's report, released late Tuesday.[13]

This practice of moving money offshore to avoid paying domestic taxes is extremely widespread. A book entitled *Treasure Islands: Uncovering the Damage of Offshore Banking and Tax Havens*[14] by Nicholas Shaxson, paints an incredible picture. He describes the techniques by which one jurisdiction after another is persuaded to provide either a special deal or total exemption for foreign money invested in their jurisdiction. The total amounts involved number in the trillions of dollars.

Shaxson asks rhetorically, "What is the largest offshore island haven?" The answer: "Manhattan."

– . –

The list of unfair tricks appears to be never-ending . In an article entitled "The Leveraged Buyout of America," Ellen Brown JD, describes a development that I consider to be totally scandalous. It reads in part as follows:

In a letter to Federal Reserve Chairman Ben Bernanke dated June 27, 2013, US Representative Alan Grayson and three co-signers expressed concern about the expansion of large banks into what have traditionally been non-financial commercial spheres.

Specifically: [W]e are concerned about how large banks have recently expanded their businesses into such fields as electric power production, oil refining and distribution, owning and operating of public assets such as ports and airports, and even uranium mining.

After listing some disturbing examples, they observed:

According to legal scholar Saule Omarova, over the past five years, there has been a 'quiet transformation of U.S. financial holding companies.' These financial services companies have become global merchants that seek to extract rent from any commercial or financial business activity within their reach. They have used legal authority in Graham-Leach- Bliley to subvert the 'foundational principle of separation of banking from commerce.'

It seems like there is a significant macro-economic risk in having a massive entity like, say JP Morgan, both issuing credit cards and mortgages, managing municipal bond offerings, selling gasoline and electric power, running large oil tankers, trading derivatives, and owning and operating airports, in multiple countries.

A 'macro' risk indeed – not just to our economy but to our democracy and our individual and national sovereignty. Giant banks are buying up our country's infrastructure – the power and supply chains that are vital to the economy. Aren't there rules against that? And where are the banks getting the money?[15]

Another article by Ellen Brown entitled "The Global Banking Game Is Rigged, and the FDIC Is Suing," exposes two other scandalous practices – interest rate swaps and rigged interest rates:

Taxpayers are paying billions of dollars for a swindle pulled off by the world's biggest banks, using a form of derivative called interest-rate swaps; and the Federal Deposit Insurance Corporation has now joined a chorus of litigants suing over it.

According to an SEIU report (http://www.seiu.org/images/
pdfs/Interest%20Rate20Swap%20Report%2003%2022%20
2010.pdf):

Derivatives ... have turned into a windfall for banks and
a nightmare for taxpayers ... While banks are still collecting
fixed rates of 3 to 6 percent, they are now regularly paying public entities as little as a tenth of one percent on the outstanding
bonds, with rates expected to remain low in the future. Over
the life of the deals, banks are now projected to collect billions
more than they pay state and local governments – an outcome
which amounts to a second bailout for banks, this one paid
directly out of state and local budgets.

It is not just that local governments, universities and pension funds made a bad bet on these swaps. The game itself was
rigged. The FDIC is now suing in civil court for damages and
punitive damages, a lead that other injured local governments
and agencies would be well-advised to follow. But they need to
hurry, because time on the statute of limitations is running out.

The Largest Cartel in World History.

On March 14, 2014, the FDIC filed suit for LIBOR-rig-
ging against sixteen of the world's largest banks – including the
three largest US banks (JP Morgan Chase, Bank of America,
and Citigroup), the three largest UK banks, the largest German bank, the largest Japanese bank, and several of the largest
Swiss banks. Bill Black, professor of law and economics and
a former bank fraud investigator, calls (http://www.youtube.
com/watch?v=Rn5JclFHglc#t=196) them "the largest cartel
in world history, by at least three and probably four orders of
magnitude."

LIBOR (the London Interbank Offering Rate) is the
benchmark rate by which banks themselves can borrow. It is a
crucial rate involved in hundreds of trillions of dollars in derivative trades, and it is set by these sixteen megabanks privately
and in secret.

Interest rate swaps are now a $426 trillion (http://www.
businessweek.com/articles/2014-02-27/interest-rate-swaps-
trading-comes-out-of-the-shadows) business. That's trillion
with a "t" – about seven times the gross domestic product of all
the countries in the world combined. According to the Office
of the Comptroller of the Currency, in 2012 US banks held

$183.7 trillion in interest-rate contracts, with only four firms representing 93% of total derivative holdings; and three of the four were JP Morgan Chase, Citigroup, and Bank of America, the US banks being sued by the FDIC over manipulation of LIBOR.[16]

The Bankers' End Game

I have enough material on the banking system to fill a whole book, but what you have read is enough to convince most impartial observers that any system that has produced 25 recessions and depressions in the U.S. since 1890 is fundamentally flawed, and must be rebuilt from the ground up. This reform becomes all the more urgent when you know what the banksters are trying to achieve – their "end game."

According to Professor Carroll Quigley, Bill Clinton's mentor at Georgetown University, it has all been part of a concerted plan by a clique of international financiers. He wrote in *Tragedy and Hope* in 1964:

> The powers of financial capitalism had another far-reaching aim, nothing less than to create a world system of financial control in private hands able to dominate the political system of each country and the economy of the world as a whole. This system was to be controlled in a feudalist fashion by the central banks of the world acting in concert, by secret agreements arrived at in frequent private meetings and conferences. The apex of the system was to be the Bank for International Settlements in Basel, Switzerland, a private bank owned and controlled by the world's central banks which were themselves private corporations.[17]

At this point I would like to assure readers that the vast majority of people working in the banking industry are just ordinary industrious and upright citizens. Few, if any, would be aware of the shenanigans perpetrated by the elite insiders of their industry. That is one of the most important reasons that the solution I propose in later chapters will preserve the jobs of the innocent.

<u>It is the system that is rotten to the core</u>!

<u>Money is the gasoline that fires the economic engine. To give private corporations a monopoly to create money is total insanity. To let them create all that money as debt that has to be repaid with interest goes beyond total insanity if that is possible. It is a crime against humanity!</u>

The giants have to be brought down to normal size and the Cartel dissolved. The big Wall Street, City of London and other giant banks can only get away with their blatant grand larceny as part of a larger group that dances to the same piper. The cartel comprises the giant banks, the Bank for International Settlements (BIS), the Bank for Reconstruction and Development (World Bank), the International Monetary Fund (IMF), and a worldwide network of central banks of which the U.S. Federal Reserve System (Fed) is the most notorious, powerful, and inimical to the public welfare – both in the U.S. and internationally. Of this list, the BIS, IMF and Fed should all be "terminated" on the basis that their net benefit to the human species is negative. I will begin with the BIS which is the nerve centre of the whole system – the switchboard through which the people who run the system disseminate their decisions.

The Bank for International Settlements – Basel, Switzerland.

Chapter Five

BANK FOR INTERNATIONAL SETTLEMENTS

To be frank, I have no use for politicians.
They lack the judgment of central bankers.

– Fritz Leutwiler, BIS president and chairman of the board, 1982-1984[1]

You might wonder why I am dedicating a whole chapter to a bank that most of my friends have never heard of. The Fed and the IMF are household words, but the BIS? What is it? It just happens to be one of the most influential and powerful institutions of the 20th century, and it played a key role in the formation of the European monetary union.

The Bank for International Settlements (BIS) was established on May 17, 1930 through an intergovernmental agreement by Germany, Belgium, France, Great Britain and Northern Ireland, Italy, Japan, the United States and Switzerland.[2,3] Its original purpose was to facilitate the payment of reparations imposed on Germany by the Treaty of Versailles after World War I.[4]

The need to establish a dedicated institution for this purpose was recommended by a committee headed by American, Owen D. Young, that had been set up to reduce the extent of reparations when it became obvious that Germany could not meet the annual payments established earlier. The Young Plan reduced further payments to 112 billion Gold Marks from the previous level of 269 billion.

I had just written a few paragraphs beyond this point when my Guardian Angel came to the rescue. A friend that I hadn't heard from for a long time sent me an e-mail to an old address where it was just discovered by accident.

He had just read a new book entitled *Tower of Basel: The Shadowy History of the Secret Bank that Runs the World*, by Adam Lebor. My friend was aware of my lifelong interest in money and banking, and thought I might be interested in reading it. That was an understatement. I devoured every word of its 272 meticulously researched pages that proved, beyond doubt, my preconceived prejudice.

I had planned to mention the BIS connection to the Nazis, and also its incredible secrecy and lack of transparency to the point that neither presidents, prime ministers nor ministers of finance can attend its meetings, leading me to conclude that the BIS should go the way of all flesh. Adam Lebor's book drove the final nail in the coffin.

I return now, to where I left off, inspired by Lebor's insights. Whereas the alleged reason for the new bank was to manage Germany's war reparations, the real purpose of the BIS was detailed in its statutes: to "Promote the cooperation of central banks and to provide additional facilities for international financial operations." It was the culmination of the central bankers' decades-old dream which was to have their own bank – powerful, independent, and free from interfering politicians and nosy reporters. Most felicitous of all, the BIS was self-financing and would be in perpetuity. Its clients were its own founders and shareholders. Most felicitous of all, the BIS was self-financing and would be in perpetuity. Its clients were its own founders and shareholders – the central banks.[5] This built-in advantage provides a significant handicap for reformers who want to see either complete transparency, or the abolition of the BIS.

"During the 1930s, the BIS was the central meeting place for a cabal of central bankers, dominated by Norman [Montagu Norman, Governor of the Bank of England] and Schacht [Hjalmar Schacht, president of the Reichsbank]. This group helped rebuild Germany. The *New York Times* described Schacht, widely acknowledged as the genius behind the resurgent German economy, as 'The Iron-Willed Pilot of Nazi Finance.'[6] During the war, the BIS became a de-facto arm of the Reichsbank, accepting looted Nazi gold and carrying out foreign exchange deals for Nazi Germany."[7]

In the pre-war period, there was solid collaboration between American and German industrialists. IG Farben, the octopus corporation, operated in the U.S. as General Aniline and Film (GAF). GAF's founding board members included Walter Teagle, president of Standard Oil; Edsel Ford, the president of Ford Motors; Charles E. Mitchell, chairman of National City Bank; and Paul Warburg, of the banking dynasty. GAF's most important partner was Standard Oil, that was also on excellent terms with the BIS.

The BIS' aid to Germany was constant. It accepted Germany's write-off of its pre-war reparation debt with barely a whimper. It accepted the Nazi annexation of Austria as routine and facilitated the transfer of both the Austrian National Bank's gold reserves and their 4,000 BIS shares to the Reichsbank. The takeover of the Sudetenland, the border province that Czechoslovakia had been forced to cede to the Nazis in September 1938, while much more complicated due to the Czechoslovaks' banks 143 branches in the province, presented no great problem to the BIS.

Another interesting point that Lebor mentions in his book is the benefit of American technology bestowed on the German war machine.

"War had brought enormous profits to the American car industry. Opel, General Motors' German division, produced the 'Blitz' truck on which the Wehrmacht invaded Poland. Ford's German subsidiary produced almost half of all the two- and three-ton trucks in Nazi Germany. There is a strong argument that without General Motors' and Ford's German subsidiaries, the Nazis would not have been able to wage war.[8] Hitler was certainly an enthusiastic supporter of the American motor industry's methods of mass production. He even kept a portrait of Henry Ford by his desk."[9]

While the pre-war and wartime activities of the various players are worrisome enough, a careful reading of what happened after the Nazis realized they were going to lose the war, and the collusion of some of the allied forces, leads to the unhappy conclusion that what is past might just be prologue. It is a suspicion that one must take seriously.

The Allies were persuaded not to bomb the IG Farben empire and reduce it to dust as they could have done. The logic was to facilitate a fast post-war recovery of Germany's industrial base as a bulwark against the Soviet Union. Plans were already underway for a post-war united Europe that would prevent Germany from ever again launching a war that would require American intervention. So, for the U.S., integration leading to some kind of political union was not an option, it was essential.

Meanwhile the Germans were exporting capital in order to flee when the war was over. Harry Dexter White, an economist, told a meeting of Treasury officials in July 1944, during the Bretton Woods conference, that Nazi leaders were preparing to flee the country or have their property confiscated. "They bought estates and industries and corporations, and there is evidence that the German corporations have been buying into South American corporations in expectation of being able to re-establish themselves there after the war."[10] The cloaking operation was extremely complex, White continued. "They are working through first, second and third fronts, so it is pretty hard to trace it without having all the data available." The Treasury officials also discussed the BIS at the same meeting, noting that out of twenty-one board members and senior officials, sixteen were "representatives of countries that are either now our enemies, or are occupied," including Walther Funk and Hermann Schmitz.[11]

"As the Allies advanced on Germany, the Nazis stepped up their plans for the post-war era. On August 10, 1944, an elite group of industrialists gathered at the Maison Rouge Hotel in Strasbourg, including representatives of Krupp, Messerschmitt, Volkswagen, and officials from several ministries. Also in attendance was a French spy, whose report reached the headquarters of the Allied invasion force, from where it was forwarded to the State Department and the Treasury. The account of the meeting is known as the Red House Report:

"Germany had lost the war, the Nazi industrialists agreed, but the struggle would continue along new lines. **The Fourth Reich would be a financial, rather than a military imperium.** The industrialists were to plan for a 'post-war commercial campaign.' They should make 'contacts and alliances' with foreign firms but ensure this was done without 'attracting any suspicion.' Large sums would have to be borrowed from foreign countries. Just as in the pre-war era, the U.S. connection and links to chemical firms, such as the American Chemical Foundation, were essential to expanding

German interests. The Zeiss lens company, the Leica camera firm, and the Hamburg-American line had been 'especially effective in protecting German interests abroad.' The firms' New York addresses were passed around the world.

A smaller group attended a second, select meeting. There the industrialists were instructed to 'prepare themselves to finance the Nazi party, which would be forced to go underground.' The prohibition against exporting capital had been lifted, and the government would help the industrialists to send as much money to neutral countries as possible, through two Swiss banks. The Nazi party recognized that after the defeat, its best-known leaders would be 'condemned as war criminals,' the intelligence report concluded. However, the party and the industrialists were cooperating in placing the most important figures in positions at German factories as research or technical experts."[12]

"Emil Puhl [vice-president of Germany's Reichsbank] discussed the Nazi leadership's post-war strategy with [Thomas] McKittrick at the BIS in March 1945, during the last few weeks of the war. The information he passed to McKittrick echoes that included in the Red House Report and Harry Dexter White's discussion at Bretton Woods. Military defeat was merely a temporary setback. The Nazis were fanatics and would never give up their ideals, Puhl explained. Instead, they would go underground. McKittrick immediately informed Allen Dulles of the conversation. Dulles sent the information on to London, Paris, and Washington on March 21, 1945. His telegram noted that Puhl had 'just arrived' in Basel:[13]

He said that the jig was up but that Nazis had made careful plans to go underground, that every essential figure had his designated place, that Nazism would not end with military defeat as Hitler and his fanatical followers would no more change their philosophy than would Socrates or Mohammed, that these men were just as convinced of their cause as ever and carried a great body of people with them. He emphasized that Nazism was like a religion, not merely a political regime."[14]

It is not surprising, given its role in providing friendly assistance to Germany both during its period of ascendance during the 1930s and then during the war years under the guise of financial neutrality, that there was a strong demand for abolition of the BIS. Henry Morgenthau, U.S. Secretary of the Treasury and Harry White both wanted it abolished. On July 10, 1944, they seemed about to get their wish. Wilhelm Keilhau, of the Norwegian delegation at Bretton Woods introduced a motion to liquidate the BIS.

No one spoke publicly in defense of the BIS. But behind the scenes its defenders – sections of the State Department, Wall Street, the Bank of England, the British Treasury, and Foreign Office – went into action. There was a bitter battle between those who wanted to see the German war machine completely dismantled after the war and those who envisaged a penitent giant re-emerging from the ashes as key players in a new united Europe.

> Harry White saw the BIS clearest. The bank's emphasis on its supposed neutrality was an alibi for its future role in reconstructing Europe, he argued:
>
> *They hope to be a moderating influence in the treatment of Germany during the peace conference. That is why Germany has treated it with the greatest of care. She has permitted her to pay dividends; she has let the people in BIS come and go across enemy territory; she has been extremely careful and well-disposed to the BIS, because she nursed that baby along in the hope that that would be a useful agency that would protect her interests beyond that of any other institution around the peace table would.*[15]

The Germans were not the only ones who recognized the future usefulness of the BIS. The same was true of powerful banking interests in the City of London and on Wall Street. These top banking barons are the ones who pull the strings to make presidents and prime ministers dance. The bankers must have believed that they could use the BIS to screen the real centers of power in the Western

World. If so, their prescience was remarkable because that is exactly how the real world has evolved.

The close connection between the banking industry and the big transnational industries is another area where close collaboration was to become the dominant factor. So the lines between justice for horrendous crimes and geo-political interests became hopelessly blurred.

In July 1945 the U.S. occupation authorities asked [Allen] Dulles to furnish a list of Germans 'eligible on the basis of ability and political record for posts in a reconstituted German administration.' The first set of lists was quickly submitted. But by autumn, Dulles, now running the OSS station in Berlin, had more detailed information about suitable German bankers. Much of this would have come from McKittrick.

In September 1945 Dulles submitted his new white list. It was divided into two categories: A and B. On the A list were three names judged suitable for 'higher posts in a ministry.' The B list contained five names that were suggested for 'lesser posts such as Bureau head or division chief.'[16] Among the names in group A was that of Ernst Hülse, the former head of the BIS banking department. Hülse, said Dulles, enjoyed 'excellent connections with banking circles abroad,' had a Jewish wife, and was definitely anti-Nazi. Hülse was appointed to the Reichsbank in the British zone and was named president of the central bank for the federal state of Nordheim-Westfalen.

The name on the B list was that of Karl Blessing, whom Dulles described as a 'prominent businessman and financial expert' with 'considerable experience in international trade.'[17]

Dulles did not mention that Blessing had been arrested and imprisoned while the Allies considered whether to charge him with war crimes consistent with his record. Nor did he say that he had supported Blessing's release.

The whitewashing of Blessing was not the exception, but the Rule. Declassified telegrams revealed that Dulles had long planned to rescue important German industrialists and scientists. In January 1945, Dulles wrote to William Casey, who was running operations inside Germany and who later served as CIA director in the 1980s:

> *My project contemplates that in normal course of events and without any prior contact with us but merely to escape impending chaos, important German industrialists, scientists, etc., will desire to find some haven, preferably Switzerland. If Switzerland is closed to them, these men might possibly turn to Russia as their only alternative…. Discreet preliminary conversations indicate some hope of securing Swiss cooperation.*[18]

Not everyone in Washington approved. The following month First Lady Eleanor Roosevelt wrote to her husband, 'Memo for the President. Allen Dulles who is in charge of Bill Donovan's outfit in Paris has been counsel, closely tied up with the Schroeder Bank. That is likely to be the representative of the underground Nazi interests after the war. There seems to be in Paris a great many people who are pretty close to the big business side![19]

The president's wife was certainly well informed about the importance of the Schroeder bank network, which reached from Germany to London and New York, and to the BIS via Kurt von Schröder. But by summer 1945, after the death of her husband, Mrs. Roosevelt's opinions counted for little in Washington.[20]

Pity! The die was cast. The vast majority of top Nazis had escaped trial and punishment. Many were appointed to important posts in their own country while others relocated to other countries in Europe and South America. The United States, thanks first to Operation Paperclip and then post-war immigration, became home to a very large contingent, many of whom were placed in positions of significant influence.

The BIS escaped the guillotine and, after a bit of a rough patch, emerged triumphant and flourishing. Its membership increased. Its influence became all pervasive. It played a significant role in the unification of Europe. Most important of all, just as the top bankers had hoped, it became a powerful vehicle for the transfer of power from democratic nation states to an unelected, unaccountable, bureaucratic institution acting on the private advice from the world's top bankers.

It has usurped the power of nation states to establish their own rules and reserve requirements for banks and used their puppet central bankers to advise their respective governments to accept BIS rules as normal in a new international world order. For this I can never forgive them.

Canada had a quite satisfactory system in place from 1939-1974 when the money creation function was shared between the federal government and the private banks. It worked well and gave us the best years of the 20th century. Then the BIS butted in and persuaded the Bank of Canada to abandon its shareholders, the Canadian people, and buy the notion that privately-owned banks were entitled to a de facto monopoly to manufacture money. But, tragically, all of it as debt that can never, ever, be repaid. Hence austerity and moribund economies operating well below their potential.

The BIS drew up a set of international rules called Basel I. These were not compulsory but were promoted as universally desirable. When the first shot proved to be less than perfect they were re-written as Basel II. The banks were still able to keep their slot-machine manufacturing capability where they put in a nickel and get a dollar back in return – plus interest, of course.

After the Wall Street meltdown of 2007-2008, from which the world is still suffering, it became obvious that BIS rules were inadequate to prevent such crimes against humanity. Consequently, the BIS scrambled to devise Basel III. I read through it recently and it still resembles Swiss cheese with holes big enough to drive a truck through. No wonder the bankers love the BIS.

To give the appearance of doing something new and helpful the BIS established an organization called the Financial Stability Board. Despite the advertising, and the gentle hand of Mark Carney, former governor of the Bank of Canada and then promoted to Governor of the Bank of England, it is still fraudulently labelled. It is still a Financial Instability Board in reality, despite the hype to the contrary.

The Bank for International Settlements is Hopeless!

In its annual report in June 2013, it said:

> Six years have passed since the eruption of the global financial crisis, yet robust, self-sustaining, well balanced growth still

eludes the global economy.... Central banks cannot do more without compounding the risks they have already created.... [They must] encourage needed adjustments of ever-larger quantities of government securities.... Delivering further extraordinary monetary stimulus is becoming increasingly perilous, as the balance between its benefits and costs is shifting. Monetary stimulus alone cannot provide the answer because the roots of the problem are not monetary. Hence, central banks must manage a return to their stabilization role, allowing others to do the hard but essential work of adjustment.

For "adjustment," read "structural adjustment" – imposing austerity measures on the people in order to balance budgets and pay down national debts. In plain English that means a kind of permanent recession that denies many millions of people the opportunity to find useful employment and the self respect of contributing to their own welfare. In my opinion this is not even worthy of discussion!

Even before reading Adam Lebor's book I was convinced that the BIS should be on the execution list. Its pre-war and post-war record is unacceptable to anyone who believes in democratic responsibility. Its love of privilege, fine dining, vintage wines and exemption from taxation provide exactly the wrong principles for a world seeking meaning and direction. Its elitist attitude is offensive to those who believe in equality of opportunity.

Most alarming of all, it aids and abets the robber barons and their Ponzi scheme which impoverishes much of the world and is undermining the very existence of Western civilization as we have known it. It has to be replaced by an institution that works for the people rather than against them. It won't be easy and probably can't be done until the Fed is nationalized and it, or its successor Central Bank of the United States casts its ballot in favor of a new World Bank for International Settlements.

I would urge anyone who is genuinely concerned about the future of planet Earth to read the *Tower of Basel*, by Adam Lebor, and make up your own mind about the nature of the crisis upon which the future of the world depends.

Chapter Six

THE IMF: IT'S TIME FOR IT TO GO!

*"To Everything There is a Season, and a Time to Every Purpose
Under Heaven: A Time to be Born and a Time to Die."*

– Ecclesiastes 3:1-2

I am somewhat ashamed to admit that for many years I did not pay much attention to what the International Monetary Fund (IMF) was doing. I knew of its origin, of course, as part of the 1944 Bretton Woods agreement designed to stabilize the post-World War II international financial system. The IMF's role was to provide member governments with short-term assistance when their foreign exchange reserves got too low as a result of propping up their currency to maintain the fixed exchange rate that had been agreed to.

Over the years, however, the system changed dramatically. The gold standard was abandoned, and many of the world's leading currencies were deregulated. Floating, rather than fixed, exchange rates became the wave of the future. That meant a reduced necessity for central banks to intervene in currency markets and consequently little need to maintain such large foreign exchange reserves. A logical consequence was that the IMF lost its *raison d'être*. Its job was redundant.

With these vague images in mind, it didn't surprise me that the IMF was seldom in the news. Since all appeared quiet on the journalistic front, I must have assumed that whatever the IMF was doing was of minor consequence and not newsworthy. This naïve assumption ended like a dream interrupted by a clap of thunder when, in 1995, I read Steven Solomon's frightening book *The Confidence Game: How Unelected Central Bankers Are Governing the*

Changed Global Economy.[1] I found that the IMF, like most big bu-reaucracies without a real mandate, had been handed a new one, and a highly questionable one at that.

The story begins with President Jimmy Carter's appointment of Paul Volcker as Chairman of the Federal Reserve Board and the latter's coronation as economic czar of the world financial system. Volcker, like most economists under the hypnotic spell of Milton Friedman, misread the economic tea leaves and decided to in-duce the worst recession since the Great Depression of the 1930s. I would like to review some of the economic consequences, and then return in the next chapter to some of the horrendous social fallout from the Fed's tight money and high interest rate policy.

Economies slowed, government deficits increased, and these were rolled over into debt and compounded at high interest rates. In the United States, the total government, corporate and person-al debt, which had been remarkably stable at about 140% of GDP, suddenly took off and headed towards 190% in less than two de-cades – the highest since before the Great Depression. Monetarism helped put the inflation genie back in the bottle but, in doing so, let the debt genie out of the bottle with a debt time bomb in its hands.

The effect on banks and banking was devastating. Led by Cit-icorp Chairman, Walter Wriston, the big international banks had decided that lending vast amounts of money to Less Developed Countries (LDCs) was an easy way to get rich. Even small banks with no expertise climbed aboard the gravy train. Between 1970 and 1982, the profits on international operations (mostly Less De-veloped Country loans) of America's seven largest banks soared from 22% to 60% of total earnings.[2]

What the banks failed to anticipate was the effect of high inter-est rates on borrowers' ability to repay. Suddenly, the poor countries found they could not earn enough foreign exchange to pay the in-terest on their external debt. Poland and Hungary had to refinance, Mexico teetered on the brink of default, and one Latin American country after another found itself in the same leaky boat and unable to meet its financial obligations. If markets had been allowed to reign supreme, virtually all of America's largest banks would have bit the dust. This didn't happen, however, and even though the entire international financial system came within a hair's breadth of collapse, that catastrophe was seemingly miraculously averted.

Actually, it wasn't a miracle. It was a wondrously complicated web of intrigue and deceit, and anyone who has the stomach for it can read the gory details in *The Confidence Game*.[3] The bottom line is that the public was kept blissfully unaware that their banks were technically insolvent until the IMF could ride to the rescue with taxpayers' money. Although there are many ordinary citizens who might applaud the bailout on the grounds that it was preferable to the alternative, it set a dreadful precedent. It telegraphed the message that banks could make irresponsible loans, willy-nilly, without fear of the consequences. They knew that taxpayers were always standing by at the ready with a life preserver handy.

The IMF as lifeguard, however, does not ride to the rescue of the countries and people negatively affected by the excesses of international capitalism. It is the banks and financial institutions that are the objects of its largesse. They are the ones who pick up their welfare checks from the taxpayers of the world.

In addition, and in a sense even worse, the IMF attaches conditions to its loan agreements requiring recipient countries to adjust their macro-economic policies in order to conform with the ideological imperatives of the Washington consensus – a lethal economic cocktail that has been totally discredited since the meltdown of 2007-2008.

As I admitted at the beginning of this section, I was not as *au courant* as someone interested in public policy should have been. Like most people in developed countries, I was too busy and too pre-occupied to keep informed. My four daily newspapers smother me with information overload, but seldom provide in-depth analyses of Third World problems. Fortunately, friends recommended that I read *The Globalisation of Poverty: Impacts of IMF and World Bank Reforms,* by Michel Chossudovsky,[4] professor of economics at the University of Ottawa, and *50 Years is Enough: The Case Against the World Bank and the International Monetary Fund,* edited by Kevin Danaher.[5]

The case histories are enough to bring tears to the eyes of anyone whose heart is not made of granite. I asked one of my sons, your average MBA, to read *50 Years is Enough*. Obviously affected, his bravest retort was, "It does go on and on." That is the truth. It goes on and on from one country to another to another, recounting in painful detail the economic and human carnage in the wake of IMF 'reforms.' In reality, an IMF reform is a synonym for disaster.

The devaluation of a nation's currency has often been a pre-condition for IMF "help." The social impact is immediate and brutal. Prices of food staples, essential drugs, fuel and other necessities increase overnight. Government subsidies for the basics have to be reduced or eliminated. IMF packages often specifically prohibit domestic wage increases to compensate for the rapid decline in purchasing power.

Borders must be opened to foreign products. Domestic industries, unable to compete with imports, must be allowed to fail. This is the exact opposite of the protectionism that allowed Germany to build a powerful domestic industrial base.

Open borders and unrestricted imports create balance of payments problems. So the IMF encourages Third World countries to concentrate on growing food and specialty crops for export, instead of food for their own people. Millions of additional people are subject to starvation diets as a result.

IMF insistence that many developing countries concentrate on commodity exports, to earn the U.S. dollars with which to pay the interest on their debts, led to a world over-supply, and consequently lower prices. That meant LDCs had even more trouble earning enough to service their existing debt, so, they had to borrow extra to pay the interest on what they already owed, and go further into debt – an inadvertent contribution to the world debt crisis.

Another condition of IMF "help" is that its central bank must be independent from political influence as a protection against the alleged inflationary bias of governments. That means that a country in financial distress cannot ask its central bank to come to its aid through money creation when that is deemed essential – as Canada and other countries did to escape the Great Depression, help finance World War II and post-war development. The

IMF effectively assumes monetary sovereignty in the countries that it "aids."

As Michael Chossudovsky points out:

> The IMF, on behalf of the (international) creditors, is in a position virtually to paralyze the financing of real economic development. Incapable of using domestic monetary policy to mobilize its internal resources, the country becomes increasingly dependent on international sources of funding which has the added consequence of increasing the level of external indebtedness.[6]

What we see here is a level of meddling in domestic affairs unequalled in modern history. It is intolerable intervention with negative consequences. If the Sub-Saharan countries had achieved higher growth, better health, higher education and better environmental protection, some applause would be in order. But, the converse is true. With the IMF, as with the Washington consensus, it is "promises, promises." Instead of short-term pain bringing long-term gain, as solemnly promised, all it has delivered is long-term pain.

All the Same Mistakes in South-East Asia

When the IMF had wreaked such havoc worldwide, you would think a different approach might have been tried in South-East Asia. No such luck! U.S. Treasury officials had regained confidence from their experience with Mexico in 1994. By July 1997, the Mexican peso had been stable for a year and this was considered a triumph for American policy. It didn't seem to matter that Mexico had endured a painful recession and that the peasants were really suffering. The peso was okay, the international investors were secure, and that's all that mattered.

The situation in Thailand was similar, but less severe, when it devalued its currency in June 1997, after running out of foreign exchange. When it turned to the U.S. for help the till was dry, but Thailand would get a $17 billion loan package for promising to impose high interest rates, restrain government spending, close floundering banks and let its currency fall in order to boost exports and reduce imports. It was the same old bitter medicine that had failed so miserably so often.

What became clear, however, was the extent to which the IMF had been reduced to a tool of U.S. foreign policy, as determined in the Treasury Department. Long suspected to be the case, any pretence that the IMF was acting independently ceased to matter. Treasury Secretary Robert Rubin and Deputy Treasury Secretary Lawrence Summers called the shots with a little private advice from the then Federal Reserve Board Chairman Alan Greenspan, and the enthusiastic collaboration of International Monetary Fund chief Michel Camdessus and his deputy Stanley Fischer, the Massachusetts Institute of Technology (MIT) economist who had been hand picked by Mr. Summers. These five men must be one of the most fearsome collection of ideologues the world has known.

They say that power corrupts, so it is not too surprising that the U.S. scuttled a Japanese proposal for an Asian Monetary Fund of about $100 billion to cope with regional crises. Mr. Rubin and Mr. Summers opposed the idea because they feared the fund would offer big loans with less stringent conditions than the IMF demanded. That was their stated objection. Skeptics suggest that the real objection was the potential loss of power and control.

The IMF has served American interests well. It has imposed the Washington Consensus on proud but helpless nations. Thus it was to be expected, when it was South Korea's turn, that the previously proud Asian Tiger would be told to toe the line. Deputy U.S. Treasury Secretary, Lawrence Summers, boasted that the IMF package did more to promote the U.S. trade agenda in South Korea than decades of bilateral negotiations.[7]

Summers did not underline the fact that of the $58 billion rescue package that the IMF and the U.S. had assembled, much of the money flowed right back out to pay Korean banks' debts to foreign banks. Once again the financial gods were appeased with a sacrificial offering of peoples' money.

Keeping the financial gods happy became standard procedure. The policy that had worked so well in Mexico, South Korea and

Thailand was ready for Indonesia in one of the most extreme examples of outside meddling ever imposed. When this led to widespread rioting, the best that IMF chief Michel Camdessus could do was express concern. He said he was worried about the social impact of economic reforms.[8]

Camdessus went on to defend IMF policy as he told a conference in Melbourne, Australia, that Asian nations being nursed back to economic health under IMF bailouts – Indonesia, Thailand and South Korea – were each responsible for their own plight.

"Sometimes a medicine creates even more pain," he said.[9] Some of us would say it was the IMF medicine that created more pain. Harvard economist Jeffrey Sachs was on target when he said: "This crisis didn't have to happen. It was not an inevitable feature of the weakness of Asia. It's a bad accident that simply keeps getting worse and worse."[10]

As the Asian crisis deepened, calls for IMF reform became widespread. Many observers called for greater transparency and accountability. Others, myself included, thought that the total package of medicine being forced down countries' throats was more likely to kill than cure. Perhaps long-term and serious disability would be more precise. In any event the "success" in South East Asia was to set stage for the next big regional crisis which was to be members of the European Union.

A Global Regulator

Meanwhile, one of the wild ideas being circulated in official circles has been a proposal to amalgamate the IMF and World Bank into one giant lender of last resort with trillions in capital – enough to cope with the largest of crises. But, if the charge sticks that the IMF has become little more than a fire brigade for private banks that make imprudent loans, increasing its capital sounds like pouring gasoline on a fire.

This fear cannot be dismissed lightly. To quote J. Richard Finlay, chairman of the Centre for Corporate & Public Governance, a Toronto-based think tank: "As things stand now, the IMF can always count on the support and lobbying clout of the global banking community. And the world's top bankers can always count on the old boys at the IMF to make them 'whole,' as U.S. Treasury Secretary Robert Rubin so quaintly put it.[11]

The IMF as Watchdog

One of the least tenable roles for the IMF is that of global financial watchdog, a kind of "supervisor of supervisors" with authority that transcends national boundaries and treats the world as one financial entity. This idea, put forward by Paul Martin, when he was Canada's Finance Minister, and endorsed by the Group of Seven (G7) countries in London, in May 1998, was overtaken by time and reality.

The real naïveté of Paul Martin and those politicians and officials who endorsed his plan to give the IMF a watchdog role, revolves around the assumption that it is possible to forecast financial crises in a fully global, unregulated financial system. It is not possible! So rather than spend taxpayers' money to establish or enhance a bureaucracy whose real role is "bailing out irresponsible banks," it is far better to consider a means of changing the banking system in a way that will provide stability and some predictability.

Wind Up the IMF

As for the IMF, it should be wound up, and the sooner the better. All the big words used by those who would reform it, words like transparency, enhanced supervision, better monitoring and greater sensitivity, are simply words. You can paint a leopard's spots but that won't change the nature of the beast. Its voracious appetite to interfere cannot be contained, so it must go.

This position has been supported by some very experienced people. Former Secretary of the Treasury, George Shultz, laid out the intellectual case in congressional testimony. He objected to "a pattern of escalation of ambition of the IMF" which would only grow if its request for increased capital was granted. The world financial system would be better off without the IMF, he argued, "because creditors would learn certain lessons. Don't loan money when there are questionable risks. Realize you'll be held accountable for your mistakes."[12]

In his appearance at a hearing of Congress's joint economic committee in May 1998, Shultz repeated and elaborated on arguments he had made earlier in an op-ed piece in the *Wall Street Journal*, which he co-wrote with former Treasury Secretary William Simon and former Citicorp Chairman Walter Wriston. "The IMF is ineffective, unnecessary and obsolete. We do not need another IMF ... Once the Asian crisis is over we should abolish the one we have."[13]

A surprising ally was Milton Friedman who endorsed this conclusion in his own op-ed article in the *Wall Street Journal* on October 13, 1998. While not blaming private lenders for accepting the IMF's implicit offer of insurance against currency risk, he did blame the international agency for offering it. Friedman shared my conviction that the U.S. and its allies are derelict in allowing taxpayers' money to be used to subsidize private banks and other financial institutions.

Other critics of the IMF include Harvard economist Jeffrey Sachs and Henry Kissinger, former U.S. Secretary of State in the Nixon era. In an article he wrote for the French newspaper *Le Monde* under the title "The IMF does more harm than good," Kissinger said: "It almost always pushes austerity measures that result in a brutal fall in standard of living, an explosive increase in unemployment and poverty." Furthermore, for him, the IMF "is always blind to the consequences of its decisions."[14]

Neither Sachs nor Kissinger recommended abolition of the IMF, settling instead for a modified and considerably reduced role. But that didn't happen. Fast forward to the 21st century and a stream of financial crises unprecedented since the Great Depression of the 1930s.

An article in the *New York Times* of October 22, 2008, headed "Scandal Hinders I.M.F.'s Role in Global Lending," a reference to Dominique Strauss-Kahn, the IMF managing director who was under investigation for alleged impropriety with a former senior official, began as follows.

> Washington – The International Monetary Fund, onetime firefighter for the global economy, is suddenly being called back into action, even as its chief stumbles on his way to the rescue.
> The fund is nearing agreements to make emergency loans to Iceland and Ukraine, and discussing aid packages with Pa-

kistan and Hungary – moves that would thrust it back into the thick of a global crisis after a frustrating period in which it was a bystander.

It is a welcome return to form for the fund, which lent billions of dollars to crisis-torn economies in Indonesia, Mexico and Argentina – and was later shunned by countries for the strict conditions that it attached to bailouts.[15]

As the size and scope of the European sovereign debt crisis became known it appeared that the IMF would need a large cash infusion to meet the demand. An article in Toronto's *Globe and Mail* on November 3, 2008 reports how the U.K.'s prime minister rode to the rescue.

A demonstration of how the financial crisis is reordering the world economy was on full display in the Middle East over the weekend.

First to Kuwait, then Saudi Arabia and then Qatar, British Prime Minister Gordon Brown went cap in hand, asking these emerging market economies for 'hundreds of billions of dollars' to help the International Monetary Fund rescue a growing number of countries from imminent bankruptcy.'

'If we are to stop the spread of the financial crisis, we need a better global insurance policy to help distressed economies,' Mr. Brown, a former finance minister, told reporters in Riyadh. 'That is why I have called for more resources for the IMF.[16]

The problem persisted and became a major item for the G20 world leaders when they met at Cannes, France in November 2011. European leaders were hoping for support in raising the $1.4 trillion bailout fund necessary to prevent countries like Italy and Spain from being part of a larger financial meltdown. But when Canadian Prime Minister Stephen Harper expressed the view that Europe was wealthy enough to solve its own problems, and President Barack Obama concurred, the Europeans were left empty-handed. As the *Toronto Star* reported:

The best that could be agreed upon was a plan to ask G20 finance ministers to look at measures to add more firepower to the International Monetary Fund, the Washington, D.C.-based institution that acts as the lender of last resort for struggling governments. The finance ministers will take up that task early next year.[17]

The bottom line is that there never will be an acceptable solution to the sovereign debt problem so long as the present insane private banking monopoly remains in place. Bailouts are debt that has to be repaid with interest. But when the IMF is involved the conditions result in more austerity and slower economic growth. Nobel Laureate Joseph Stiglitz, one of the few economists I have heard of who deserves to be read, calls them "beggar-thy-neighbor policies."

> Of all the mistakes the IMF committed as the East Asian crisis spread from one country to another in 1997 and 1998, one of the hardest to fathom was the Fund's failure to recognize the important interactions among the policies pursued in the different countries. Contractionary policies in one country not only depressed that country's economy but had adverse effects on its neighbors. By continuing to advocate contractionary policies the IMF exacerbated the *contagion*, the spread of the downturn from one country to the next. As each country weakened, it reduced its imports from its neighbours, thereby pulling its neighbors down.[18]

Sovereign countries (outside the Eurozone) can print their own money which doesn't have to be paid back. That is a better solution than letting private banks print (computer entry) each country's annual shortfall putting citizens in the hopeless situation of spending the rest of their lives trying to pay it off, with interest.

What the world needs now is not a reformed IMF, even if that were possible; it needs a massive relief from unsustainable debt. Certainly, it does not need an IMF whose principal function is to pass the tin cup for needy banks and financial institutions. The time has come for a clean start without the IMF and without any of the conditions it has imposed on the poorest of the poor. In addition, all of its outstanding loans should be forgiven and written off. For some countries, at least, it would be a small nudge back along the road to prosperity.

PRESIDENT'S SIGNATURE ENACTS CURRENCY LAW

Wilson Declares It the First of Series Constructive Acts to Aid Business.

PRESIDENT WOODROW WILSON.

Makes Speech to Group Democratic Leaders.

Conference Report Adopted Senate by Vote of 43 to 2

Banks All Over the Country Haste Enter Federal Reserve System

Gov-Elect Walsh Calls Passage of A Fine Christmas Present.

WILSON SEES DAWN OF NEW ERA IN BUSINESS

Aims to Make Prosperity Free to Have Unimpeded Momentum.

HOME VIEWS OF CURRENCY ACT

"A Christmas present to the people of the country," is the name Gov-Elect David I. Walsh gives to the Currency act.

"I think," he said last night, "that President Wilson and the National Congress are to be congratulated upon the enactment of the Currency bill.

"The purpose of the act is one

FOUR PENS US BY PRESID

WASHINGTON, Dec 23—Pr Wilson signed the Glass-Ow rency bill at 6:01 o'clock in the presence of members of inet, the Congressional Cu on Banking and Currency a ocratic leaders in Congress ally.

With a few strokes of the President converted into

Newspaper report of the enactment of the Federal Reserve Act, December 24, 1913.

Chapter Seven

THE BIGGEST HEIST
IN HISTORY

*"The Federal Reserve (privately-owned banks) are one of the most
corrupt institutions the world has ever seen."*
– Senator Louis T. McFadden (For 22 years Chairman of the U.S.
Banking and Currency Commission)

The Fed, as you may not know, but might guess from the haste with which it rides to the rescue of the big New York banks when they are in trouble, was the brainchild of the barons of Wall Street. Taking a leaf from the memoirs of John D. Rockefeller Sr., who loudly proclaimed that he didn't like competition and proved the validity of his thesis by buying up or making deals with his competitors, the heads of New York's most powerful banks concluded that genuine competition was not a profitable policy. So they decided to do something about it.

A small, select group organized a very secret meeting at the private resort of J.P. Morgan on Jekyll Island, off the coast of Georgia. There, in the atmosphere of a mystery thriller, they agreed on an audacious plan. Their scheme, devised by Paul M. Warburg, and subsequently adopted by Congress, was the creation of a legal private monopoly to control the U.S. money supply for the benefit of the few under the guise of protecting and promoting the public interest.

"The seven men who attended the secret meeting on Jekyll Island, where the Federal Reserve System was conceived, represented an estimated one-fourth of the total wealth of the entire world." The group comprised of: Nelson W. Aldrich, Henry P. Davison, Charles D. Norton, Abraham P. Andrew, Frank A. Vanderlip, Benjamin Strong and Paul M. Warburg as recorded on page 24 of *The Creature from Jekyll Island: A Second Look at the Federal Reserve* by G. Edward Griffin.[1] Even a quick scan of the names and their connections is enough to convince one that their "creation" was not designed to be in the interests of the American people.

It is a tribute to the skill of the international bankers that they were able to draft a bill, revise it, change its name and make the few window-dressing compromises necessary to get it adopted by Congress just before Christmas when quite a few Representatives must have been dreaming of sugar plum fairies instead of exercising due diligence. Only Congressman Charles Lindberg Sr. seemed to grasp the essence of what was going on.

To put it bluntly, the Congress transferred its sovereign constitutional right to create money to the sole custody of a small group of private bankers. The magnitude of the heist is unprecedented in the history of the world – the numbers now are in the high trillions.

If, instead of copying some European experiments, the U.S. had established a publicly-owned central bank mandated to serve the interests of the American people, the U.S. federal debt could have been zero today, instead of $16 trillion and rising. There would have been no interminable wrangling about increasing debt limits, and budgets could have been addressed rationally. But that is what might have been. This book is dedicated to what has to be done to reverse the damage before it becomes fatal.

Soon after the Federal Reserve bill was passed, the magnitude of the tragedy began to be recognized. William Jennings Bryan, who acted as Democrat whip, later said: "In my long political career, the one thing I genuinely regret is my part in getting the banking and currency legislation (Federal Reserve Act of 1913) enacted into law."[2] President Woodrow Wilson, just 3 years after passage of the Act, wrote: "A great industrial nation is controlled by its system of credit. Our system of credit is concentrated (in the Federal Reserve System). The growth of the nation, therefore, and all our activities are in the hands of a few men .... We have come to be one of the worst ruled, one of the most completely controlled and dominated governments in the civilized world."[3] But the bill was not repealed; now, more than 100 years later, the sell-out is still the law. This makes you wonder what the people's representatives have been doing to earn their salaries.

The people in charge of the original deception were very far-seeing. They realized that when future governments had to borrow from them they would need a constant income stream to pay the interest on the bonds. So they persuaded the government to introduce income taxes, first as a temporary measure, but later permanently, so that it would be able to meet its obligations to the bondholders. In fiscal year 2005, total individual income taxes in the U.S. totalled $927 billion. Of that amount $352 billion, or 38%, was required just to pay interest on the federal debt. The figure would be higher now. The tragedy is that probably not one cent of that $352 billion was necessary.

It wasn't long after the ink had dried on the Federal Reserve Act before the banksters, as they are often called by people who really understand how the banking system works, decided that an independent press might catch on to the chicanery. Oscar Calloway, is reported in the Congressional Record of February 9, 1917, as follows.

> In March 1915, the J.P. Morgan interests, the steel, shipbuilding, and powder interests, and their subsidiary organizations, got together twelve men high up in the newspaper world, and employed them to select the most influential newspapers in the United States and a sufficient number of them to control generally the policy of the daily press of the United States.... They found it was only necessary to purchase the control of 25 of the greatest papers. The 25 papers were agreed upon; emissaries were sent to purchase the policy, national and international, of these papers; ... an editor was furnished for each paper to properly supervise and edit information regarding the questions of preparedness, militarism, financial policies, and other things of national and international nature considered vital to the interests of the purchasers [and to suppress] everything in opposition to the wishes of the interests served.[4]

World War I was a boon for the banking interests which created tons of money in exchange for government bonds. When the war was over, the money supply was great enough to sustain the house of cards and create a credit bubble which burst in 1929. Sadly, it was Wall Street insiders who inserted the needle after ensuring that they would emerge from the disaster with their wealth intact, and their power enhanced. Seldom in history have an elite few been able to inflict so much pain and misery on millions of innocents.

In the wake of the Great Depression, the U.S. Senate Banking and Currency Committee Report that became widely known as the Pecora Report on the Practices of Stock Exchanges, indicated that there were insiders who benefited from the crash.

"Legal chicanery and pitch darkness were the banker's stoutest allies," Pecora wrote in his memoir.[5]

To make matters worse, the Fed adopted policies that lengthened and deepened the extent of the crisis. I agree with the observation Milton Friedman and Anna Jacobson Schwartz made in their epic *A Monetary History of the United States, 1867-1960.*[6]

When the Federal Reserve Banks closed their doors on March 4, 1933, "The central banking system, set up primarily to render impossible the restrictions of payments by commercial banks, itself joined the commercial banks in a more widespread, complete, and economically disturbing restriction of payments than had ever been experienced in the history of the country. One can certainly sympathize with [President] Hoover's comment about the episode: 'I concluded [the Reserve Board] was indeed a weak reed for a nation to lean on in time of trouble.' "[7] Not only has there been little change in attitude since the 1930s, it appears that little has been learned from the experience. Americans still put their trust in a system regulated by a Fed which gives the interests of the banks and the money-lenders a higher priority than the interests of the country.

Admittedly, the Fed, like most central banks, provided some assistance in helping to provide low-cost money for use by the federal government in financing World War II. Soon after the war, after a successful battle with President Truman, it reverted to its policy of serving the interests of the descendants of the families responsible for its birth, to the near total exclusion of the average American.

Worse, it officially adopted the policies of Milton Friedman and his colleagues at the University of Chicago, and became an active participant in the monetarist revolution. This was mandated by the Policy Committee of the Bank for International Settlements in 1974 with the active support of Fed Chairman Paul Volcker, a disciple of the Nobel Laureate and his philosophy of a self-regulating banking system in which governments would play no part. It proved to be one of the most disastrous ideas in the history of economics.

Dr. Friedman based his ideas on his study of 100 countries over 100 years which showed that prices were directly related to the growth of the money supply. I contend that his conclusion, while technically correct, was comparable to finding that in 100 countries, for 100 years, summer followed winter. What this truism does not explain is whether the summers were hot and dry, or cold and wet – weather that produced bumper crops or a drought-induced wipeout. Similarly the Friedman analysis completely ignores the most important development in post-World War II economics which was the wage-price spiral caused by the market power of big business, big labor and big government. In *Free to Choose*, where he discusses how the labor market operates, he says: "Here, too, interference by government, through minimum wages, for example, or trade unions, through restricting entry, may distort the information transmitted or may prevent individuals from freely acting on that information."[8]

Quite so! But having observed and objected to the rigidities in the labor market due to government intervention, he proceeds to ignore the connection between wages and prices by denying the existence of cost-push inflation. He pretends that the system is self-regulating and that equilibrium will be restored by some invisible hand.

This blind spot has been noted by many critics. In *Capitalism's Inflation and Unemployment Crisis*, Sidney Weintraub says: "To interpret money wages as 'simply another price' is to mistake flies for elephants." A general wage rise "comprises about 55% of gross business costs, closer to 75% of net costs, and probably even more of variable costs."[9] In fact, money wages constitute the major factor in the economic equation; they far out-shadow any other price.

In view of this, one should not underestimate the significance of Dr. Friedman's unsubstantiated contention that "wage increases in excess of increases in productivity are a result of inflation rather than the cause.[10] This proposition appears to fly in the face of the data. The Economic Report of the President 1995, shows that wages outstripped productivity in the United States every year from 1964 to 1994. Therein lies the principal source of the inflation for that period.

Not only have wages moved up faster than productivity, they outpaced prices in 18 of the 21 years prior to the time Milton and Rose Friedman first published *Free to Choose* in 1980 – the exceptions being '70, '74 and '79. The wage index for the entire 1964-1991 period kept ahead of the price index.

The principal cause of inflation in the western world was not, as Dr. Friedman insisted, classic inflation, i.e. too much money chasing too few goods! It was primarily cost-push inflation, i.e. nominal wages that were a multiple of productivity for 25 consecutive years. This was a new phenomenon that classical economists have not yet incorporated into their textbooks. (For a much more comprehensive analysis of where Friedmanites went wrong see my book *A Miracle in Waiting: Economics that Make Sense*).

Incorrect Diagnosis, Disastrous Treatment

As any good doctor will attest, a wrong diagnosis can result in prescribing medicine with side effects that are far worse than the disease. So as soon as the Bank for International Settlements decided that central banks worldwide should transplant Milton Friedman's classroom abstractions into the real world economy rough waters were inevitable. The cure would indeed be far worse than the disease.

The man of the hour was Paul Adolph Volcker, President Jimmy Carter's nominee who took the helm at the Fed on August 6, 1979.

Volcker was a big man physically, 6' 7," with big plans for change. A devoted Friedmanite he believed that inflation could be licked and stability achieved by simply limiting the growth in the money supply to the same percentage as the growth in the real economy.

When Volcker told the then Treasury Secretary, George Miller, and the President's Council of Economic Advisers' chairman, Charles Schultze, that he proposed to apply strict monetary targets to the banking system they were strongly opposed because they thought that was the road to recession. They were right, and the subsequent recession was a contributing factor in Carter's electoral defeat in November 1980. But Volcker was undeterred by politics.

Social Consequences

The social devastation caused by the 1981-82 recession has been widely discussed. This included massive unemployment on a scale unknown since the Great Depression; tens of thousands of people lost their homes because they couldn't pay the new, higher interest rates on their mortgages; and thousands of bankruptcies occurred when struggling companies couldn't cope with a combination of slack demand and sharply higher interest payments on their bank loans. The inhumane consequences of the Fed's action should have been enough to signal that the cure was as bad or worse than the disease. But there were other economic consequences that were even more far-reaching. The world financial system was rocked to its core and changed in ways that haven't yet been reconciled with the real world of political economy.

The Fed – A Law Unto Itself

When I read that the Fed had never been properly audited I thought of that Biblical adage about "the sins of the fathers being visited on future generations." That certainly is true of the Federal Reserve Act adopted in 1913. The Congress of that year licenced a handful of the richest people in the world to rob the workers of America of a significant slice of their salaries and wages, and to do so silently without sirens screaming, and guns blazing as might happen if any one of us was foolish enough to try robbing a bank.

We, on the other hand, are robbed by people trained as magicians capable of taking money out of our pockets without a real awareness of what is happening to us. In Canada we know, if only after the fact, what our central bank is doing to us. The Bank of Canada, which is 100% owned by Canadian taxpayers, must keep proper accounts, have its books audited by an accredited firm, and make the results available for anyone to see. The Fed has long operated under the conjurer's cloak.

It required a lifetime campaign by former Congressman, Ron Paul, who made the unwarranted power and secrecy of the Federal Reserve his passion from the 1970s until it finally became a national issue, to peel the first layer from the veil of secrecy. His stubborn insistence that the public had the right to know how much their currency was being diluted, and who was benefiting from it, finally paid off despite the opposition of Ben Bernanke, Alan Greenspan and various other bankers who vehemently opposed the audit and lied to Congress about the effects an audit would have on markets. Nevertheless, the results of the first audit in the Federal Reserve's 100-year history were posted on Senator Bernie Sanders' webpage on Saturday, September 1, 2012. The story as reported in *Before Its News*, reads as follows:[11]

What was revealed in the audit was startling:

$16,000,000,000,000.00 had been secretly given out to US banks and corporations and foreign banks everywhere from France to Scotland. For the period between December 2007 and June 2010, the Federal Reserve had secretly bailed out many of the world's banks, corporations, and governments. The Fed likes to refer to these secret bailouts as an all-inclusive loan program, but virtually none of the money has been returned and it was loaned out at 0% interest. Why the Federal Reserve had never gone public about this, or even informed the United States Congress concerning the $16 trillion dollar bailout is obvious – the American public would have been outraged to find out that the Federal Reserve bailed out foreign banks while Americans were struggling to find jobs.

To place the $16 trillion into perspective, remember that the GDP of the United States was only $16.77 trillion in 2013. The entire national debt spanning its 200+ years' history was $19.3 trillion. The latest budget to be debated so vigorously in 2015 was $3.8 trillion and the deficit was $43.5 billion – lower than the year before. So it seems incongruous that there was no debate whether $16,000,000,000,000 would be given to failing banks and failing corporations around the world.

In late 2008, the TARP Bailout bill was passed and loans of $800 million were given to failing banks and companies. That was a blatant lie considering the fact that Goldman Sachs alone received 814 billion dollars. As it turns out, the Federal Reserve donated $2.5 trillion to Citigroup, while Morgan Stanley received $2.04 trillion. The Royal Bank of Scotland and Deutsche Bank, a German bank, split about a trillion and numerous other banks received hefty chunks of the $16 trillion.

This is a clear case of socialism for the rich and rugged, you're-on-your own individualism for everyone else.' Bernie Sanders (Independent, Vermont)

When you have conservative Republican stalwarts like Jim Demint (South Carolina) and Ron Paul (Texas) as well as self-identified Democratic socialists like Bernie Sanders all fighting against the Federal Reserve, you know that it is no longer an issue of Right versus Left. When you have every single member of the Republican Party in Congress and a progressive Congressman like Dennis Kucinich sponsoring a bill to audit the Federal Reserve, you realize that the Federal Reserve is an entity unto itself, which has no oversight and no accountability.

Americans should be swelled with anger and outrage at the abysmal state of affairs when an unelected group of bankers can create money out of thin air and give it out to megabanks and supercorporations like Halloween candy. If the Federal Reserve and the bankers who control it believe that they can continue to devalue the savings of Americans and continue to destroy the US economy, they will have to face the realization that their trillion dollar printing presses will eventually plunder the world economy.

The list of institutions that received the most money from the Federal Reserve can be found on page 131 of the GAO

Audit and are as follows:

Citigroup: **$2.5 trillion** ($2,500,000,000,000)
Morgan Stanley: **$2.04 trillion** ($2,040,000,000,000)
Merrill Lynch: **$1.949 trillion** ($1,949,000,000,000)
Bank of America: **$1.344 trillion** ($1,344,000,000,000)
Barclays PLC (UK): **$868 billion** ($868,000,000,000)
Bear Sterns: **$853 billion** ($853,000,000,000)
Goldman Sachs: **$814 billion** ($814,000,000,000)
Royal Bank of Scotland (UK): **$541 billion** ($541,000,000,000)
JP Morgan Chase: **$391 billion** ($391,000,000,000)
Deutsche Bank (Germany): **$354 billion** ($354,000,000,000)
UBS (Switzerland): **$287 billion** ($287,000,000,000)
Credit Suisse (Switzerland): **$262 billion** ($262,000,000,000)
Lehman Brothers: **$183 billion** ($183,000,000,000)
Bank of Scotland (UK): **$181 billion** ($181,000,000,000)
BNP Paribas (France): **$175 billion** ($175,000,000,000)

And many many more including banks in Belgium of all places. (Google: Government Accountability Office audit of the Federal Reserve, July 21, 2011 to read the 253-page report.)

The list goes on and on!

Wow! Aren't these figures enough to rot your socks? Imagine the Fed diluting the money supply by trillions and without any authority other than its own. The Congress, and as far as we know, the White House, were kept completely in the dark.

Quantitative Easing (QE)

What is Quantitative Easing?

Quantitative easing is a cute and less offensive way of saying "printing money."

Well not actually printing money in the way they show it on television to catch people's attention. There is very little paper money in existence. Nearly all of the money supply, or money-base as it is sometimes called, is simply virtual money – a computer entry to be more specific.

So if the Fed, or any other central bank, wants to increase the supply of (virtual) money, it simply buys government securities, or perhaps even bundles mortgages of uncertain value (who knows?), books them as an asset, and then with a flick of the computer keys creates the (virtual) money to pay for them. It is a kind of Wizard of Oz magic that the banking fraternity has managed to convince themselves, and nearly everyone else, is perfectly legitimate. They can get away with it because no one has looked behind the curtain to check the real credentials of the Wizard.

The stated object of the policy is to increase the cash reserves of the banks and financial institutions, so that they can increase their loans to business and individuals, thus stimulating the economy and providing new jobs for the unemployed. That is the theory, but it works only if you have both willing lenders and borrowers. In the absence of either one or both the medicine creates more questionable side effects than the intended recovery.

In a weak economy with high unemployment and high personal debt loads, there are few people willing or able to take on additional debt. There is a comparable reticence on the part of the lenders, whose alternatives are too attractive when compared to taking on a bundle of high-risk loans.

It is obvious that much of the money – albeit by an indirect route – found its way into the stock market to purchase blue chip securities with higher yields than government treasury bills and bonds. The Dow Jones Index hit an all time high in the Fall of 2013 in the absence of sufficient real economic growth to justify the trend. The small economic advantage comes from the so-called "wealth effect," that makes people who are lucky enough to own a few stocks feel better, and more likely to spend. That is a plus but a small one.

Apologists for QE may be correct when they say that economic growth has been higher since 2007-2008, when Wall Street banks crashed the system, than it would have been otherwise. But critics suggest that the negative consequences outweigh the advantages.

In a May 22, 2013 *Wall Street Journal* article by Andy Kessler titled "The Fed Squeezes the Shadow-Banking System," he argues that QE3 has backfired. Rather than stimulating the economy by expanding the money supply, it has contracted the money supply by removing the collateral needed by the shadow banking system. The shadow system creates about half the credit available to the economy but remains unregulated because it does not involve traditional bank deposits. It includes hedge funds, money market funds, structured investment vehicles, investment banks, and even commercial banks, to the extent that they engage in non-deposit-based credit creation. Kessler wrote:

> "[T]he Federal Reserve's policy – to stimulate lending and the economy by buying Treasuries – is creating a shortage of safe collateral, the very thing needed to create credit in the shadow banking system for the private economy. The quantitative easing policy appears self-defeating, perversely keeping economic growth slower and jobs scarcer."

That explains what he called the "great economic paradox of our time":

> Despite the Federal Reserve's vast, 4½-year program of quantitative easing, the economy is still weak, with unemployment still high and labor-force participation down. And with all the money pumped into the economy, why is there no runaway inflation? ... The explanation lies in the distortion that Federal Reserve policy has inflicted on something most Americans have never heard of: 'repos,' or repurchase agreements, which are part of the equally mysterious but vital 'shadow banking system.' The way money and credit are created in the economy has changed over the past 30 years. Throw away your textbook.[12]

Critics of QE also charge that a lot of it is circulating as "hot money" that is beginning to create inflationary bubbles in several countries around the world. So, you have to wonder about the judgment of Fed leadership. It must have been aware that QE was first used by the Bank of Japan (BOJ) to fight domestic deflation in the early 2000s – officially on March 19, 2001[13] – without noteworthy success. Why copy an experiment that failed to resurrect a flagging Japanese economy?

The bottom line, it appears, is that QE has been good for the banks but not for the people. It is the same old story. Shovel the money into the banking system without any guarantee that it will flow through to the unemployed and underemployed people who are desperate for relief. For the people of the U.S. where money has been so diluted by QE, the whole policy has been one gigantic flop!

There are some profound questions! Why did the Fed create trillions of U.S. dollars to assist U.S. banks that we thought had already been "rescued" with taxpayer's money? Why did the Fed come to the aid of foreign banks, privately-owned corporations and financial institutions? We will probably never know the answer to these questions because there is no law requiring it.

What we do know is that the Fed was subversive to American interests from the outset, and it has to be nationalized or wound up and replaced by a legitimate Bank of the United States that would secure the interests of American taxpayers rather than those of a toxic international banking cartel.

This inestimably important action must be undertaken now – at once! The project will provide a non-partisan litmus test for voters as to whom they should trust. Politicians who enthusiastically support winding up the Fed and replacing it with a genuine people's bank will be worthy of re-election. Foot draggers will deserve to be defeated and wind up in the dustbin of political chicanery.

One final point. The fed has long provided much of the sinuous-muscle power of the international banking cartel which, like a serpent, has been coiling itself ever more tightly around Western civilization, while squeezing the life blood from the hopes and aspirations of millions of increasingly helpless people.

It is well known that the only way to relax a serpent's deadly grip is to cut its head off. That done, all that remains is to administer the life-giving serum essential to restore the patient's health and sanity. Fortunately such a serum can be quickly provided. It is called government-created money (GCM).

Greenback to Federal Reserve Notes.

Chapter Eight

GOVERNMENT-CREATED MONEY

"Whoever controls the volume of money in any country is absolute master of all industry and commerce."

– President James A. Garfield

The right to create money belongs to federal governments. It was once the exclusive prerogative of Kings, Queens and Emperors. When the people rebelled and forced the monarchs to cede much or all of their power to elected representatives, sovereignty with respect to money flowed with it. People and their representatives own the "patents" to create money.

Banks, on the other hand, have no rights. They have only privileges granted by legislatures. Their charters give them privileges that are not available to ordinary people; these can be altered or revoked by the granting authorities. Regretfully, most amendments have been to benefit the banks at the expense of the people they should serve.

The United States created a dreadful problem a little more than 100 years ago when it transferred its sovereign rights to a small group of erudite but ruthless private bankers who have created inestimable loss and heartache for the American people. The only remedy, as I pointed out earlier, is to shut the Fed down and start over again with a publicly-owned central bank.

The Eurozone countries have also created a problem for themselves by transferring their monetary sovereignty to the European Central Bank. This is not a problem that can't be solved by political will based on a much better understanding of what the money-shortage problem really is.

The problem, in a nutshell, is a monetary system in which nearly all "money" is created as debt. Worse, it is all debt that has to be repaid with interest. But no one creates any money with which to pay the interest. The net result is a worldwide sea of debt in which the economies of most countries are drowning beneath the waves of bank-created (debt) money (BCM).

Before recommending the only solution that makes any sense to me, I decided to look at alternatives being espoused by others. The first and easiest is Bitcoins.

Bitcoins

For several months I received e-mails suggesting that I get on the Bitcoin bandwagon. The idea was an innovation – a very successful one for the originators and early subscribers – but I resisted because I had not checked them out against the criteria that must be applied. When I did, I found that Bitcoins are digital, electronic money – phantom money, if you like. They have that characteristic in common with money created by the chartered banks. Consequently, they too, will not contribute to public debt reduction, or play any significant role as an economic stimulus.

Finally, they appear to be subject to price manipulation. On May 28, 2014, Coin Desk, the voice of digital currency, reported that the Bitcoin Price Index (BPI) "recently crossed back above $590 on the 27th of May, representing a 64% gain from 10th April when the price was as low as $360."[1]

A currency with this kind of volatility should be eschewed and allowed to fade away as a footnote to history.

The Gold Standard

Another solution that is being touted in several quarters is a return to currencies that are convertible into gold or silver at a fixed rate. Some monetary reformers have a romantic attachment to this system which has been tried more than once. It did appear to work for short periods, but always had to be abandoned when its fundamental weaknesses created too much strain on the real economy.

There are several fundamental weaknesses. The first and most obvious is that some countries are blessed with significant reserves of gold among their natural resources. Other countries have little gold, or none. This provides a natural and virtually insurmountable handicap.

The second major problem is caused by trade imbalances. Countries with large trade deficits (the U.S. for example) would have to export their gold in payment, on demand. They would then have to shrink their money supply proportionate to the loss of gold, which would cause a recession or depression. (The U.S. at the time of the War of Independence is a classic case.)

Countries with very large trade surpluses, as has happened with Japan and then China, would suffer the opposite problem. If their currencies were based on an ever-increasing gold inventory, rampant inflation would result. The bottom line is that tying the currency supply to the random incidence of one or two commodities doesn't make any sense.

The only common sense solution is the one proposed by the late Yale economics professor Irving Fisher who suggested that the money supply should be tied to a basket of goods and services that comprise the broad range of items that most individuals might want to purchase from time to time. In the real economy that means the money stock should be increased in direct proportion to the increase in goods and services available for purchase.

People often ask if "printing" money isn't inflationary. The answer is "not if it results in the production of additional goods and services." I sometimes compare the real economy to a giant pot of Irish stew that comprises copious quantities of meat, potatoes and diverse vegetables floating in just enough water to provide the perfect consistency. As it is consumed the pot can be replenished by adding additional water and more meat and vegetables in the same proportion. Too much water makes it a thin gruel (inflation) while too little reduces it to mush (high unemployment and economic stagnation).

Returning to the real economy, there are millions of unemployed men and women who ask nothing more than the opportunity to provide the additional goods and services to meet their own needs, and contribute to the general welfare. The only obstacle is an acute shortage of money.

So, what the world desperately needs is a massive infusion of government-created, debt-free money (GCM) to dilute the debt and stimulate economic growth. The actual amount can only be a guess because there is no formula, and only observations after the fact will show how much is required to jump- start the economies that have been in the doldrums since 2007-08. I am suggesting the equivalent of at least $10 trillion U.S. dollars for the first round.

The United States alone should create at least $2 trillion. People all over the world are sick to death with hearing about the U.S. budget and debt ceiling. It is difficult to conceive of two more useless and self-destructive debates. There are other equally or more urgent issues to be addressed.

The difference between bank-created money (BCM) and government-created money is profound. All BCM has to be repaid with interest whereas GCM can be put into circulation debt-free and remains in the money supply permanently. GCM doesn't disappear in times of recession as much of the BCM does. Private banks create "virtual" money out of thin air when they make loans; the opposite occurs when loans are repaid either voluntarily or at the call of the banks. It is just like shovelling the equivalent into a furnace and burning it. When this happens, of course, the money supply decreases, purchasing power disappears and jobs are lost, because money is the life-blood of the economy.

There are, of course, people who insist that all money should be created as debt. This is as obtuse as the assertion that the world was created in six 24-hour days. How does anyone think the existing debt can be paid off if the only way you can coax an economy to grow is to borrow more debt money into existence and go deeper into debt? Anyone who has studied eighth grade mathematics should be able to detect the folly of that myth.

Even conventional economists admit that money is the fuel essential for an economy to grow. That gives us two choices. We can borrow more and go further into debt, which is the only game in town at the moment, albeit a painfully slow game because there is a shortage of credit-worthy borrowers. In my country, Canada, the average household debt is currently 165% of disposable income. Consequently, borrowing more to buy more isn't a good option – especially in view of an inevitable rise in interest rates that will pinch disposable income even more.

The other option is the infusion of large sums of GCM to stimulate the economy and stop the debt curve from rising even further. There are so many real needs that could be addressed if it were not for a shortage of money. There are old neglected bridges and antique sewer and water lines to be replaced, roads to be repaired, new hospitals to be built to provide better health care, and myriad steps to be taken to preserve our ecological heritage.

Myths aside, government expenditures in these areas would create thousands of new jobs – lead to more people paying taxes to increase government revenues and, eventually, to reduce public debt. Where will the money come from? If the Fed can use its computers to create trillions of dollars for the exclusive benefit of bankers, it is surely possible for governments, whose right it is to create money, to use its power to enhance the health and welfare of its citizens. I know this will work because I have personally observed the principle being put to the test.

The Canadian Precedent

In 1938 there were no job openings in Canada – none! Then, in 1939, World War II began and it wasn't long until everyone was either in the armed forces, or working in factories to build the tanks, trucks, airplanes and ships required to support a really magnificent war effort. Unemployment dropped to an historic low of one percent.

You may wonder where the Canadian government got the money to initiate this unprecedented economic miracle. The answer is that the Bank of Canada printed it. The Bank bought government of Canada bonds and paid for them with newly minted cash. The government paid the Bank interest on the bonds which then, because the government owned 100% of the Bank shares, was returned as dividends, with only the cost of administration deducted. In effect, it was near zero cost money that produced such wondrous results.

The newly created money that the government spent into circulation wound up in the private banks where it became what the economists called "high-powered money." High-powered money was really "legal tender" money or "real money" that the banks could use as "cash reserves" which the law allowed them to leverage into bank loans equal to 12½ times their reserves. So if $10 million of what was literally government-created money was ultimately deposited in one of the commercial banks, the banking system was able to create an additional $125 million in book-entry or "virtual" money.

The commercial banks were able to lend this money to help businesses build factories, develop essential products, buy "War Bonds," etc. These large infusions of first government-created cash, followed by bank-created credit, made it possible for Canada to be transformed in a few short years from a largely agricultural and resource-based economy into a significant mixed economy that included a strong manufacturing, industrial and scientific base.

What made this all financially possible was a sharing of the money-creation function between government and the commercial banks. That enabled Canada not only to play a larger-than-life role in the war effort, but also to extend the miracle into the postwar years.

Government-created money played a key role in many of our infrastructure projects like the great St. Lawrence Seaway development, the Trans-Canada highway, new airport terminals and port facilities. It also enabled the federal government to assist the provinces and municipalities with many of their major public works ranging from bridges to sewage-disposal systems.

Another marvellous benefit that government-created money helped make possible was the establishment of a social security network to help citizens in times of distress. Some of us who had lived through the Great Depression of the 1930s were determined that never again would someone lose their home, farm or life savings due to a serious illness of one of the members of the family. Nor would someone be left destitute because he or she was unemployed.

This system of money-creation sharing between the government and private banks worked splendidly for 35 years until 1974, when the Bank of Canada unilaterally changed the rules. As far as I know – and I and others have spent many hours in research without finding any evidence that would refute it – this was done without either advising or obtaining the consent of the Canadian government that owns 100% of the shares on behalf of Canadian taxpayers.

The Governor of the Bank of Canada, Gerald K. Bouey, simply announced that the Bank was adopting monetarism.[2] There was no mention that this was being done to conform to a policy of the BIS, in Basel, Switzerland. Of much greater significance was the failure to disclose that the Bank was adopting the BIS' prohibition of providing low cost money to governments. In future, we would have to borrow in the market, and pay market rates.

This fundamental change in policy was to cost Canadian taxpayers dearly. From fiscal 1974/75 to fiscal 2010/11 we paid one trillion, one hundred million dollars in interest on federal debt alone – almost all of it totally unnecessary. Just imagine what that much money could have accomplished if spent for useful purchases!

Our American cousins fared even worse. Soon after the end of World War II, Wall Street took President Truman on for size, and guess who won? The easy money of the wartime years ended, and Washington had to go cap-in-hand to the banking cartel for its inevitable budget shortfall and pay market rates as high as 18% (set by the Fed) to balance many of its budgets. There is little doubt that the accumulated interest to the present would be in excess of the entire federal debt – in excess of $19 trillion. It is sad to reflect that every cent of the $19 trillion is due to the naivety of U.S. politicians who gave the people's right to create money to a handful of the richest, most cunning men on earth – the wealthiest 1/10 of one percent. When you add to this insult the fact that Wall Street is responsible for the seemingly endless current Great Recession, it is easy to conclude that enough is enough! The gigantic fraud must end! Sanity must prevail!

What To Do?

A group of monetary reformers, predominantly Canadian, have prepared and submitted a plan to our government that could be a model for a new world banking order. The objectives are quite universal:

1. Inject very large sums of government-created, debt-free money into every national economy suffering from high unemployment and low growth. This includes the Eurozone where the actual mechanics are a bit more complicated due to existing treaties. The goals would include reducing the level of world unemployment by half in less than two years. Increased activity on this scale should provide new hope to the middle class who have been subjected to systematic reduction.

2. Provide nation states with the fiscal flexibility to address global warming pretty damn quick before the magnitude of the damage becomes calamitous.

3. First cap and then reduce federal net debt as well as those of states, provinces and municipalities.

4. End immediately the power of the BIS, IMF, World Bank, the Fed and other central banks to destroy democratic institutions and "in the process" Western civilization.

5. End the power of the BIS and the international banking cartel to run the world and, in particular, reduce the leverage of private banks from their present larcenous levels, often equal to 20/1 or more, to 2/1 over a period of 7 years. That means banks would be able to create $200.00 in loans or acquire that amount of interest bearing assets for every $100.00 in cash that they have in their vaults or on deposit with their central banks.

6. Replace an unstable and unsustainable monetary and financial system with one that is both stable and sustainable.

7. Revive the concept of government of, by and for the people before it is snuffed out completely.

We then demanded that our government abandon its austerity budget – an idea that was tried in the 1930s and failed miserably – and adopt a new deal for Canadians. Then, so that they would know exactly what we meant, we spelled it out for them, as follows:

A Social Contract Between
the Government and People of Canada

In view of the fact that our present banking and financial system is unstable, unsustainable and basically immoral, we, the undersigned, on behalf of all Canadians, demand that the federal government use its constitutional power over all matters pertaining to money and banking by forthwith taking the following action to benefit all Canadians:

1. The government of Canada should print fifteen non-transferable, non-convertible,non-redeemable $10 billion nominal value Canada share certificates.

2. Simultaneously, the Justice Department should be asked for a legal opinion as to whether the share certificates qualify as collateral under the Bank of Canada Act. If not, legislation should be introduced to amend the Act to specify their eligibility.

3. The government should then present the share certificates to the Bank of Canada that would forthwith book the certificates as assets against the liability of the cash created, and deposit $150 billion in the government's bank accounts. The federal government should immediately transfer $75 billion to the various provinces and territories in amounts proportional to their population, with the understanding that they would help the municipalities, as appropriate, so that there would be no need to cut back on essential services, or to sell valuable assets.

4. Amend the Bank Act to reverse the 1991 amendments that eliminated the requirement for the Canadian chartered banks to maintain cash reserves against their deposits, and provide the Minister of Finance, or someone acting on his or her behalf, the power to set the level of cash reserves for banks and other deposit-taking institutions up to a maximum of 34%, provided the increase is not less than 5% per annum until the

new 34% base has been established in 7 years. <u>This will ensure that there will be no inflation resulting from the government-created money</u>.

5. The government should repeat the action prescribed in Sections 1 and 3 every year for 7 years or until bank cash reserves reach 34% of their total assets.

6. Once the transition has been made the Governor of the central bank shall, each year, estimate the amount of increase in the money stock required to keep the economy growing at its optimum with the number of job openings being roughly equal to the number of job seekers. He/she shall then acquire, on a predetermined schedule, shares from the federal government in exchange for cash up to 34% of that amount.

7. In the event of a disagreement between the Governor and the Minister of Finance in respect of the amount by which the money supply should be increased, or the rate of interest to be charged by the bank for overnight lending, the view of the Minister shall prevail. In any such case, however, a direction from the Minister shall be in writing and made public forthwith. This procedure is consistent with the principles of democracy, and should eliminate future cases of monetary and fiscal policies being at odds rather than working in harmony.

This formula can be applied to any country that owns its central bank outright, like Canada, or the U.K. Other countries, especially the United States, must reclaim control of their sovereign right to create their own money. In view of the fact that immediate action is essential for the average citizen, the President of the United States can take advantage of a legislative anomaly and have the Treasury mint two trillion-dollar platinum coins to begin the process of economic stimulation, and end the debt ceiling barrier. If the Secretary of the Treasury objects, the President should fire him and appoint a replacement who understands what "public service" means.

This expedient would buy enough time for Congress to remedy its 100-year-old blunder of giving the people's birthright to a handful of wealthy bankers. The Fed must be wound up because there will be no peace on earth to people of goodwill until it is. Total reparations for the damage done will be impossible. Action now, however, will end the carnage, and the establishment of a wholly owned central bank along the lines of the Canadian model will provide a ray of hope for a better, fairer world for all humankind.

The Eurozone has created its own problem resulting in horrendous hardship for some of its member states. If the general welfare of all its citizens is given the highest priority, however, there is no reason why a formula cannot be devised that would allow the European Central Bank to create debt-free money for each of the member countries in exchange for non-transferable, non-convertible, non-redeemable shares in those countries, in direct proportion to their population. There is no impediment except the political will, even if it means amending the provisions of a treaty.

As a life-long monetary reformer, I have been seeking a solution that would clip the wings of the elite robber barons who have been ripping off ordinary citizens for centuries, produce a just, workable and stable financial regime worldwide and, most important, transfer control of the most powerful tool in the economic arsenal from private hands to those of the elected representatives of the people. Although this is not an easy task, it is entirely feasible and absolutely essential – the most urgent reform facing humankind today!

Still there are a number of obstacles to be overcome. The first, and most formidable, is the nearly universal ignorance about the nature of money, what it is, and who prints (creates) it. Only about one percent of the population is aware that almost all money is "virtual" – nothing more than a computer entry.

It is little wonder, then, that the private banks' "licence to steal" has become so much a part of our everyday life that it is seldom questioned. When the G20 world leaders met in Toronto in June 2010, they spent much of their time discussing how to prop up the unstable, debt-based system that has produced twenty-five recessions and depressions in the U.S. since 1890, and totally devastated millions of lives in the process. There was no discussion, at least none reported, of the urgent need for a fundamental change in the system.

So, the balance of power worldwide is very much on the side of the bankers who, apparently, have the politicians – thanks to the advice of their principal economic advisers – in their pockets. The politicians, in turn, have the armed forces and police under their control, so that even a peaceful protest faces monumental odds.

Yet, what monetary reformers are asking is only that sovereign governments, that have inherited the right to create money, exercise that right on behalf of all the people who are equal shareholders of that right, instead of borrowing it from licensees who don't even pay a royalty for using someone else's patent. There is absolutely no excuse for sovereign governments to balance their books by borrowing money from private bankers who create it out of thin air – a computer entry! Sovereign governments should have no sovereign debt in their own currency. None! They have been taken to the cleaners by the rich, elite bankers who constantly outwit them.

Assuming that one day soon politicians should see the "light," and start doing what is best for their electors, instead of digging themselves deeper and deeper into the quagmire of partisan politics, there is still the problem of what, specifically, to do. In principle, they have the right to exercise one hundred percent of the money-creation function and leave the private banks with none. But, would that be prudent? Would some kind of compromise that incorporated checks and balances result in both a better system and a much smoother transition?

Monetary reformers are their own worst enemies when they consider that question. Each of us has his or her own preferred solution. When I broached the subject with one of America's most knowledgeable reformers, he said something like, "This time we've got them (presumably meaning that the banking cartel was vulnerable following the 2007-2008 catastrophe for which it was directly responsible) so, we're going to go for the jugular." (Meaning 100% government-created money.)

I have never been able to convince myself that this is the preferred solution. It would mean that private banks would have to have one dollar in their vaults, or on deposit with the central bank, for every dollar they lent out. This was the solution Milton Friedman favored all his life but that he finally abandoned because he concluded it was politically impossible.

I agree that it is politically impossible, but I am far from convinced that it would be the best solution, even if it were possible. To be blunt, I don't trust politicians with that much power. It is a kind of absolute power that would inevitably lead to corruption. We have already seen the kind of total chaos that the bankers have created by abusing their power. They have been directly responsible for both the Great Depression and the current Great Recession. We would not want to see a system where very different but similarly corrupting practices might evolve.

My reservation applies both to the principle of 100% reserves and to the potentially negative consequences of its implementation. A well-known Canadian monetary reformer recently circulated an e-mail to about a dozen of his friends who support the 100% reserve system and asked them how fast they would implement their proposal if given the choice – in effect, how fast they would print enough money to buy all of the federal government's outstanding debt. The response ranged from "immediately" to "12 months."

To my mind, they have not adequately considered the total chaos that would ensue. Insurance companies, retirement funds and some wealthy individuals would be awash with cash but with extremely limited opportunities for investing it. Their actuarial tables would be in tatters. Worse, if banks were suddenly required to convert from nearly zero cash reserves to 100%, they would have to call almost all of their loans and bring on the worst depression the world has ever seen. That is a result that can and must be avoided.

The criterion for any worthwhile reform must be a fast, smooth transition to full employment and the transfer of the ultimate power over interest rates and the rates of growth of the money supply from unelected, unaccountable bankers to the elected representatives of the people who, in theory at least, should operate the system in the interests of their electors.

This is not just an academic issue. It means that the whole notion of "capital adequacy" has to be abandoned. There is no such thing as "capital adequacy" because it is just a benchmark, someone's best guess as to a line that might reduce the number of bank insolvencies under "normal" circumstances.

"Capital adequacy" is the open door through which the banking fraternity galloped following Milton Friedman's curious flip-flop from being a proponent of 100% cash reserves to zero percent for no better reason than "to get the government out of the business of having anything to do with the lending and investing activities of private financial entities. Either 100 percent reserves, i.e., a narrow banking system, which is what I would prefer, or zero percent reserves so government has no supervisory power over banks has that result," as he told me in a letter dated October 15, 1998.[3]

One has to question the judgment of an economist who went from one extreme to the other without considering the merit of 25% reserves, or 50%, or 75%. One also has to question the judgment of anyone who believes that the financial system can operate independently of government. That point was proven beyond question in 2007-2008 when governments had to intervene with massive amounts of taxpayers' money to prevent the whole international house of cards from collapsing. So governments must, if they have any independence at all, renounce the capital adequacy expedient and re-introduce the requirement for cash reserves as the regulator of monetary aggregates.

For many years, I opted for a 50% cash reserve system. It was just an arbitrary figure – one that seemed reasonable. Dr. Douglas Peters, former chief economist of the Toronto-Dominion Bank, as it was then, who has been a good friend and adviser over the years, complained that at a 50% reserve rate the banks would have to call all of their loans.

I did an exercise based on his own former bank's balance sheet for the previous year. The bank would not have had to call any loans but would have been required to sell all of its other assets including stocks, bonds, and real estate, etc., many of which they really had no business buying and owning in the first place. A factor that I did not consider at the time was that the bank would be left with no margin for expanding its loan portfolio even if that should be in the public interest.

In my book, *A Miracle in Waiting: Economics that Make Sense*, I changed the ratio from 50% cash reserves to 34%; that would leave the banks with a multiplier of two. Even that, of course, is a drastic reduction from the current levels of ten, fifteen, twenty or more. A leverage of two to one would still leave the banks with sufficient capacity to finance new commercial and industrial development, as well as increased consumption. It would deprive them, however, of their ability to engage in all of the risky gambling games they have developed in the last few decades. There would be no proprietary trading as set out in the so-called Volcker rule; no money for hedge funds; no money for exotic derivatives; no money for margin purchases of stocks and bonds. It would be back to basics. Banks should be little more than public utilities offering essential banking services.

The seemingly miraculous flipside is that the 34% annual creation of new money by governments would allow them to balance budgets at all levels, federal, state and municipal with reasonable tax levels – significantly lower than they are at present. This ability to get by with lower taxes would be augmented by the fact that very significant amounts of existing public debt would be monetized over the period of time banks were allowed to achieve their 34% cash reserve levels. With an approximate reduction of sovereign debts by one-third worldwide, the interest components of taxes should be dramatically reduced. This could be augmented if government budgets included provision for perhaps a 1% or 2% a year reduction in outstanding debt as part of their new regime. Right now, however, the world economy needs a massive infusion of government-created money. Then pump-priming should be reduced, as appropriate, until normal, balanced budgets were adequate.

So what I am proposing is a staged transition involving a massive quick start for the world economy, the establishment of cash reserve requirements that would sterilize the huge amounts of money created for this purpose, a subsequent division of the money creation function that would see governments creating 34% of all new money put into circulation each year, and the reduction of bank-lending ratios from their current larcenous levels to a modest two to one.

The new system would be one of checks and balances where governments would be key players in the rate of expansion of their economies; and business cycles, as we have known them, would become a thing of the past. The banking industry would survive as profitable businesses that would be good investments for anyone, including individuals and retirement funds. Most of the people working in the industry, with the exception of the rogue traders and others who have caused so much trouble, would preserve their jobs. The plan would in no way preclude the establishment of state banks or other competition. In fact, the big monster banks should be broken up to the extent that the failure of one would not and could not disrupt the entire financial system. Entry into the banking system should be encouraged, and small banks should be able to survive much more easily because the rules would be the same for both the small and the large.

Finally, the urgency for action cannot be over-emphasized. Millions of people who are unemployed have lost confidence in their leaders and are losing hope in the future. They represent a very volatile element in world society. Their needs have to be met and their futures assured in order to create stability as a by-product of justice.

Government-Created Money is Not Inflationary!

The idea that government-created money is inflationary is just not true. It is just a myth – actually a very big lie – that bankers and bureaucrats rely on to prevent thinking people from examining the international banking system, and the extent to which we have been robbed generation after generation.

As anyone in the business should know, it is the amount of money created that determines prices, and not who prints it. Money is money whether it is government-created money (GCM), or bank-created money (BCM).

Government-created money would be inflationary if the banks were allowed to use it as a lever –"high-powered money" – to increase their production of virtual (debt) money. But, that can not happen with the proposed system because the expansion of bank credit will be directly related to the amount of cash a government makes available to the banking system – an amount governed by the capacity of the economy to produce real goods and services.

In fact, that is the only kind of control that is even designed to work credibly. Under the current system of so-called "capital adequacy," the banks are free to increase their capital, print more money, and create an inflationary bubble, as they have on many occasions.

The current system, under which privately-owned banks create about 97% of the total money supply, and all of it as debt on which interest has to be paid, while no one creates any money with which to pay the interest, is inherently inflationary. This is due to the fact that to keep the economy growing it is necessary to create (a) enough new money each year to pay the interest on the existing debt and (b) enough additional debt money to keep the economy growing, however slowly.

The failure of the present system to maintain the value of money can be illustrated by the fact that one U.S. dollar at the time that the Federal Reserve System was established 100 years ago is worth only five cents today. Talk about inflation!

Look at the Canadian precedent. Canada actually used the equivalent of government-created money from 1939 to 1974. The Bank of Canada created very large sums of near zero cost money for the government to spend into circulation. That was essentially government-created money, and it was not the cause of the inflation of the late '60s and early '70s, which was occurring simultaneously in other countries. In both cases rising oil prices was a factor but the principal cause in every case was wages rising out of sync with productivity.

So, to achieve full employment – the number of unemployed job seekers roughly equal to the number of job openings – requires some mechanism to prevent the wage-price cycle from reoccurring. I have written extensively on this subject and will not repeat it here. In principle, however, it has to be a solution that does not employ interest rates as a lever of control. That is far too blunt an instrument that creates collateral damage worse than the problem being addressed.

Historians play down the role of money creation as a causal factor in bringing about the U.S. War for Independence. We are led to believe that it was all about tea and taxes. But there were more important reasons, as James Ferguson explains, "[Benjamin] Franklin cited restrictions upon paper money as one of the main reasons for the alienation of the American provinces from the mother country."[4] This point of view was confirmed by William F. Hixson in *Triumph of the Bankers*. "To a significant extent, the war was fought over the right of the Colonists to create their own money supply. When the Continental Congress and the states brought forth large issues of their own legal-tender money in 1775, they committed acts so contrary to British laws governing the colonies and so contemptuous and insulting to British sovereignty as to make war inevitable."[5]

This was a clear case of the banks versus the people. When the colonists started to create their own money, and London banks became aware of it, they realized that a vast new market for loans was being lost. Furthermore, they didn't want other parts of the world to adopt the same radical practice. So, they persuaded the parliament at Westminster to pass a law prohibiting it. This meant that instead of looking after their own financial needs, the colonists had to borrow from the London banks and repay, principal and interest, in gold that they didn't have. This led inevitably to a bad recession and increased unemployment – setting the stage for war.

Victory of the Bankers

It was the Civil War in the United States that had the greatest impact on the system. Although Abraham Lincoln had not been a proponent of GCM, he certainly recognized its usefulness in times of emergency. In his December 1862 message to Congress, Lincoln made the following reference to the failure of the banks and the need for GCM. "The suspension of specie payments [their failure to provide gold or silver coins in exchange for their bank notes] by banks soon after the commencement of your last session, made large issues of United States Notes [greenbacks] unavoidable. In no other way could the payment of the troops, and the satisfaction of other just demands, be so economically or so well provided for. The judicious legislation of Congress, securing the receivability of these notes for loans and internal duties, and making them a legal tender for other debts, has made them a universal currency; and has satisfied, partially, at least, and for the time, the long felt want of a uniform circulating medium, saving thereby to the people immense sums in discounts and exchanges."[6]

While the immediate need had been to meet the exigencies of war, President Lincoln had also recognized the long-standing necessity for a "universal" or national currency to replace the hodge-podge of bank notes existing at that time. One historian estimated that in 1860 there were "7,000 kinds of paper notes in circulation, not to mention 5,000 counterfeit issues."[7]

From the time greenbacks first came into circulation in 1862, they carried the words: "The United States of America will pay to the bearer five dollars ... payable at the United States Treasury." In fact, however, they were government-created inconvertible money until 1879 when they first became convertible into gold at face value. It will come as no surprise that this switch in policy was engineered by Hugh McCulloch, a former banker and gold monometallist who became secretary of the treasury in 1865. He sold bonds in exchange for greenbacks and then destroyed the greenbacks. In this way he managed to load the government – people – up with debt for no good reason except to reinforce the concept of a bankers' monopoly to create money.

The Guernsey Success

When skeptics ask for an example in real life where government-created money has been utilized consistently and effectively for an extended period, it is only necessary to look at the history of the Isle of Guernsey, beginning in the early 19th century. At that time, the island boasted natural beauty, but little else. There was nothing to attract visitors or to keep residents from moving to the mainland. There was no trade nor hope of employment for the poor. The market was open and needed a cover, and the shores were eroding due to the sorry state of the dykes. What to do? Why, set up a committee, of course.

Finally, as Olive and Jan Grubiak report in *The GUERNSEY Experiment*, "after grave deliberation, the Committee reported in

1816 with this historic recommendation – that property should be acquired and a covered market erected; the expenses to be met by the Issue of States Notes to the value of £6000."[8] The story, as related by the Grubiaks in their well documented pamphlet, is well worth reading for anyone interested in the subject.

The experiment had its ups and downs, as the banks made a valiant, but in the end unsuccessful, effort to put an end to the practice. Consequently, it has persisted to this day with the result that the island has modern infrastructure, no unemployment to speak of, very low taxes, and no debt. If you contrast this extremely successful policy with that of the United Kingdom with its enormous debt, and taxpayers still paying interest on money borrowed to fight the American colonists in the War for Independence more than 200 years ago, it will be hard to escape the conclusion that there is a better system and that we should be well advised to adopt it.

Finally, I had some econometric studies done by Informetrica of Ottawa in 1993. They proved conclusively that judicious use of government-created money by the government of Canada would be beneficial across the board. Compare that with the trillions of dollars of quantitative easing that the Federal Reserve System in the U.S. has pumped into the banking system in the U.S. and Europe without accomplishing much of anything of significance, except to line the pockets of the bankers.

It is no wonder that Henry Ford Sr. said that if people understood the banking system, there would be a revolution before morning. People have to educate themselves as to how the system really works, and then demand a revolutionary change under which governments share the money-creation function with the private banks in a way that would guarantee full employment and steady growth from year to year, without fear of recessions and depressions that have been such a curse for so long.

Chapter Nine

Visitors From
Starry Realms

"The most important decision we make is whether we believe we live in a friendly or hostile universe."

– Albert Einstein

It is a fact that the quick demise of the highly leveraged banking system is the most urgent issue facing the human species at this time. But, there are other issues of primal concern. The first, and most important, is global warming. I will return to this subject in a later chapter.

The third major issue, one that is not well known by the majority, is the extraterrestrial presence and technology. Approximately 50% of Americans think that their government is withholding the truth about the Star Visitors but have no idea of how much has been withheld. The other half are blissfully unaware that the reality is stranger than science fiction, and that they have been consistently misinformed and lied to by a government that has engineered one of the most successful cover-ups in history.

In fact, much of the information is in the public domain. That is the source of what I will be saying in this chapter and then again in a later one. The problem is that the government of the U.S., in particular, has encouraged the idea that anyone attempting to expose the facts is either an addict or a lunatic. I must admit that I have become an addict of seeking the truth because the alternative is much too dangerous for all humankind.

My concern has changed to passion as I have become increasingly aware that the three subjects – the banking cartel, global warming, and the extraterrestrial presence and technology – are all inextricably interconnected. Consequently, in order to "get the picture" you can't study just one, you have to understand them all. This is possible if you abandon the mass media as your principal news source and do your own digging in relevant books and the internet.

One of the many books crammed with useful information is *The Secret History of Extraterrestrials: Advanced Technology and the Coming New Race* by Len Kasten. It was not the first book on the subject of ETs that I read, as you will learn later in this chapter, but one of the best. It also has a section on Recommended Reading that lists most of the important books published before 2010. Two early stories confirm that the subject of ETs and the Visitors from other realms is not really new. It is the rapidly increasing awareness that is new.

Many of us who have seen the world famous pyramids and Sphinx have wondered how it was possible for the ancient Egyptians to erect such magnificent structures. Kasten has concluded that they must have had help. He writes as follows:

> The 'ancient astronaut' hypothesis seems to have become an established concept, rapidly gaining mainstream acceptance. Thanks to the groundbreaking work of Erich von Däniken and Zecharia Sitchin, among other notable writers and researchers, it is becoming clear that high-tech visitors from distant stars have stopped here at our little planet at various times since prehistory. For most of the researchers on this subject, the largest and most obvious clues have been in Egypt. When, in the early 1990s, Robert Bauval discovered that the three pyramids at Giza, when viewed from the air, were aligned exactly as the three stars in the constellation of Orion, an unmistakable link was established between Orion and Giza.... this link probably means that spacefarers from Orion built the pyramids and the Sphinx.[1]

Another story was of specific interest to me as a former Minister of Defence. The following is a summary gleaned from Kasten's book and other sources:

On February 2, 1961, an armada of about 50 UFOs flew south from Russia and then turned around and headed for the North Pole just in time to avoid the panic button being pushed by the headquarters of the Supreme Headquarters of the Allied Powers in Europe (SHAPE) which might have triggered another world war. Once the crisis was recognized as a false alarm, SHAPE ordered an investigation into the UFO phenomenon that was titled *An Assessment: An Evaluation of a Possible Military Threat to Allied Forces in Europe*, and written over a three-year period from 1961-1964. The conclusions of the study were earth-shattering. The authors determined, with absolute certainty, that we have been actively visited by representatives of at least four extraterrestrial civilizations for thousands of years.

> Some of the events reported in the book were so open that there was no question of their authenticity, such as the case where a disc landed on a runway in Italy and a very human-looking ET emerged and spoke to the traumatized Italian soldier on duty in perfect Italian. In another case, a Danish farmer interrupted his dinner to run out into his backyard to check on a noisy ruckus by his animals, to discover a large disc sitting there on three legs. Then a door in the craft opened, and (again) a humanlike alien invited him, in perfect Danish, to take a ride. The excited farmer didn't hesitate. He threw down his napkin and scooted aboard. His incredulous wife watched as it took off, and then she called the police, who called in the military. When the joyride was over, they all watched with mouths agape as the ecstatic farmer bounced out of the craft and it closed up and zoomed into the sky. The couple was debriefed for three days. It was cases like these, involving ETs that were human look-alikes, that really electrified the military. That meant that aliens could be walking down the corridors of the Pentagon unrecognized.[2]

It was a near miracle that the public has learned of the existence of *An Assessment*. Our benefactor is retired Army Command Sergeant Major, a decorated Korean War veteran, who was given what we call a "plum assignment" at SHAPE just outside of Paris where he worked as an intelligence analyst and was given a Cosmic Top

Secret clearance, the highest in the Command. It was there that his profound inner transformation from innocent "good soldier" to disillusioned, concerned citizen took place.

His story, as he tells it, is as follows. Late one night when he was working the graveyard shift, he was bored to distraction. The colonel in charge thought he would enjoy shocking Dean by giving him a Cosmic Top Secret document to read. It was *An Assessment*. "By the time Dean finished reading that book, the old, highly structured, and predictable world he had taken for granted all his life was in shambles all around him as he contemplated an entirely new, incredible reality."[3]

Dean observed his oath of secrecy while he was in the military, but once he was fully retired he became one of the most important whistleblowers in the 1990s. Now he is in his 80s and unable to participate as he once did but it is important that his testimony be given the mainstream exposure it deserves. Before doing my bit I tracked him down by contacting his wife, Marcia Schafer, who guaranteed the authenticity of his incredible revelation.[4]

It is obvious that there is a lot of history relating to flying saucers, or UFOs as they are commonly called, that predates the crashes at Roswell, New Mexico, in 1947. But, that became the key starting point for my interest in these matters, so that is where I shall begin.

On Tuesday, July 8, 1947, at 11:00 a.m. Mountain Time (MT), Roswell Army Air Field commanding officer, Colonel William Blanchard, announced (in a press release) the recovery of a flying disc.[5] THAT WAS THE TRUTH!

Later that same day, at approximately 4:30 p.m. Central Standard Time (CST), Brigadier General Roger Ramey, the commander of the Eighth Air Force, and Blanchard's supervising officer, presented to the press an alternative story. He claimed the army had recovered a rawin target device suspended by a Neoprene rubber balloon.[6] (Rawin is a method of determining wind speed and direction using a radar-sensitive target or radio transponder.) THAT WAS A LIE!

The information provided by Brig. Ramey was not only a lie, it became the cornerstone lie on which has been built a monstrous skyscraper of lies and deceit spanning more than sixty years during which the American public, press and Congress have been deliberately not informed and systematically misinformed about the subject of the Extraterrestrial presence on and around our planet, and the extent to which some of their vastly superior technology has been replicated for military and industrial use.

I have to admit that my interest in ETs and their relationships with us only began in the 21st century. It is true that when I was Minister of National Defence (Canadian spelling) for Canada I received UFO sighting reports. About 80% of those could be explained as natural phenomena with the balance being "Unidentified Flying Objects" in the literal sense.

If I had known then even a fraction of what I know now, I would have asked some very pointed questions of scientists and senior officers in my own department. My curiosity would have included questions of my U.S. counterpart who had said that he would "tell me anything I wanted to know." It was a great opportunity lost because I suspect he was one of the few Secretaries of Defense who was really in the loop. Unfortunately, I was far too busy unifying the three individual Canadian armed forces into a single Canadian Armed Forces to be interested in anything as esoteric as UFOs.

Decades later, a young bilingual chap from Ottawa, Pierre Juneau, began sending me information on the subject. I told him honestly that I didn't have time to read his material, but he was very patient and suggested that I just put it on a shelf and wait for that proverbial rainy day when I might find time.

Meanwhile he asked me to make time to watch a two-hour ABC special by Peter Jennings that included testimony by retired Air Force pilots, commercial airline pilots, air traffic controllers, police officers and others. There were the usual debunkers, but these were far less convincing than the witnesses with first-hand experience. I couldn't fathom any reason why they would go on air and say they had seen one or more UFOs if that was not the truth.

Pierre also sent me a book entitled *The Day After Roswell*,[7] by Lt. Col. Philip Corso, a retired U.S. Army intelligence officer. It looked intriguing; so I decided to put it on my list for holiday reading. I couldn't find it when I looked in 2004, but the following summer when I was trying to find another book, there was Corso's *The Day After Roswell* staring me in the face.

So, I took it with me to Arundel Lodge, the old farm house and cabins that my late wife of fifty-nine years and I had run as a tourist resort for forty-five years while she was alive. I found Corso's book both interesting and compelling. A couple of times I asked myself if it could possibly be fiction, as was the case with *The Life of Pi*,[8] the substitute book I had read the summer before. The answer was a firm no. I recognized too many names of military bases and generals to leave me in any doubt as to the book's authenticity.

Before I reached the final pages, my nephew Philip, who was also vacationing at "The Lodge," came past and asked me what I was reading. "Well, I'm a skeptic," he informed me. "It's a free country," I responded, "you are entitled to think what you want." That afternoon Philip left for home, but a couple of days later he called me. "I phoned the general and told him what you were reading and he said, "Every word is true, and more! Where can I get a copy of the book?" I gave him the name of a bookstore that had copies in stock.

By a curious coincidence, or was it serendipity, just before leaving for the Muskoka Lakes District where our Arundel Lodge was located, I had been asked by Victor Viggiani and Mike Bird to speak at their Exopolitics Toronto Symposium on UFO Disclosure and Planetary Direction, on Saturday afternoon, September 25, 2005. I had absolutely no intention of accepting because I was not, and still am not, a ufologist and had nothing to say. After reading *The Day After Roswell*, however, I concluded that there were huge issues involved that should be in the public domain. How much had we learned from back-engineering the alien craft that had crashed? Was there a possibility of future star wars? Were the American taxpayers aware of what was going on, and the cost involved?

These questions and more raced through my head, and I felt a profound responsibility to speak out in the hope of generating a serious debate. Before doing so, however, I needed confirmation from the retired United States Air Force general personally. Philip had introduced us a year or so earlier at an aeronautical show, so I asked for a heads up to the general that I would be calling.

When he picked up the phone, he didn't even give me the opportunity to say, "Hello, how are you?" before saying, "Every word is true, and more." We then spent the next 20 minutes talking about the "and more," to the extent possible consistent with his oath. He confirmed that there had been crashes at Roswell (there were actually two, almost simultaneously), that the U.S. had long been working on back-engineering the technology, and that there had been face-to-face exchanges between the Star Visitors and U.S. officials.

Only one hurdle remained before going public. I was getting married to Sandra Bussiere, widow of my best friend ever, on October 1st, one week to the day after the conference. I phoned Sandra, explained the situation, and she gave me a reluctant green light after I assured her it would be a "one off" affair. Little did I dream the extent to which that well-intentioned promise would be broken.

I phoned Viggiani and Bird and told them that I accepted their invitation and would show up at Convocation Hall, University of Toronto, on September 25th, at the appointed hour. I was the last speaker, after Stanton Friedman, Richard Dolan and Stephen Bassett, all distinguished ufologists; and after a few preliminary remarks, I said, "UFOs are as real as the airplanes flying overhead." This gave me the dubious distinction of being the first person of cabinet rank in the G8 group of countries to state categorically, without any reservation, that UFOs are real.

As soon as news of my categorical statement of September 2005 was in the public domain, corroborating material of all kinds began to flow in like a mighty river. I received more than a dozen books and countless memos, magazines and documents of all kinds, including many that had been highly classified.

I soon found – and I don't know why it should have been a surprise to me – that whereas I had been disinterested and consequently uninformed, there was a small army of dedicated ufologists who had been painstakingly researching the subject for years, and in some cases decades, who had already discovered relevant information and documentation of diverse sorts, and who had recorded much of it in book form. They have been the pioneers paving the path of discovery for the much larger army of skeptics and naysayers who have yet to be exposed to what I like to call "the broader reality."

One of the most illustrious of these pioneers is Dr. Steven Greer, M.D., who gave up a lucrative medical practice because he was so concerned about the secrecy surrounding the whole question of the extraterrestrial presence and technology, and the implications of what that means for all humanity. When Dr. Greer visited Toronto in May 2006, we arranged to meet for lunch at one of Toronto's waterfront cafes where he gave me a three-hour briefing of what he had learned in the course of his research. He had talked to about 400 former military officers, scientists, civil aviation officers, policemen, pilots and others and managed to film and record about 100 who revealed in detail what they knew about important subjects that the U.S. government has been deliberately hiding for as far back as 60 years or more.

Not only was I struck with the depth and diversity of the testimony Dr. Greer had assembled for his "Disclosure Project," I was alarmed by some of the testimony of witnesses who confirmed my suspicions of American military plans including the militarization of space, that I consider highly questionable and not necessarily in the best interests of either the U.S. or the world. The peaceful uses of space should be open to all humanity, a frontier as challenging and thrilling as climbing Mount Everest, and even more wondrous.

The following month, in June 2006, I delivered the keynote address at the Extraterrestrial Civilizations & World Peace Conference at Kona, Hawaii, at the invitation of Dr. Michael Salla, head of the Exopolitics Institute, and his wife Angelika Whitecliff, co-organizer of the conference. In addition to the pleasure of spending a few days in such a delightful part of the planet, I had the opportunity to listen to a number of speakers, all of whom knew far more about the subject than I did. My role was to expand on my concerns about the military and political implications of visitors from other planets; subjects on which my long years of experience served as a useful backdrop.

The principal advantage of the conference, however, was not having a platform to express my concerns, it was the knowledge I gained from listening to the presenters and the invaluable contacts that I made when I was there. Two, in particular, have become friends and our paths have crossed many times in the intervening years. The first of these very interesting people that Sandra and I met in Kona was Paola Harris, a well-respected ufologist who had expected to be on the platform in Toronto when I first went public, but had to cancel for health reasons. Paola subsequently flew from Rome, where she was residing, to Toronto for an interview that she managed to have aired in several languages and jurisdictions. She gave us a copy of her book, *Connecting the Dots*,[9] that I found every bit as interesting as I would expect from the exuberant Paola.

The contents included a lengthy interview with Monsignor Corrado Balducci. Two things became obvious from the clergyman's answers to Paola's questions. He was well versed in the subject; and although he was speaking as an individual, and not as an official Vatican spokesman, his superiors were well aware that he was speaking with their full knowledge, at least, if not their unofficial blessing. The following is from their dialogue:

> The acronym UFO is used here in a wider sense to include the existence of living beings on other planets. The aim of my intervention, and speaking out, is to underline that something real *must* exist in the phenomena, and that this does not conflict at all with the Christian religion, and is considered positive, even among theologians.
>
> First, something real *must* exist. Secondly, I have made some theological considerations on the habitability of other planets. Thirdly, much witness testimony favors it. Conclusion: Something real *must* exist.
>
> Paola Harris: Is it a grave mistake to think that you are the *official* voice of the Vatican?
>
> Monsignor Balducci: 'These ideas are mine, and I do not represent the Vatican. However, I am told that the Holy Father, John Paul II, has seen me on Italian TV several times and follows my radio homilies. If there were some objection, I'm sure I would know. I believe there to be no problem here.'[10]

His candid comments lend credence to unofficial information to the effect that the Vatican may have had direct contact with at least one species of Visitors, and that the Holy See may have been in the know from the early days when General Eisenhower was alleged to have had direct contact with the Visitors at what is now known as Edwards Air Force Base, in the company of several witnesses including Bishop MacIntyre of Los Angeles who, despite official objections, would have reported directly to the Holy Father.[11]

We had another lucky break at the conference. Mike Bird, one of the two Canadians who had been responsible for getting me involved in the first place, acted as our unofficial mentor and guide. When we asked if he knew a nice place to have dinner he recommended a nearby restaurant. We took his advice and asked him to join us.

When we arrived at our destination, and the maître d' was about to seat us, Mike recognized one of the presenters, Capt. Robert Salas, and his wife Marilyn; so, we persuaded them to join the party. Not only were they delightful dinner companions, the story that the Captain told bordered on science fiction, but it was real – only too real – because he was there. The following is a very brief summary based on that conversation, his presentation, his book *Faded Giant*,[12] and the evidence he provided Dr. Greer as part of the Disclosure Project.

The incident occurred on the morning of March 16, 1967. Capt. Salas and his commander, Fred Mywald, were on duty at Oscar Flight, a part of the 490th strategic missile squad. It was still dark, and they were sixty feet underground, at the ICBM launch control facility. Early that morning Salas received a call from the topside security guard who said that he and some of his colleagues had been watching some strange lights flying around the site launch control facility. The guard said it was quite unusual, because they were just flying around. "You mean a UFO," Salas asked? The guard didn't know what they were; they were not airplanes, but there were lights, and they were just flying around. They weren't helicopters, either, but they were making some strange maneuvers that he couldn't explain. Salas says that he just shook his head and said: "Call me if anything more important happens."

Some time later the guard called again and this time he appeared to be very frightened. Salas could tell by his voice that he was "very shook up." "Sir," the guard said: "There's a glowing red object hovering right outside the front gate – I'm looking at it right now. I've got all the men out here with their weapons drawn." The Capt. didn't know what to make of it and was somewhat uncertain as to what order he should give in the face of unprecedented circumstances. Salas thinks he said something like: "Make sure that the perimeter fence is secure." At that point the guard said he had to go because one of his men had been injured climbing the fence.

Salas went over to his commander, who was taking a nap during a rest period, and started relating the information he had received; and, as he spoke, the missiles – Minuteman One missiles with nuclear-tipped warheads – started shutting down, one by one, as a result of guidance system failures. At the time, Salas recalls, he felt that they were losing them all; but later, in reviewing the incident with Fred Mywald, his commander, they concluded that only seven or eight had been rendered inoperable.

The Air Force did an extensive investigation of the entire incident and was not able to come up with a probable cause of the shutdowns. Each missile was independently controlled and the system was very reliable. Failures were rare and seldom, if ever, had there been more than one shutdown at a time. Weather was not a factor, and power surges were ruled out. A Boeing engineer who did some laboratory tests thought that some kind of electromagnetic force or field might have caused the signal to go. Needless to say, as with all other matters related to the Extraterrestrial presence, the whole incident was kept secret without any public awareness.[13]

My exposure in these early days was primarily to American ufologists and UFO devotees. I had been too busy to look in my own backyard. Often I was asked if I knew Wilbert Smith, a Canadian pioneer who seemed to have achieved the status of an icon. I felt some shame when I had to admit that I had never heard of him. When I began my research in earnest I found that I had no further to look than in my own files where there were several articles about or written by Smith that various people had sent me to read but were just put away for that day of leisure that never came.

Worse, Wilbert Smith had been a senior employee of the Canadian Department of Transport (DOT) where I became minister not long after his retirement. My predecessor, a close friend, had left all his personal files for me. In a Top Secret memorandum to the Controller of Communications, dated November 21, 1950,[14] Smith recommended that a project be set up by DOT to study certain aspects of the Saucer phenomenon, particularly those in the electromagnetic and radio wave areas. Part of the case he made reads as follows:

> While in Washington attending the NARB Conference, two books were released one titled *Behind the Flying Saucers*,[15] by Frank Scully, and the other, *Flying Saucers from Outer Space*,[16] by Donald Keyhoe.
>
> Both books dealt mostly with the sightings of unidentified objects and both books claim that flying objects were of extra-terrestrial origin and might well be space ships from another planet. Scully claimed that the preliminary studies of one saucer which fell into the hands of the United States Government indicated that they operated on some hitherto unknown magnetic principles. It appeared to me that our own work in geo-magnetics might well be the linkage between our technology and the technology by which the saucers are designed and operated.
>
> If it is assumed that our geo-magnetic investigations are in the right direction, the theory of the operation of the saucers becomes quite straightforward, with all observed features explained qualitatively and quantitatively.
>
> I made discreet enquiries through the Canadian Embassy staff in Washington who were able to obtain for me the following information.
>
> (a) The matter is the most highly classified subject in the United States Government, rating higher even than the H-bomb.
> (b) Flying saucers exist.
> (c) Their modus operandi is unknown but concentrated effort is being made by a small group, headed by Doctor Vannevar Bush.

(d) The entire matter is considered by the United States authorities to be of tremendous significance.

I was further informed that the United States authorities are investigating along quite a number of lines which might possibly be related to the saucers such as mental phenomena, and I gather that they are not doing too well since they indicated that if Canada is doing anything at all in geo-magnetics they would welcome a discussion with suitably accredited Canadians.

While I am not yet in a position to say that we have solved even the first problems in geo-magnetic energy release, I feel that the correlation between our basic theory and the available information on saucers checks too closely to be mere coincidence. It is my honest opinion that we are on the right track and are fairly close to at least some of the answers.

Smith apparently succeeded in persuading his superior to cooperate, for early in 1951 Project Magnet was set up. Smith sought and obtained the cooperation of the Chairman of the Canadian Defence Research Board, Dr. Omond Solandt, who allowed him to use the radar facilities at Shirley's Bay, not far from Ottawa. As I indicated earlier, I was totally unaware of this activity and I doubt that my immediate predecessor, Hon. J.W. Pickersgill, knew much more.

Wilbert Smith himself summed up the government's position. In an address to the Vancouver Area UFO Club on March 14, 1961, he stated the following:

Project Magnet was not an official Government project. It was a project that I talked the Deputy Minister into letting me carry out by making use of the extensive field organization of the Department of Transport. Unfortunately the gentlemen of the press climbed on this and made a big deal of it.... However, we carried the project through officially for about four or five years and then went underground because of press interference ... [17]

The balance of the speech was much more fascinating. Smith makes it very clear that he – and some others – obtained a lot of important information from the Extraterrestrials – presumably from contacts that were checked out for accuracy. In addition to the vast array of scientific knowledge acquired, Smith gleaned enough information concerning the nature and intent of the Visitors to develop his own personal philosophy concerning them. I am sure he would like me to share a couple of paragraphs.

Furthermore, when the material given to us through the many channels is all assembled and analyzed, it adds up to a complete and elegant philosophy which makes our efforts sound like the beating of jungle drums. These people tell us of a magnificent Cosmic Plan, of which we are a part, which transcends the lifetime of a single person, or a nation, or a civilization, or even a planet or solar system. We are not merely told that there is something beyond our immediate experience, we are told what it is, why it is, and our relation thereto.

Many of our most vexing problems are solved with a few words, at least we are told of the solutions if we have the understanding and fortitude to apply them. We are told of the inadequacies of our science, and we have been given the basic grounding for a new science which is at once simpler and more embracing than the mathematical monstrosity we have conjured up. We have been told of a way of life that is utopian beyond our dreams, and the means of attaining it. Can it be that such a self-consistent, magnificent philosophy is the figment of the imagination of a number of misguided morons ... ?

We may summarize the entire flying saucer picture as follows. We have arrived at a time in our development when we must make a final choice between right and wrong. The people from elsewhere are much concerned about the choice which we will make, partly because it will have its repercussions on them and partly because they are our blood brothers and are truly concerned with our welfare. There is a cosmic law about interfering in the affairs of others, so they are not allowed to help us directly even though they could easily do so. We must make our own choice of our own free will. Present trends indicate a series of events which may require the help of these people and they stand by ready and willing to render that help. In fact, they have already helped us a great deal, along lines that do not interfere with our freedom of choice. In time, when certain events have transpired, and we are so oriented that we can accept these people from elsewhere, they will meet us freely on the common ground of mutual understanding and trust, and we will be able to learn from them and bring about the Golden Age all men everywhere desire deep within their hearts.[18]

***

At that point I had not yet talked to anyone who had actually seen a flying saucer close up. My long-time friend, and former Canadian Forces Information Officer, Ray Stone sent me an e-mail from one of his friends, Nickolas Evanoff, who had seen the real thing. It reads as follows:

In the late 1970s, or perhaps 1980 or 1981, I was visiting a certain USA Government organization in Virginia, which I cannot disclose, when I was asked if I wanted to see a real UFO. Of course, I said, so I had to go through a series of documents and had to sign them, mostly for non-disclosure. Because I was in the Emergency Preparedness Organization they said it would be of great help to me and our organization if such an incident happened in Canada. I was not allowed to inform my bosses when I got back, or anyone else.

Next I was on board a USA Gov. aircraft and flown to the midwest of the USA which I think was either Arizona or Nevada and we landed at a US Air Force Base which I cannot disclose.

Then we went into a humongous hangar and there was a damaged UFO. The interior size of it was about that which we saw at Local Heroes Bar side. When it crashed it had eight aliens on board and six of them died on impact and the pilot and co-pilot survived for a couple of days. The USAF doctors didn't know how to treat them because they were from another planet so they died. I didn't see the bodies but I was shown some photographs of them and they were similar to us humans but thinner, had a head and arms and legs and a torso along with five digits on their hands and feet. On board was a nuker for cooking food and a supply of water along with two bathrooms. The manuals were in hieroglyphics and no one could read them including folks from Alaska (Eskimos), India and Egypt. Berkeley University was awarded a contract to photocopy and try using their computers to read them but were unsuccessful.

The reason this UFO crashed was no different from youngsters (18 to 22 years of age) driving cars at excessive speeds on the 400 series highways in Canada or Interstate highways in the USA. The pilot and co-pilot who were young were not aware of the earth's gravitational pull and it was too late to slow down when they reversed their thrusters so they crashed. Most of the craft was not seriously damaged but the collision caused havoc on board.

I asked why didn't the President of the USA inform the public of this incident and I was told it was because of Religion and possible panic amongst Americans and other citizens around the world. I was also informed about a two passenger (pilot and co-pilot) UFO that crashed outside of Helsinki, Finland in 1952 and was published in newspapers around the world and the next day no more information was allowed. Bizarre!

That is pretty much it and when we left the hangar got back on board the aircraft and flew back to Virginia. I was frustrated for years because I couldn't tell anyone what I saw, including my wife.

Nick[19]

I wanted to get the story from Nick personally; so Ray Stone set up an interview for a Sunday afternoon in October 2007. Before the day came, Ray advised that if I wanted to talk to Nick, who had Lou Gehrig's Disease, before he died, I had better telephone him, which I did, at once, on October 7. He confirmed the story and identified "Virginia" as CIA Headquarters in Langley. He also told me about a UFO landing near Winnipeg, Manitoba, that had not been publicized. A few days later he passed to his reward.

***

The biggest surprise I have encountered in the course of my research for this chapter was to find a file amongst my own papers going back to my days as Minister of Transport. It contained a 15-page booklet, including several pages of photographs, entitled "Description and Performance of Unidentified Flying Objects from 1947-1967," as taken from newsstand sources, compiled by Malcolm McKellar, of Vancouver, British Columbia. Sightings were reported from Brazil; Perth, Australia; Salem, Oregon; Queen's, New York; Danville, Virginia; Santa Ana, California; Zanesville, Ohio; Melbourne, Australia; and Rouen, France, to mention only a few where the best photos were taken. All of the descriptions are interesting, but I am including only one that paints a precise portrait of one of the early-type space ships.

In 1952, "Oscar Linke and daughter, reporting to NANA, Berlin, stated that before their escape from Russian-held Germany, they used to take frequent motorcycle rides toward the border. On one such trip, the daughter called attention to a phosphorescent object in a small forest. From a distance of one hundred feet, the object appeared to be a disc, twenty-five feet across, resembling a huge warming pan without a handle. In the center of it, there seemed to be a sort of upper works which rose out of the top of the craft. It was darker than the rest of the object, which was the color of aluminum, well polished.

> Two small figures – like tiny humans about four feet tall – were seen wearing shiny one piece garments, silver in color. On the chest of one of these creatures was a box or package about the size of three packs of cigarettes, and on the front of the package was a bright, blinking blue light. They did not seem to be using this box. Both figures were standing outside the UFO.
>
> Suddenly one tapped the other on the helmet (shiny, glasslike) and both climbed hurriedly into the spacecraft through a porthole on the top of the square part of the upper-works aforementioned. The object was seen to have two rows of circular portholes around the edge, about the size of portholes on a ship. As father and daughter watched, the square upper works began to retract into the dome and simultaneously the UFO started to rise from the ground slowly. It rose to a hundred feet, hovered for a moment and then sped away.[20]

***

The Rendlesham Forest Case

This has become one of the best known cases in the annals of ufology. It was first brought to my attention by Nick Pope who was, at the time, the officer in charge of the UFO desk at the U.K.

Ministry of Defence and, following his retirement from that post, is now a star witness at almost every major conference on the subject. We first met over lunch in London not long after I first became engrossed in the subject of UFOs.

As we parted, he handed me two files that looked especially interesting. One related to the Rendlesham Forest incident just outside the US Air Force's twin NATO bases at Bentwaters and Woodbridge, Suffolk, in 1980. Unlike most sightings, this one had been widely reported due to a memorandum sent to the U.K. Ministry of Defence by Lieutenant Colonel Charles I. Halt, who was Deputy Base Commander RAF Woodbridge at the time. Pope thought that Halt might be willing to talk to me. So, that fall, I wrote to the Colonel, who lived in Virginia, and asked if he would see me when I was in Washington for the National Prayer Breakfast in early February 2007. He replied that he didn't usually respond to correspondence on that subject, but that because he knew and trusted Nick Pope, he would be happy to see me.

On February 2, 2007, I hired a car to take me to the gated city that the Colonel runs, and we had lunch at their country club. He told his story candidly in an interview that lasted more than an hour. It was so fascinating and included so many significant points including the inevitable incredulity, the attempt by officialdom to discount what happened, and other aspects of the UFO saga, that I recounted the interview in full in *"Light."* I decided not to repeat it here, but to give you another source of information on this classic case.

Meanwhile, I found the verbatim report from a tough, no-nonsense U.S. Air Force Colonel totally compelling. It was also very revealing in the sense that it underlined the Visitors' pre-occupation with our nuclear capability. I have read that the ETs have carefully surveyed every military base worldwide where nuclear weapons are either installed or stored. And for a very good reason. Their use could create a nuclear winter that would end human habitation.

Contact with some Celebrities His Serene Highness Prince Hans-Adam of Liechtenstein

The first Monday after Sandra and I returned from our honeymoon, I received an e-mail from a complete stranger, following up on a telephone conversation first-thing that morning. He wishes to remain anonymous, so I will just call him George. "Further to our telephone discussion of this morning, I am confirming details via this e-mail. H.S.H. The Prince indicated to me his interest in discussing with you certain aspects of how to formulate global policy in response to ET involvement in human affairs, past, present and in the future, after learning about your recent presentation at the U. of Toronto Exopolitics Symposium. He will be in Memphis, TN attending to business matters, arriving in the late afternoon of Monday November 14. He is free all day Tuesday, Nov. 15, with the exception of a few hours of meetings which can be rearranged that day to suit your schedule…. I would be happy to book a flight for you if you wish."[21]

I was flattered and immensely interested by the invitation but, regrettably, our availability didn't match. I don't know how my schedule becomes so complex, but often it does, and a couple of alternate dates were equally untenable. So, I had to settle for a telephone call, which was pretty general in nature, and at the end of which the Prince issued an invitation to stay at the castle on my next visit to his principality. To date, I have been unable to accept his kind hospitality despite the magnetic attraction.

A substitute was the opportunity to read a manuscript that the Prince had written for publication but which had been turned down as being too esoteric and theoretical. It is probably another case of the Prince, like other pioneers in the subject, being too far ahead of his time. It may be a while, however, before the majority of us are sufficiently informed about the subject for it to become cocktail or dinnertime conversation. I hope that day will come. Meanwhile, "George" has become a mentor who advises me how to avoid the many land mines and improvised explosive devices that await people who speak too openly on the subjects of this chapter.

Shirley MacLaine

At suppertime on Thursday May 11, 2006, the phone rang. Our inclination was not to answer because the majority of calls during the dinner hour are telemarketers and it taxes our sense of restraint to get rid of them without appearing obviously rude. Sandra decided that she would take the risk in case it was her daughter Wanda, who was calling. So she said hello, and told me that it was a lady asking for me.

"Hello Professor Hellyer," she said, "this is Shirley MacLaine." After explaining that I was not a professor, but that I was Paul Hellyer, she asked about dinner, Saturday or Sunday. I said that Saturday was out because I was taking the family to the Stratford Festival that day to see "Hello Dolly," but I would take her number and get back to her about Sunday, when Sandra planned to be in Montréal visiting her mother on Mother's Day. Sandra gave me her blessing to accept – provided I reported in full – so I made a reservation for two and called Ms. MacLaine to finalize the arrangement.[22]

I was not totally surprised to receive the call because Shirley – it was first names from the outset – had tried to track me down through the Canadian Action Party head office in Vancouver, which is probably where she got my phone number. The attraction, I knew, was my well-publicized interest in UFOs, a subject that was both old hat and of deep concern to her. When Sandra revealed the news to the family at dinner, after the Saturday matinee, conversation with Grandpa gained a new and brighter currency.

When I met Shirley at the Park Hyatt Sunday night, she decided that it would be preferable not to go out – it was not a nice evening – so the concierge canceled the reservation I had made, and we dined in the hotel restaurant that was well and favorably known to me. We got along well from the start. Shirley proved to be quite charming, and very down-to-earth, which was reassuring for an actress of such wide renown.

For about three hours, we carried on a wide-ranging discussion, mostly about UFOs and her life-long interest in the stars and the possibility of life on other planets that began when, as a child, she was given a telescope for Christmas. She would spend hours gazing at the heavens and wondering. Then on Saturday night, July 19, 1952 (she remembered the date because she had recorded it in her diary) just after she had graduated from high school, a pilot reported seeing UFOs over Washington and two Air Force jets took off in hot pursuit. A week later more UFOs buzzed the White House knocking the Korean War and the presidential campaign off the front page. Shirley recalled that a few days later Air Force Intelligence Chief, Major General John Samford, speaking for President Truman, told his television audience that the crafts were not from the Soviet Union, though he couldn't say where they were from.

These events confirmed for Shirley that there is "life out there" and that she should seek all the information possible on the subject. So, through the decades she has built up a truly impressive roster of witnesses and informers from across the political and diplomatic spectrum. It was a very candid exchange that was as fascinating as it was informative.

She must have enjoyed the encounter as much as I did because on Tuesday, Sandra phoned my office to tell me that Shirley MacLaine had called and invited us both to have dinner with her Thursday evening at six o'clock. I said, "Sure, why not?" When the time came, Shirley was wearing a shawl and prepared to go out, so we went around the corner to Roberts Steak House. The place was packed and we didn't have a reservation but they quickly "found" a suitable table.

This time she really let her hair down and talked about personal and family matters, which was good because Sandra believes that UFOs are real but doesn't enjoy spending a lot of time talking about them. We also talked about Faith. I told her that my God was the God of Abraham, Isaac, Jacob and Ishmael, and that Jesus was my role model. She wanted to know if I would go to the cross, and I admitted that I would probably "chicken out." It was a wonderfully revealing evening, but she wanted us to keep mum about the details. I am respecting that undertaking.[23]

Before we parted, she invited the two of us to visit her ranch in New Mexico, with its twelve dogs, four horses, numerous cats and assorted other animals. She is going "off the grid" in favor of wind and solar power in conformity with her concern about the future of the planet. It sounds like a wonderful spot that would be nice to visit, but for now, at least, that is in the future. Meanwhile, we have maintained the relationship based on common interests.

Edgar D. Mitchell, Apollo 14 Astronaut

There is something quite exciting about getting a call from a friend saying that Apollo astronaut Edgar Mitchell will be speaking in Toronto soon and has indicated an interest in meeting you, if that can be conveniently worked into both of your schedules. Sandra, good scout that she is, said: "Why don't we invite him to dinner?" So that is what we did. He was to arrive in Toronto the evening before his speech on July 8, and would come directly to our place from the airport.

The plan was simple and straightforward, but sometimes the unexpected can intervene. As his flight approached Lester Pearson International Airport the pilot reported a cracked windshield. So, instead of landing, he turned the plane around and went back to Pittsburg to get a new one installed. So we were "in the dark," so to speak, until the plane returned to Toronto and Mike Bird, who had been the go-between, finally delivered Mitchell and his traveling companion, Susan, an hour and a half later than expected. Mike and his friend Susan – later to be his wife – made up the balance of the sextet.

There was much joy and relief when everyone was well and truly settled in. I poured drinks and put the salmon in the oven only to find that, due to its size, the fish took twice as long to cook as I had estimated. But, no one complained, and the delay provided a head start with the fascinating and quite unusual conversation that ranged from Earth to the far reaches of the Cosmos and back again. Ed expressed the unique view that the universe may be flat, and we see it as a hologram – a proposition that few of his colleagues agree with.

I started dinner with grace, which led to a discussion of the nature of God. Ed described some of the transcendent experiences he and others had encountered. When Sandra asked if he didn't think that God had something to do with this, he said it depended on how you define God. He does not believe in a grandfather God with long gray whiskers sitting in the heavens. Rather, he defines "deity" in general – the universe as God's body, with a collective mind.

Ed denied having seen UFOs on his trip to the moon, an answer that I had to respect. But at one point, when he mentioned the alleged crash at Roswell, I interjected: "Why do you use the word 'alleged?' " A tell-tale smile a mile wide came across his face. Shortly after that he asked me how many species (of Visitors) I thought there were. I replied, "Somewhere between two and twelve." "That's what I think, too," Ed said in response.

An important area of agreement came when we discussed possible reasons for the extended cover-up. The two most obvious were religion and economics, and the power base associated with each. In Ed's words:

> You can make a good argument for that; it's hard to decide which, but it's certainly entrenched power in any of these areas. It's putting self-interest ahead of the common interest, and that is exactly the mission we have (to overturn). I try to work at it every damn day.

The one question Ed dislikes most is: "What does it feel like to set foot on the moon?" When one is in a critical survival mode, as he was, you don't have time to think about "feel." Fortunately, Ed was willing to stay with us long enough for a great journey of discovery with an amazing man who is going all out in an effort to help save our beautiful planet. It was a privilege to have him with us and we follow his endeavors with much interest.[24]

Edgar is the founding chair of the Institute of Noetic Sciences (IONS), a non-profit membership organization exploring the frontiers of human consciousness. It is hard to imagine a more fascinating and significant area of exploration. In his case, too, we kept in touch, in mutual support, until his death on February 4, 2016.

Update 2007

I read numerous books on various aspects of the "broader reality" that we humans must adjust to, and each one helped my understanding in one way or another, although I must admit that the boundaries of my "broader reality" kept getting stretched like a scroll being opened in both directions from the center. So, even though I had moved from about grade one to the grade four or five level in two years, I decided that before beginning to write about the subject I would go to another symposium and just listen to the experts, in order to ensure that there were no dramatically new developments of which I was unaware.

I signed up for the 5th Annual UFO Crash Conference at Las Vegas, Nevada, held in November 2007. The conclave was sponsored by Ryan Wood, and his father Dr. Robert Wood. Ryan had sent me a copy of his book *Majic Eyes Only*[25] that told the stories of seventy-eight UFO crashes over a period of about a century beginning in 1897. Wood admitted that the evidence was stronger in some cases than in others, but if even half of them were adequately authenticated, and that would be on the conservative side, there had been a large number of crashes. At the conference he told me that since the book had been published he had learned of fifteen more cases, and I had one additional new one from the Canadian experience.

Equally important as the information about government crash retrievals, and their extensive cover-up, was the revelation of allegedly authentic information concerning the Top Secret/Majic Eyes Only, or MJ-12 as they are more popularly known, the small group originally established by President Truman to monitor and exercise control over the whole spectrum of the Extraterrestrial presence, and the exploitation of their technology. The MJ-12 document purports to show the extraordinary lengths that were to be taken to keep the public in the dark.

The conference also gave me the opportunity to renew acquaintance with two additional pioneers, Stephen Bassett, executive director of Paradigm Research Group, sponsor of the X-Conferences, and Richard Dolan, author of *UFOs and the National Security State*.[26] Both of these men had presented in Toronto, in September 2005, where we had appeared at a joint press conference at the end of the program. I also had the good fortune to break bread with Danny Sheehan, the Keynote speaker, who had defended the Berrigan brothers as well as the late Dr. John Mack, the Harvard psychiatrist, and author of *Passport to the Cosmos*,[27] who became one of the world's top experts in the field of human-extraterrestrial contact.

Another rare opportunity occurred when I had lunch with Linda Moulton Howe, author of *Glimpses of Other Realities*,[28] Emmy

Award winning TV producer, and acknowledged to be one of the world's most thorough and successful investigators. Her presentation at the conference was limited to a single recent case, but that didn't disguise the fact that her contacts in government, the military, and among abductees are probably without parallel.

While planning the trip to Las Vegas I had managed to work in another important experience at the same time. Except for a very brief exchange in Toronto the day I went public, I had never spoken at length to an abductee, and I decided it was important for me to do so, and make up my own mind concerning their authenticity, before sticking my neck out on the subject. My Guardian Angel cooperated, and I managed to arrange two significant meetings by simply extending my time in Vegas by one day.

Travis Walton

A U.S. Navy veteran, Ed Cochrane, who had phoned me about UFOs on several occasions, told me about his friend, Travis Walton, who had been the subject of a movie, Paramount's *Fire in the Sky*.[29] His friend knew about my interest in matters extraterrestrial, and would be willing to meet and talk to me. Ed gave me Travis' phone number and when I contacted him I found that he lived in Snowflake, Arizona, not far from Vegas by plane. So he and his wife Dana agreed to meet me there on the weekend.

We were able to spend quite a bit of time together, and I interviewed him at length about his story – one that may be the best documented case of alien abduction ever recorded. On the evening of November 5, 1975, Travis and his six co-workers were returning home after a day's work in the Apache-Sitgreaves National Forest not too far from where they all lived. As they drove along they saw an unusually bright light shining through the forest gloom and decided to follow it. Eventually they got close enough to observe this incredible object in the sky.

Travis, his curiosity piqued, recklessly left the safety of the old truck in which they were riding to take a closer look. He was soon knocked to the ground by a blast of mysterious energy that left him motionless. When they realized what had happened the other near-hysterical men took off in fright. Eventually they decided that they were morally obliged to go back and see if there was any trace of Travis; but, when they reached the clearing where the episode had occurred, there was no sign of him.

They had to report their stories to the authorities who were understandably incredulous. They then were interrogated at length and when there was no sign that alcohol might be the source of the mystery, a hint of foul play became inevitable. The interrogations and lie detector tests had spanned five and a half days until the space ship dropped Travis off not too far from the scene of his disappearance. His next problem was to walk to a pay phone and face the unenviable task of convincing his brother-in-law that his return was real, and not just another hoax, so that he would agree to come and get him.

There was general rejoicing that Travis was back alive but there was not universal acceptance of his incredible story. He told me that his friends and acquaintances were divided about fifty-fifty between believers and skeptics. The effect on his psyche was severe; it took years for him to fully recover and to be able to hold his head up high. Speaking personally, I am totally convinced of his truthfulness and anyone who is interested in the drama and the trauma of this stranger-than-fiction story should read Travis' book *Fire in the Sky*, and skip the movie of the same name that contains a nightmare scene that must be part of the "jazzing up" that Travis admitted had been done to make it more saleable. It may have filled seats in the theater, but if the Visitors had legal rights on Earth they could launch a big class action suit against Paramount Studios for the monstrous misrepresentation of what the Visitors are really like.

Jim Sparks

The other abductee that I met and interviewed at length was Jim Sparks, who has the distinction of being one of the best-informed "experiencers," as Dr. John Mack liked to call them, anywhere. I was fascinated by his early encounters with his abductors – he has been abducted dozens of times – but I was even more interested in what he had learned from the Visitors in the later years, after he had accepted the fact that he had some kind of role to play and that he might just as well relax and enjoy it. So, he eventually became comfortable in their presence. Jim has the added distinction of having been conscious throughout most of his encounters, whereas the majority of abductees recall significant details only under some form of hypnosis.

The ETs have a message for us that should make headlines in every newspaper and magazine in every language in the world – *"We are hell bent on the destruction of our planet as a hospitable place to live or visit."* The ETs may have an agenda or agendas of their own; but what the Visitors have in common is the concern that we are in the process of making our planet uninhabitable and that is not in their interests or ours.

On one occasion they showed Sparks and other abductees a video of sparkling streams and lakes teaming with fish, beautiful forests, blue skies and snow-capped mountains. Then the scene slowly changed and the same streams and lakes had dead bloated fish floating on the surface, the skies were darkened with smog, the forests were dying or being cut down at such a pace that they no longer had the capacity to renew the atmosphere. It was a chilling scenario but no different from the one we see in our newspapers daily as we slowly but surely adjust to the reality that we are rapidly destroying the Earth's ecosystems.

Another of the ETs' preoccupations, as I have already mentioned, is our military's love affair with nuclear weapons. They rightly anticipate that if we don't reduce our stockpiles dramatically, and soon, that some megalomaniac will opt to bring about a nuclear Armageddon that will reduce the planet to a barren wasteland. This just confirmed my earlier suspicion, based on the incidence of sightings, that there is a direct connection between their concerns and our intransigence.

Their greatest revelation to Sparks, however, is that they have met with humans and collaborated in sharing technology. The deal, however, included specific timing for the release of this information to the public. This treaty, like many others, has been observed in the breech. The excuse for continued secrecy is that the public couldn't handle the truth. That is the same old nonsense that we get from the ruling elite. Admittedly, there would have to be major adjustments to accommodate the new and broader reality. But, at the same time, that broader reality offers attractive and exciting opportunities, including the possibility of saving this marvelous planet for the benefit of generations to come.

One interview Jim had with a group of Visitors was so powerful in its message to us Earthlings that I asked permission to reproduce it verbatim here, a wish to which Jim cheerfully agreed. The excerpt from his book *The Keepers*[30] follows:

***

It was night, but I wasn't frightened for some reason. In fact, I was so calm and relaxed that I was enjoying the ride. Twenty feet from the ground, I started to rock slowly back and forth several times like a pendulum, almost as if I were being guided to a target and this was the final adjustment. The transport method was the same, but the technology was notably much more gentle. When I was a few feet from the ground, I saw the profiles of about a dozen large creatures standing in a semi-circle, and then I blacked out.

WE WOULD HAVE GIVEN IT TO YOU, BUT WE KNEW IT WOULDN'T HAVE MEANT ANYTHING UNLESS YOU EARNED IT. IT WAS THE ONLY WAY

YOU COULD POSSIBLY UNDERSTAND WHAT YOU HAVE BEEN A PART OF AND WHAT YOU HAVE TO DO.

The message came to me loud and clear as I began to regain consciousness and opened my eyes. I later understood that by "IT" the Voice meant knowledge.

I found myself standing in that abandoned carnival yard, clear-headed and fully conscious. There were those creatures again, and I could see that holograms of human faces were cast over their faces, to disguise their true appearance and make me feel less apprehensive.

I noticed that each alien seemed to be concentrating and communicating or transmitting its thoughts to the creature to my left. They seemed to be of like mind, as though combining their consciousness into one telepathic Voice. They continued:

THERE ARE SOME THINGS YOU NEED TO UN-
DERSTAND.

YES, IT'S TRUE THAT WE HAVE BEEN IN CON-
TACT WITH YOUR GOVERNMENT AND HEADS OF
POWER.

IT IS ALSO TRUE THAT AGREEMENTS HAVE
BEEN MADE AND KEPT SECRET FROM YOUR PEO-
PLE. IT IS ALSO TRUE THAT IN THE PAST SOME OF
YOUR PEOPLE HAVE LOST THEIR LIVES OR HAVE
BEEN BADLY HURT TO PROTECT THIS SECRET.

OUR HANDS HAD NO PART IN THIS.

WE CONTACTED YOUR LEADERS BECAUSE YOUR
PLANET IS IN GRAVE TROUBLE. YOUR LEADERS
SAID THE VAST MAJORITY OF YOUR POPULATION
WASN'T READY FOR ANYTHING LIKE US YET, SO WE
MADE TIME AGREEMENTS WITH YOUR LEADERS AS
TO WHEN YOUR PEOPLE WOULD BE MADE AWARE
OF OUR PRESENCE. THIS PART OF THE AGREEMENT
HAS NOT AT ALL BEEN KEPT.

IT WAS ALSO AGREED THAT IN THE MEANTIME
STEPS WOULD BE TAKEN TO CORRECT THE ENVIRON-
MENTAL CONDITION OF YOUR PLANET WITH OUR
ADVICE AND TECHOLOGY. WE SAY 'ADVICE' BECAUSE
WE RESPECT THE FACT THAT THIS IS YOUR PLANET,
NOT OURS. THEY ALSO BROKE THIS AGREEMENT.

I felt an awful wave of emotion from them – the feeling of
abandonment. To feel any emotion from them at all was amazing, but this was quite overwhelming.

You aren't giving up on us, are you?" I asked.

There was a long silent pause and I received the transmitted feeling of tremendous loss.

Well, are you?" I asked.

NO."

I felt an immediate sense of relief – straight from my own
emotions!

YOUR AIR, YOUR WATER, ARE CONTAMINATED.

YOUR FORESTS, JUNGLES, TREES AND PLANT
LIFE ARE DYING.

THERE ARE SEVERAL BREAKS IN YOUR FOOD
CHAIN.

YOU HAVE AN OVERWHELMING AMOUNT OF NUCLEAR AND BIOLOGICAL WEAPONS, WHICH INCLUDE NUCLEAR AND BIOLOGICAL CONTAMINATION.

YOUR PLANET IS OVERPOPULATED.

WARNING: IT IS ALMOST THE POINT OF BEING TOO LATE, UNLESS YOUR PEOPLE ACT.

THERE ARE BETTER WAYS OF DERIVING ENERGY AND FOOD NEEDS WITHOUT CAUSING YOUR PLANET ANY DAMAGE.

THOSE IN POWER ARE AWARE OF THIS AND HAVE THE CAPABILITY OF PUTTING THESE METHODS INTO WORLDWIDE USE.

I let this digest for a moment. I definitely had the feeling that these creatures were speaking as one.

Then I asked, "Why aren't we doing that now?

Silence. I was willing to wait. I had come a long way to be treated like this by them, to have this kind of meeting. Apparently I had earned their respect and trust. The best part was that I was getting direct, truthful answers to my questions. I decided that I would milk this rare situation to its fullest, asking as many questions as I could get away with, even personal questions.

I repeated my question, and they answered.

THOSE IN POWER VIEW IT AS A MILITARY AND SECURITY THREAT.

That upset me. "You mean to tell me the people in power have the ability to save and better this planet, and they aren't doing it?

AMNESTY.

What do you mean?

COMPLETE AMNESTY TO THOSE IN POWER, GOVERNMENTS AND LEADERS WHO HAVE BEEN SUPPRESSING THE TRUTH. THEY CAN'T BE HELD LIABLE FOR ANY PAST WRONG DEEDS. IT IS THE ONLY WAY THESE LEADERS CAN COME FORWARD WITH THE TRUTH. IT IS NECESSARY THAT YOU DO THIS IN ORDER TO WORK TOGETHER AND SURVIVE.

Of course, they were suggesting forgiveness. My anger at all this faded as I thought about it. It made sense. Heads roll whenever cover-ups are exposed. And this was a cover-up of galactic proportions – no pun intended.

If anyone had a good reason to hate their government for covering up this information, it was me, and others like me. Most abductees still consider themselves victims who constantly suffer ridicule. When your government's policy is to say, 'You're just plain crazy, it only deepens the pain.

I let my intelligence rule over my emotions and calmed down.

How do I fit in all this? What can I possibly do?

WHAT YOU ARE DOING ALREADY. WE WILL SHARE MUCH MORE KNOWLEDGE WITH YOU IN THE FUTURE. ALTHOUGH YOU UNDERSTAND A LOT, WE WILL SHOW YOU MUCH MORE.

CONTINUE TO WORK WITH PEOPLE THAT COME TO YOU. WE ARE AWARE OF THE SMALL GROUPS THAT ARE FORMING AROUND THE WORLD AND WE HAVE ADVICE. YOU WILL RECEIVE MORE KNOWLEDGE IN THE NEAR FUTURE.

These were not the exact same aliens who had worked with me all those years – but there was a link between them, and the pain and learning I went through all led up to this.

I asked my questions and they continued to give me some personal advice. They also said:

CONTINUE TO WORK WITH PEOPLE WHO COME TO YOU. THESE GROUPS FORMING AROUND THE WORLD ARE PEOPLE WHO ARE PREPARED TO LEARN. CONSIDER THEM THE CORE. THEN YOU WILL HAVE THOSE WHO WILL SEEK YOU OUT, WHO ARE STILL IN FEAR. ONCE THEY ARE OVER THE FEAR, THEN THEY WILL BE READY FOR THE CORE GROUP.

MOST IMPORTANT IS THE CONDITION OF YOUR PLANET. THE FIRST STEP IN SOLVING THIS SERIOUS PROBLEM IS AMNESTY.[31]

Prophecy

When much of this material was written in 2009, I was convinced that Earth had been visited for millennia by EBEs

(Extraterrestrial Biological Entities) from other star systems. I was less certain about our own solar system. I had heard many rumors but hadn't seen enough convincing evidence to repeat any in print. Since then my total knowledge has increased almost exponentially, and I am persuaded that several planets in our own celestial backyard are inhabited. My library contains many cases but due to space restraints I will only mention one, briefly, by way of example.

This story is taken from the book *Sowers of Life*, written by Charlie Paz Wells (aka Veronica Paz Wells).

The time was 1974, and the place was Lima, Peru. Two ordinary teenagers, Charlie and Sixto Paz Wells, along with several of their friends, traveled out to the Santo Domingo de los Alleros mountains along the Peruvian coast and experienced what they claim was contact with extraterrestrials. This extraordinary event was not limited to a one-time sighting, but became an 8-month-long odyssey, witnessed by more than 100 people, that tested the bounds of their sanity, their families and their friendships and became known as a UFO movement called "Rama."

During that period that changed their lives forever, they claim – in remarkable detail – that they witnessed alien space ships, had physical contact with extraterrestrial beings, and were teleported to distant planets within and outside of our solar system. As word spread of these encounters, it became clear that something transformative was happening, and it was impossible to deny the messages that were being transmitted – frightening to some, reassuring to others ... we are not alone.[32]

The Beings communicated with the boys through telepathy. They would establish initial contact by downloading to the boys the location, time and the date of an upcoming sighting of their ships. If the entire group received the same information, they knew it was real. Often the sightings took place 60 km outside of Lima in an area called Chilca. This form of "proof" was how the ETs established a relationship and a level of trust with the young group.

They would not be harmed. This experience would prove to be different than their other sightings. This time they were invited into a ship. According to Charlie, they were greeted by a Being standing in front of the craft who looked quite human, yet was much taller, with long straight blond/white hair and slightly almond-shaped eyes. He claimed to be from the planet Apu, from the constellation of Alpha Centauri. There were five extraterrestrials on the ship – three men and two women.

Inside, the group was led to a screen embedded in the ship's wall. Pointing to the screen the extraterrestrial told them, "This is the future of your planet …" An image appeared on the screen, showing desert and barren, dry plains. He explained that humans are part of an immense universe consisting of many different civilizations and planets. But humans have lost their way, and have become a threat to themselves and to the other civilizations that exist in our solar system and beyond. He said that the aliens' recent contact with the boys was an experiment – a test to see how the boys reacted to their presence. Could they be trusted? He insisted they were there to help. The reason they reached out to the boys was that they are young and open-minded. "It is the youth who will make the changes necessary to ensure human survival. You can decide to continue or end this experience. If you choose to continue, we will meet again." He walked them to the door and said goodbye.

In July of 1974, their experiences became more intense. The extraterrestrials introduced the group to a powerful light called a "Xendra," or inter-dimensional portal – a doorway between our world and theirs.

The extraterrestrials explained that there are more than 80 different extraterrestrial civilizations interacting within our solar system, all of which have gone through an evolutionary process. Now there is peace in the universe – and they want to keep it that way. Earth and human beings are going through their own evolutionary process and are unstable. Human's obsession with nuclear and atomic energy risk destroying themselves and their planet. Humanity is not in balance with the universe and the universal laws that control it. The guides explained that they want to help us realize we are not alone, and that there is a better way of living and evolving that is sustainable. But, before they give us the tools and technology to continue our evolution, they need to be assured that whatever they do for us will be for the benefit of ALL humanity, not just those in power who will use it to further their own agendas.

The young group struggled to process what they were told and shown by the extraterrestrials. How would anyone possibly believe what they had experienced? They began to take detailed notes of each encounter, writing down everything the extraterrestrials told them. These notes would one day form the foundation of a global UFO movement called "Rama," based on many books written by both Charlie and his brother Sixto about their experience.

I talked to the adult Charlie Paz Garcia a few weeks before this section was written. He explained that he and his brother had been teleported to Ganymede, one of Jupiter's moons, where they had seen a city of incredible beauty and Charlie was transported to Apu in Alpha Centauri. In Apu the people live underground because the surface is uninhabitable.

While Charlie was there, he was briefed on the future of our planet if we don't change our ways. His core message was that we have been incredibly bad stewards of our Earthly home, and will have to change our way of life dramatically in order to survive and live in peace both on Earth and with our celestial neighbors. This is the same message that has come from so many sources that I wanted to underline it here!

I will return to this subject briefly in Chapter 12.

Chapter Ten

THE MILITARY-INDUSTRIAL COMPLEX
(Currently Known As "The Cabal")

In the councils of government, we must guard against the acquisition
of unwarranted influence, whether sought or unsought, by the mili-
tary-industrial complex. The potential for the disastrous rise of mis-
placed power exists, and will persist.[1]

– President Dwight D. Eisenhower

This chapter heading comes from the famous warning President Dwight D. Eisenhower included in his farewell address. It was a "heads up" that Americans and the world ignored, at incredible cost and imminent peril. To quote the general:

This conjunction of an immense military establishment and a large arms industry is new in the American experience. The total influence – economic, political, even spiritual – is felt in every city, every State house, every office of the federal government. We recognize the imperative need for this development. Yet we must not fail to comprehend its grave implications. Our toil, resources and livelihood are all involved; so is the very structure of our society.[2]

Wikipedia has this to say in conjunction with President Eisenhower's plea in respect to the military-industrial complex:

The term is sometimes used more broadly to include the entire network of contracts and flows of money and resources among individuals as well as corporations and institutions of the defense contractors, the Pentagon, the Congress and executive

145

branch. This sector is intrinsically prone to principal-agent problem, moral hazard, and rent seeking. Cases of political corruption have also surfaced with regularity. A parallel system is that of the military-industrial-media complex, along with the more distant politico-media complex and prison-industrial complex.

A similar thesis was originally expressed by Daniel Guérin, in his 1936 book *Fascism and Big Business*, about the fascist government support to heavy industry. It can be defined as, 'an informal and changing coalition of groups with vested psychological, moral and material interests in the continuous development and maintenance of high levels of weaponry, in preservation of colonial markets and in military-strategic conceptions of internal affairs.' An exhibit of the trend was made in Franz Leopold Neumann's book, *Behemoth: The Structure and Practice of National Socialism* in 1942, a study of how Nazism came into a position of power in a democratic state.[3]

I emphasize these historical references because all too often history repeats itself and we fall into the same trap unaware that the same tricks have been used to deceive us as with previous generations. I will attempt to make the case that we are headed down that same slippery slope, and that it is long since time to put on our climbing boots before we reach the abyss.

When I read the complete text of President Eisenhower's farewell address – which I highly recommend as worth the effort, I found a beautifully crafted catalogue of high principles and noble aspirations tinged with a touch of melancholy. I got the impression that he felt betrayed, and that there was an unspoken concern about the extraterrestrial presence and technology, given the inevitable consequences for good or for bad.

Ufologist Michael Salas gave me a copy of his excellent book *Exopolitics* that contains much of the political background relating to the subject, and how the U.S. government and Congress lost control of the ET file. He explains how Nelson Rockefeller, as adviser to President Eisenhower, reorganized the control mechanisms for reverse engineering and essentially placed them in the hands of the military-industrial complex. Eisenhower recognized what had happened before he left politics, and this led to his classic warning.

One of Dr. Steven Greer's witnesses for his "Disclosure Project," Brigadier General Stephen Lovekin, a military officer who served directly under Eisenhower, confirmed the basis of the General's concern.

> But what happened was that Eisenhower got sold out. Without his knowing it he lost control of what was going on with the entire UFO situation. In his last address to the nation I think he was telling us that the Military Industrial Complex would stick you in the back if you were not totally vigilant … And I think that he realized that all of a sudden this matter is going into the control of corporations that could very well act to the detriment of this country. This frustration, from what I can remember, went on for months. He realized that the phenomenon, or whatever it was we were faced with, was not going to be in the best hands. As far as I can remember, that was the expression that was used, 'It is not going to be in the best hands.'[4]

The general's instinct was prophetic. It was authenticated by Dr. Wernher von Braun, the world-famous German rocket scientist who came to the United States immediately after World War II as part of "Operation Paperclip." He may have been sympathetic to the Hitler regime when he was involved in the German war effort, but his views mellowed as the years passed, and his major concern became the military-industrial complex of which his work made him an integral part.

Dr. Carol Rosin, who worked with von Braun for several years, noted his dismay at the fact that such a large part of the U.S. budget was allocated to the military machine. This was only possible when a clear majority of the American people were convinced that there was an enemy to be feared. So, when the Cabal, which controlled the major U.S. media outlets, wanted to influence public opinion, all they had to do was pick an "enemy" and exaggerate the degree of the threat it posed in order to justify their vast expenditures on armaments.

Von Braun told Rosin that there would be a succession of "enemies." "First it will be the communists, then it will be the terrorists, and after that it will be the extraterrestrials."[5] As the succession of "enemies" appears to be coming on stage exactly as planned, I should like to examine each one in somewhat greater depth than I have done before.

Our Communist "Enemies"

This one was an easy call. Even though the Union of Soviet Socialist Republics had wound up on the side of the Allies in World War II, and suffered incredible losses during the Siege of Leningrad, they were always suspect. We only accepted them as "friends of convenience."

The anti-Soviet propaganda machine went into overdrive. Our precious freedoms were threatened by an evil empire under the control of iron-fisted atheists. So there was no alternative but to mobilize against this all-pervasive threat if we did not want to lose everything that our valiant soldiers, sailors and airmen had fought and died for in World War II. At least that was the official line of those invisible hands that control our destiny, and I have to admit that I swallowed it hook, line and sinker.

Cold warriors were popular in the period of my ascendancy as a young politician. I was never an extremist, so I eschewed U.S. Senator Joseph McCarthy's career-wrecking crusade, and considered it quite abominable. Still, I was a convinced anti-communist, and did what I could to keep the Soviet menace at bay. This included strong support for the formation of the North Atlantic Treaty Organization which seemed like an honorable and practical way of preventing the spread of communism across Europe.

Consequently, when I became Minister of National Defence for Canada in 1963, one of my first actions was to visit our troops in Europe in order to assess their battle readiness. I was appalled by what I found. Our highly rated Brigade Group in Europe was limited to using trucks for battlefield deployment rather than armored personnel carriers. The artillery was of World War II vintage with no new self-powered howitzers. The Long John battlefield missiles had warheads filled with sand, rather than the nuclear warheads for which they were designed. I resolved on the spot that my first priority would be to provide the most up-do-date possible equipment necessary for our troops to fulfill their assignments.

I might not have been quite as enthusiastic about my black and white reading of the choice between Soviet state capitalism and Western "market" capitalism if I had been aware of the extent to which Wall Street had financed the Bolshevik revolution. Anyone who still believes that the revolution was spontaneous should read Chapter 22, "Bolsheviks' Benefactors," in *The True Story of the Bilderberg Group*, by Daniel Estulin. You will find there the key to much that is going on in the world today. I will quote just two or three paragraphs that should be sufficient to encourage you to read the whole sordid affair.

> Even though channels linking the Rockefellers and the Soviets have been largely censored, Antony Sutton's detailed document, *Wall Street and the Bolshevik Revolution*, exposes how John D. Rockefeller and American super capitalists financed the Bolshevik Revolution in Russia. At the outset of his investigation, he found 'virtually nothing written on the close relationship over the past century that the Rockefellers have had with its supposed arch-enemies, the Communists. [Nevertheless,] there has been a continuing, albeit concealed, alliance between the international political capitalists and international revolutionary socialists to their mutual benefit.'[6]

> For example, Simpson, Thacher and Bartlet, the leading Wall Street law firm specializing in reorganization and mergers was firmly behind the Bolshevik regime in Russia. 'As one indication of their support,' writes Sutton, 'partner Thomas D. Thacher wrote a report which became decisive in gaining British cabinet support for the Bolsheviks ... This memorandum not only made explicit suggestions about Russian policy that supported the pro-Bolshevik position of William Boyce Thompson, the then director of Chase, now Chase Manhattan Bank, but even stated that the 'fullest assistance should be given to the Soviet government in its efforts to organize a volunteer revolutionary army.'

> It is worth noting that one of Simpson, Thacher and Bartlett's alumni was the young Cyrus Vance, who would later be-

come President Carter's Secretary of State and, following that, a senior director of the Rockefeller Foundation. Small world indeed.

One of the Wall Street firms involved with the Bolsheviks was J.P. Morgan, as was revealed in Harold Nicholson's biography of Morgan partner Dwight Morrow, the father-in-law of Charles Lindbergh, Jr.

Another mega-organization supporting the Bolshevik cause was the Federal Reserve Bank of New York, controlled by the five principal New York banks. In *The Unknown War with Russia*, Robert J. Maddox noted in 1977, 'William Laurence Sanders, chairman of Ingersoll Rand, and deputy chairman of the Federal Reserve Bank of New York, wrote to President Wilson, on October 17, 1918, 'I am in sympathy with the Soviet form of government as the best suited for the Russian people.' George Foster Peabody, also deputy chairman of the Federal Reserve Board of New York since 1914, and noted philanthropist, who organized the General Education Board for the Rockefellers, stated that he supported the Bolshevik form of state monopoly.'

The scam boggles the mind when we consider that three of the top officers of the Federal Reserve Bank of New York publicly supported Bolshevism – Sanders, Peabody and William Boyce Thompson.[7]

The story raises the ugly truth about international banks assisting in the creation of a formidable enemy and then making tons of money financing an American war machine capable of containing it. This "they win, the people lose" formula has become the one that has now set the world on its calamitous course.

It may have been partly luck that the Soviet Union decided not to test the United States by starting a war that might quickly have presented the NATO Allies with the option of either losing all Europe to the Soviet system, or of pursuing a nuclear escalation leading to the virtual annihilation of both the U.S. and the U.S.S.R. It was the French fear that, given that option, the U.S. would "chicken out," and sacrifice Europe to save its own skin, that led the French to develop their own independent nuclear capacity.

In any event, the deterrent worked and the stalemate continued for decades. In many ways this was good for the world because both communists and capitalists curried the favor of Third World countries, and presented their most benign and attractive face.

No one could have been happier than I when the Berlin Wall came down on November 9, 1989. The elation on our side of the curtain was near universal, and very significant on the other side as one country after another regained its freedom. Nearly everyone believed that these historic events signaled the dawn of a new era of peace and prosperity for people everywhere.

There was much talk of a peace dividend. Without any enemies of military significance, the Western countries, and the U.S. in particular, could reduce expenditures for armaments and divert the savings to myriad essential priorities including health care, education, environmental protection including sustainable growth, and the development of new sources of energy to replace fossil fuels. There would also be more money for the arts and the alleviation of poverty and illiteracy on a global basis. The prospects were dazzling in their scope and diversity. It was a unique and God-given opportunity for a new, braver and fairer world.

We blew it! We blew the chance of a lifetime to do good things!

A small group of zealots undermined our golden opportunity to pursue peace, not war. Little did we dream that they had a vastly different "vision" of the New World Order. That group included U.S. Vice-President Dick Cheney, former Defense Secretary Donald Rumsfeld, former Deputy Secretary of Defense Paul Wolfowitz, Douglas Feith who held the number three position at the Pentagon, Lewis "Scooter" Libby, a Wolfowitz protégé, who later served as Cheney's Chief of Staff before his dismissal, John R. Bolton who was assigned to the State Department to keep Secretary of State Colin Powell in check, and Elliott Abrams, appointed to head the Middle East policy at the National Security Council. Apparently all envisioned a world dominated by the U.S. – economically and militarily.[8]

Their plan, now commonly known as "The Project for a New American Century," included preventive wars (in clear violation of international law), regime change wherever and whenever the U.S. desires, and if they can get away with it without excessive casualties, and the establishment of a kind of economic and cultural hegemony with America acting as "constabulary" (their word) globally.

This was to be accomplished without authority of the United Nations and without the restraint of existing international treaties. It would involve a military buildup unprecedented in "peacetime" history and could trigger an arms race which is precisely the opposite to the peace dividend that the world had rightly looked forward to.

The Machiavellian scheme involved secret police, the curtailment of civil liberties in defiance of the U.S. Constitution, and a moribund economy, operating way below its potential – exactly those features for which the Soviet Union was held in contempt.

One distinction may be that the "vision" was "on the record." Not since *Mein Kampf*, in the 1930s, had anyone been so open about their intentions. The problem, as it was in the 1930s, is that decent people refuse to believe that such far-fetched belligerence is planned, even when they see it in cold print.

To those of us who have been around long enough to put things in historical context there is no disguising the nature of the beast. The Project for a New American Century was a plan to establish an American Empire unprecedented since the fall of the Roman Empire; and with consequences more devastating and demoralizing for greater numbers of people than the Evil Empire from which we thought the world had been liberated.

I have decided to include excerpts from the original PNAC for the simple reason that a test sample of U.S. tourists visiting my small resort in Muskoka, Ontario, revealed that not one of them had ever heard of it. Not one. One can only conclude that the majority of Americans didn't know what was really going on in their own country, and the far-reaching consequences for them both individually and collectively.

Project for a New American Century

The initial draft of the Pentagon document "Defense Planning Guidance" on Post-Cold War Strategy was dated February 18, 1992. Some of the key sections are as follows:

    1. Our first objective is to prevent the re-emergence of a new rival, either on the territory of the former Soviet Union, or

elsewhere, that poses a threat on the order of that posed formerly by the Soviet Union. This is a dominant consideration underlying the new regional defense strategy and requires that we endeavor to prevent any hostile power from dominating a region whose resources would, under consolidated control, be sufficient to generate global power.

2. The U.S. must show the leadership necessary to establish and protect a new order that holds the promise of convincing potential competitors that they need not aspire to a greater role or pursue a more aggressive posture to protect their legitimate interests. In non-defense areas, we must account sufficiently for the interests of the advanced industrial nations to discourage them from challenging our leadership or seeking to overturn the established political and economic order. We must maintain the mechanisms for deterring competitors from even aspiring to a larger regional or global role.

3. Like the coalition that opposed Iraqi aggression, we should expect future coalitions to be ad hoc assemblies, often not lasting beyond the crisis being confronted, and in many cases carrying only general agreement over the objectives to be accomplished. Nevertheless, the sense that the world order is ultimately backed by the U.S. will be an important stabilizing factor.

4. While the U.S. cannot become the world's policeman by assuming responsibility for righting every wrong, we will retain the preeminent responsibility for addressing selectively those wrongs which threaten not only our interests, but those of our allies or friends, or which could seriously unsettle international relations.

5. We continue to recognize that collectively the conventional forces of the states formerly comprising the Soviet Union retain the most military potential in all of Eurasia; and we do not dismiss the risks to stability in Europe from a nationalist backlash in Russia, or efforts to reincorporate into Russia the newly independent republics of Ukraine, Belarus, and possibly others ... We must, however, be mindful that democratic change in Russia is now irreversible, and that despite its current travails, Russia will remain the strongest military power in Eurasia and the only power in the world with the capacity of destroying the United States.

6. In the Middle East and Southwest Asia, our overall objective is to remain the predominant outside power in the region and preserve U.S. and Western access to the region's oil.[9]

When a leaked copy of the document, prepared under the supervision of Paul Wolfowitz, then the Pentagon's Undersecretary for Policy, was disclosed by the *New York Times* in May 1992, the negative reaction from both the White House and foreign capitals was so strong that it had to be redrafted.

The new sanitized version adopted a much more conciliatory note. It stated: "One of the primary tasks we face today in shaping the future is carrying long-standing alliances into the new era, and turning old enmities into new cooperative relationships."[10]

The document made a small bow in the direction of a leveling of military investments coupled with greater economic and security cooperation. The bottom line remained unchanged, however. "It is not in our interest or those of the other democracies to return to earlier periods in which multiple military powers balanced one another off in what passed for security structures, while regional, or even global peace hung in the balance."[11]

As someone who has long observed the techniques of creating politically acceptable language, and has sometimes been a practitioner of that craft, I would say that the principal difference between the first and the revised draft is in the weasel words. You can't change a tiger by whitewashing its stripes. The men responsible for the first draft had changed little, if at all. That conclusion can be substantiated by their actions in office; the abrogation of the anti-ballistic missile treaty, the vast buildup in military expenditures at the expense of other priorities that the majority might consider more important; the installation of a world-wide system of regional defense commands, and the insistence on developing weapons of incredible destruction for use in space.

One has to ask how such a small group of neo-conservative ideologues could take over the U.S. administration as a first step towards an expanded empire. In a stroke of good luck for them, and bad luck for nearly everyone else, including the vast majority of the American people, George W. Bush chose Dick Cheney as his running mate. The die was cast.

Once the U.S. Supreme Court decided that George W. Bush would succeed Bill Clinton as the 43rd President of the United States, the President-elect put the former defense secretary in charge of his transition team. Cheney slotted one after another of his Pentagon team for the New American Century into key posts to the point where they had the balance of power in the incoming administration. Overnight, the long-standing tenet that defense should be an extension of foreign policy was reversed.

It may have been relatively easy to persuade President Bush to abandon his stated policy of not getting America more deeply involved in international affairs, but persuading the American people would be more difficult. Sophisticated Americans would question such a giant sea change in policy.

The authors of "Rebuilding America's Defenses: Strategy, Forces and Resources for a New Century" recognized this difficulty from the outset, for their document contained the following sentence. "Further, the process of transformation, even if it brings revolutionary changes, is likely to be a long one, absent some catastrophic and catalyzing event – like a new Pearl Harbor."[12] (Since deleted from the text.)

Well, it wasn't too long before they got their catastrophic and catalyzing event. Terrorists struck the World Trade Center in New York, and the Pentagon in Washington.

September 11, 2001

I wept internally when the full impact of what was happening penetrated my consciousness. I was at the office when one of the staff said they had just heard over the radio that the World Trade Center in New York had been attacked. We turned on the TV and saw a spiral of flame and smoke escaping from one of the towers. It took a few seconds to absorb the fact that what we were seeing was genuine and not some Orwellian computer creation. As we watched in silent horror we could only imagine how awful it really was.

It was a long day and night that no witness could ever forget – the reports of casualties followed by images of the dead and the dying. Firemen trapped inside the buildings, in the course of duty. Occasionally, there was a good luck story of someone who had escaped or, blessed by fortune, had missed his or her train, and been spared.

Almost the whole world mourned. Canada mourned. The overwhelming majority of Muslims condemned the treacherous attacks. A vast crowd of 80,000 assembled on Parliament Hill in Ottawa in an outpouring of love and affection for our American friends and neighbors. Many of us attended special remembrance services in our respective churches as an expression of deepest concern and sympathy. A group of people from Toronto organized a weekend pilgrimage to New York to demonstrate their support and empathy.

My sympathy for the friends and families of the injured and dead was genuine and continues unwavering to this day. My sympathy for the U.S. government began to grow a bit thin, however, when I heard President Bush cite the reasons for the attack. "Why do they hate us?" he asked rhetorically in an address to the Congress. "They hate what they see right here in this chamber: a democratically elected government. Their leaders are self-appointed. They hate our freedoms: our freedom of religion, our freedom of speech, our freedom to vote and assemble and disagree with each other."[13]

I felt sad when I heard the President's words. I assumed that he believed what he was saying, but if that were true, he was profoundly ignorant of the real thoughts and feelings of people in other parts of the world. If he wanted to hear the truth, he should have listened to Osama bin Laden, leader of al-Qaeda, who was well-informed concerning the origins of the kind of fanatical hatred of the U.S. which had led to such treachery. This is his version of events:

> Every Muslim must rise to defend his religion. The wind of faith is blowing and the wind of change is blowing to remove evil from the Peninsula of Muhammad, peace be upon him. As to America, I say to it and its people a few words: I swear to God that America will not live in peace before peace reigns in Palestine, and before all the army of infidels depart the land of Muhammad, peace be upon him.[14]

That is clear enough. The dislike of America has nothing to do with democracy versus dictatorship, or wealth, or freedom of

religion and assembly. It is directly related to American foot-drag-
ging in stick-handling a just settlement of the Palestinian question,
while continuing to meddle in Middle Eastern affairs, including the
stationing of troops on soil considered sacred to Islam. In short,
American foreign policy was the root of the conflict.

You would think that someone in the State Department, the
CIA, or the FBI, if not all three, would have briefed the president
on such critically important issues. Perhaps someone did, but the
American people were never let in on the secret. To do so would
have created too much disillusionment. More importantly for the
Bush administration, it would have undermined plans to implement the Project for a New American Century which ignores the
sensibilities of all outsiders.

Months later the president was forced to admit that he had been
forewarned of a possible al-Qaeda hijacking plot nearly a month
before September 11, 2001. "U.S. National Security Adviser Condoleezza Rice acknowledged that the White House was alerted that
'something was coming' and that Mr. Bush was alerted to the possibility of hijackings in a written 'analytical' briefing delivered to him at his
ranch in Crawford, Texas, on August 6."[15] She went on to insist that
there was no information about the time, place or method of attack,
this despite the fact that the word hijackings was used in the briefings.

One would have thought that the warning would have been sufficient for the U.S. forces to go on high alert and especially the two
squadrons of fighter jets at Andrews Air Force Base assigned to defend the White House. There was another mystery. Why did the president pretend that he had first learned of the attacks in that classroom,
when he had actually been briefed as he left his hotel that morning?[16]

It is doubtful that how much the president actually knew will
ever be known, and it has ceased to be relevant except to historians. What is relevant is the reaction to the attack and the brand of
terrorism it represented. The administration was faced with three
options. (a) It could accept the real reasons for the fanatical hatred
and take the necessary steps to remove the causes of it. (b) It could
accelerate the police and intelligence campaign necessary to locate
and neutralize the very limited threat from a handful of al-Qaeda

operatives with the active cooperation and assistance of just about everyone in the world including Muslim countries. (c) It could launch an all-out war on terrorism, the only option of the three that was destined to fail from the outset.

Not too surprisingly, option (c) was the administration's choice. An all-out war on terrorism was the only choice that fit the strategy of the military-industrial complex as reflected in the Plan for a New American Century. It is, unfortunately, a war that will never end until we see the end of the people who made the fateful and tragic decision to launch it.

The Truth About 9/11 Leaking Out

> Did you see these buildings turn to dust or do you 'believe' they collapsed because you were told that they collapsed? Whoever controls the energy controls the people.
>
> But whoever controls their perception controls everything.[17]

– Eric Larsen

In "Light," I expressed the view that, although doubts had been raised about the official story concerning 9/11, it was likely that the truth might never be known. I now believe that I was wrong and that the cloak of deception has slowly but convincingly unravelled.

I was personally suspicious early on when quite legitimate questions were being raised without any reasoned response. If Condoleezza Rice had warned the president on August 6th that something ominous was in the wind, why wasn't the whole east coast on high alert? There were myriad questions that just wouldn't go away.

Privately, I encouraged the researchers in their endeavors. The evidence began to emerge and accumulate as the months and years passed by. A book by a well-known and highly respected Canadian journalist, Barrie Zwicker, was a milestone. His *Towers of Deception: The Media Cover-Up of 9/11*, published in 2006, couldn't be dismissed given his reputation as a passionate and intellectually honest sleuth.[18]

In 2010, I received a copy of First Edition: v.1.1 of the *9/11 Investigator: Exposing the Explosive WTC Evidence*. A headline article entitled "1,000 Architects & Engineers Challenge Official Report of WTC Destruction" by Rich Caragol, architect, began as follows:

> Welcome to Architects & Engineers for 9/11 Truth. We are a non-partisan association of more than 1,000 A/Es, with about 10,000 affiliates from all over the world. We are technical professionals representing more than 25,000 years of collective experience. We do not offer conspiracy theories. We do have serious questions about the official reports of the destruction of all three World Trade Center skyscrapers on 9/11. We are calling for a new independent investigation that includes all of the evidence that is missing from these building reports. We, along with other researchers and groups in the growing international 9/11 truth movement, have compiled critically important eyewitness testimony, photo, video, and scientific forensic evidence that has been ignored, falsified, or destroyed by individuals and agencies that were responsible to the public for a thorough transparent investigation.
>
> Our website, AE911Truth.org documents much of this important work. Our online store hosts several books, DVDs, technical papers, and other effective tools such as brochures, cards and vinyl banners, for use in educating the public."[19]

A page 4 "Summary of Evidence: A Call to Action" by Pete Denney follows:

> The destruction of the Twin Towers and WTC Building 7 were the largest structural failures in modern history. The official story, as told by the 9/11 Commission and NIST, claims that fires weakened the structures, causing all three buildings to collapse. However, the evidence, most of which was omitted from official reports, supports a very different conclusion: explosive controlled demolition.
>
> Summary of the evidence:
>
> 1. Rapid onset of destruction with unnatural symmetry of debris.

2. Constant acceleration at or near free-fall through the path of what should have been greatest resistance.

3. 118 witnesses to explosions and flashes of light, and foreknowledge of WTC 7's collapse.

4. Lateral ejection of multi-ton steel sections 600 feet at more than 60 mph.

5. Mid-air pulverization of 90,000 tons of concrete, and massive volumes of expanding pyroclastic-like dust clouds.

6. Isolated explosive ejections 20-60 stories below 'crush zone.'

7. Total destruction of all three buildings, with 220 missing floors from the Twin Towers – each an acre in size.

8. Several tons of molten steel/iron found in the debris pile.

9. Evidence of thermite incendiaries on steel beams.

10. Nanothermite composites found in WTC dust.

11. Destruction of evidence by those in charge of the investigation.

The above constitutes overwhelming evidence supporting the hypothesis of engineered destruction. Demolition experts agree that the preparation to execute the controlled demolition of a high-rise building takes months to plan and carry out. Several credible reports of foreknowledge have come forth. It is only reasonable to suspect that powerful insiders, not just the 19 alleged hijackers, were behind the destruction.

We at AE911Truth believe that it is time for every American to face the facts and their own conscience. Almost 3,000 people were murdered at the WTC on the morning of September 11, 2001. The United States has invaded two countries under cover of the rhetoric of the War on Terror, resulting in massive casualties and unprecedented deficit spending. We have lost many of our civil liberties as a result of the PATRIOT Act, the Military Commissions Act, and other laws enacted in reaction to 9/11.

Once you, too, investigate the evidence we believe that you will want to take action.[20]

In the course of writing this book, I came across a YouTube by Major General Albert Stubblebine III, who left no doubt where he stood. His final assignment before retirement was responsibility for all of the U.S. army's strategic intelligence forces around the world. He and his wife were in Hawaii attending a conference when the 9/11 attack took place around 3:00 a.m. local time.

At about 3:30 a.m. the general, by then retired, got a phone call from one of the officers who had served under him. The general's recollection is as follows: She said: "Sir, the United States is at war." I said, "What are you talking about?" "The United States is at war." I said, "Come on, what have you been drinking?" She said, "Listen to me, go turn on the television, the United States is at war." I still didn't believe. I go turn on the television and I see the towers. I still didn't believe. I said, "That's a joke." I switched channels, a tower is going down, I switched channels, a tower is going down. I said, "Oh my God." So I thanked her for the information. I turned to Rima and I said, "You watch, I guarantee you right now that the information about that attack was in the system and somebody missed it. The information was there … that that attack was coming. Somebody didn't see the signals. That's my own personal intelligence background, although my experience after that … the intelligence world tells me that when something that big goes by somebody missed the information. So, I was a believer, absolute believer that the attack was a terrorist attack. That it was all done by other forces and after that … my wife began to put the pieces together. She said: "I don't think that attack was done by the enemy, the terrorists that you indicated." I said, "You're wrong. I don't believe it. It's unbelievable." And so she began to find bits and pieces of information and she would present them to me. And I said, "No, no, no. Not my government. My government would not tell a lie like that." I was in disbelief. I was so ingrained in my belief system that I could not believe. I literally could not believe that anybody but a sort of Arab terrorists could do something like that.

> Then one day I saw a picture. It was a photograph of the Pentagon and the hole in the Pentagon. I looked at it and I said, 'Wow.' I looked at it again, there's something wrong with this

picture. Then I kept looking ... then I began to not to look at it ... but to study the photograph itself ... what's wrong with this picture ... why is your belly saying ... my kinesthetic aspect of my processing system ... saying there's something wrong with that picture. There was something wrong.

So I analyzed it, not just photographically, I did measurements, I did all kinds of things. I checked the plane ... the length of the nose ... where the wings were ... I did all of the measurements ... took the measurements of the Pentagon ... the depth and destruction of the plane ... *conclusion* ... *that airplane did not make that hole.*

I went public. At the time I am the highest-ranking officer, I believe, that has ever gone public. Whatever that story was, the official story, was not true. Now, I was very careful to not say what it was because I couldn't prove it. I was careful to say it was not the airplane that did that, because I can prove it was not the airplane.

In the hole, however, was a turbine that looked like a turbine from the missile ... I can't prove that. I don't know, but there was something that did not look like the engine from airplane, but did look like a turbine from a missile.

Later, I saw another photograph by one of the sensors on the outside of the Pentagon. Now, all of the sensors had been turned off, which is kind of interesting, isn't it. That day, why would all of the sensors around the Pentagon be turned off? That's strange. I don't care what the excuse is. That's strange. There happened to be one that did not get turned off. And in that picture, coming in, flying into the Pentagon, you see this object, and it obviously hits the Pentagon. When you look at it, it does not look like an airplane. Later, sometime later, after I'd gone public, that imagery was changed. It got a new suit. It now looked like an airplane. But, when you take the suit off, it looks more like a missile.

Let me go back to the next very important piece of information. The amount of energy required to melt the girders, the steel in the tower, can not be gotten to a melt point with the fuel that was in the airplane. Not possible! So, any melting did not occur as a result of the hit from the airplane. Point. I call it dot. OK! Dot!

When you look at the tower coming down, what you see at each floor, successive puffs of smoke – puff, puff, puff, puff ...

all the way down. Where are the puffs of smoke coming from? Well, they claim that they are from the collapsing floors. Uh, Uh! ... No, No, No! Those puffs of smoke are controlled demolitions. That's exactly what they are, because that's exactly how they work. And so, the fact that the airplane hit it, did not cause that collapse of the building. **The collapse of the building was caused by controlled demolition.**

Fact – Building 7 – Silverstein, I believe is the name of the owner. He was on video and you could see Building 7 ... you could literally see it. And there was a fire in Building 7 ... there is no doubt about that. No airplane hit it. I assume that the fire came from some debris, but I'm not even sure of that. But in the lower right-hand corner of the building was a fire ... not a very big fire. It didn't appear to be out of control. It certainly was in a small part of the building. But then he is heard on the video ... okay ... he says, "pull it" and then the building collapsed. What does pull it mean? What are the words pull it mean? Let me tell you. That's the order for controlled demolition. That is their phraseology that's used for blowing up something. And that's when Building 7 blew up.

All of the air defense systems in that part of the country had been turned off that day. All of the air defense systems had been turned off. Why? Apparently because the vice-president was out in Colorado and he ordered them turned off. Why would you turn off all of the air defense systems on that particular day unless you knew something was going to happen? It's a dot. It's information. But strange that everything got turned off that day. Dot!

There was an exercise that was designed for the air defense systems that was attack on the towers by airplanes. Isn't that strange that we had an exercise that mimicked what really happened? Strange that we had planned an exercise that was exactly what happened. And, at the same time, the air defense systems were turned off. Did you find that strange? I find that really strange. Dot. Just a piece of information.

But how does it correlate with everything else? So, you see the dots. You have all of these dots. They're just bits of information. But that's exactly how the intelligence world works. You get a bit of information here. You get a bit of information here. A bit here and a bit here. And pretty soon you get a picture. To me, what does the picture say? The picture says that what we heard and were told in the newspapers, the media, was not the real story. There's enough doubt in the official story, where the stories were absolutely not consistent with what happened. They paint a different picture than the one that was given to the media.

How easy is it for you to shift your belief system from, I totally believe in my government to, oh my God! What's going on? That's exactly where I went in all of this. Because my belief system was so strong from age five when I could remember standing on a parade ground at attention, with not anybody telling me to do that – at West Point. I did it because I wanted to do it. Because I believed. And, then going to the military academy and serving, defending ...

The real story was ... I have a question, I guess. The real story to me is, who was the real enemy? Who participated in this? Who planned this attack? Why was it planned? Were the real terrorists the people in Arab clothing? Or were the real people that planned this, the people sitting in authority in the White House?[21]

The Clincher

For some years I have been convinced in my heart that 9/11 was an "inside job," a "False Flag Operation" as they are called by historians, but I studiously avoided exposure to the evidence in order to claim lack of sufficient information as justification for not getting involved. That long-time comfort zone was lost in November 2012, not by design, certainly, but because, no doubt, it was meant to be.

I had been invited by Jeroen van Straaten and his incredibly dedicated team of futurists to speak at their conference, Breakthrough Energy Movement, in Hilversum, the Netherlands, the weekend of November 9-11, 2012. New Energy is not my expertise, but the meeting offered a platform for me to flog a "State of the World" address, while providing the opportunity for me to learn more about breakthrough energy, a subject of intense interest. The time and location were also positive factors. My wife, Sandra, and I planned to visit Turkey with a group of former Canadian parliamentarians, and so all we had to do was stop over in the Netherlands for a few days on our way home to Toronto.

After a night in Amsterdam, our hosts offered to pick us up at the hotel and drive us to Hilversum. We accepted their kind offer, and readily agreed when we were asked if we would mind sharing the car with a couple of other presenters, one of whom was a delightful Judy Wood, who would be talking about 9/11. Sandra and I both decided that she was one person to whom we must listen.

Her PowerPoint presentation was mind-boggling. She dispelled any notion that the two tall towers could have been taken down by fires started by the two terrorist aircraft that had ploughed into them. The towers were designed to withstand more stress than the suicide attack could have created.

Judy hadn't quite finished her presentation when her time ran out; so, a second hour was scheduled for that purpose. During the question period, Judy refused to say who was responsible for the heinous crime, probably because she didn't know. The answer has to be one of America's most closely guarded secrets. All she would say was, "Look at the evidence" – evidence that clearly and unequivocally refuted the official version.

When the session ended, everyone I spoke to was convinced. Even my wife Sandra, who automatically tunes out at the slightest whiff of the notion of conspiracy, was convinced that Judy had it right. We decided to buy a copy of her book; but it was sold out by the time we got down to the book table, and we were left empty-handed.

Fortunately, Lady Luck came to the rescue. Within days of starting to write this chapter, a friend mailed me a copy of *Where Did The Towers Go? Evidence of Directed Free-Energy Technology on 9/11*, by Judy Wood, B.S., M.S., Ph.D. I was soon engrossed in 500 pages of the most meticulously researched and photographically prepared account of a major historical event that I have ever seen.

I will quote only one paragraph under the heading, "What Debris Pile?," and one eyewitness account in support.

> The WTC towers did not collapse. They did not collapse from fire nor did they collapse from "bombs in the buildings" (or conventional controlled demolition.) They were turned to dust. They were turned to powder in mid-air. The majority of the building mass did not slam to the ground, as evidenced by the

seismic data. Nearly all of each tower was turned to dust in mid-air and either floated to the ground or blew away. The majority of what remained of the towers was paper and dust. A gravity collapse (with or without bombs in the building) cannot turn a building into powder in mid-air.[22]

I looked and said, 'Guys, there used to be 106 floors above us and now I'm seeing sunshine.'... 'There's nothing above us. That big building doesn't exist.'... These are the biggest office buildings in the world and I didn't see one desk or one chair or one phone, nothing. – Jay Jonas, (firefighter, survivor in stairwell B).[23]

While there are thousands of experts who reject the official version of 9/11, and they should be applauded for their pains-taking research, Dr. Wood appears to me to be the only one to conclude that something new and very different from previously known technology was involved. It is a key point of fundamental importance so I asked her if she would write a short summary for me to include here, and she graciously agreed.

Dr. Judy Wood

"Many people will be surprised to learn that it was not just three World Trade Center (WTC) buildings that were destroyed on 9/11, but all seven, much of their mass turned to dust. This was done in broad daylight in front of virtually the entire planet, yet few people realized this. How was such a thing possible? People prefer to believe what they are told over what they observe. Before noon on 9/11/01, we were all 'told' *who* had done '*it*' and *how* '*it*' had been done, this before any investigation had even been conducted to determine *what* '*it*' was that had been done.

"The order of crime solving is to determine:

1. WHAT happened, then

2. HOW it happened (e.g. by what weapon), then

3. WHO did it. And only then can we address

4. WHY they did it (i.e. motive).

"If you begin with anything other than *what* happened, you are only addressing an imagined problem, not a real one. Because of people's skipping that first step, what happened on 9/11 became a belief, even though the evidence contradicted this 'belief.'

"The book *Where Did the Towers Go?*[24] allows the reader to review a wide variety of evidence gathered in one place. This is a full-color 540-page book that includes over 860 images and diagrams. The book takes the reader through this evidence in a methodical way – *showing* them what happened rather than asking them to believe a theory. When we know for ourselves what happened, it grounds us to reality and we can understand what is at stake.

"The reader will learn that the towers did not burn up nor did they slam to the ground. Mostly, they turned into dust in mid air. The evidence for this is irrefutable. If the buildings had slammed down to the ground, there would have been appropriate seismic signals, and the underground of lower Manhattan would have been flooded due to a ruptured slurry wall. But none of this happened. Not only that, but the ground shook for only 8 seconds during the demise of WTC1, although a billiard ball dropped from the roof of WTC1 would take 9.22 seconds to reach the ground – in a vacuum, with no air resistance. There were 14 survivors in Stairway B of WTC1 during the demise of WTC1; when the dust cleared, they looked up to see blue sky and walked out on their own. If the building had collapsed, they would have been crushed. If fires or high heat had caused all the destruction, they would have been cooked to death and people in southern Manhattan would have been blinded by the light from the tremendous heat required to destroy the buildings. Heat weakens steel, but it does not cause steel to turn to powder in mid air. The lack of appropriate seismic signal eliminates the possibility that **Kinetic Energy** destroyed the WTC. The lack of appropriate heat eliminates the possibility that **Thermal Energy** destroyed the WTC. That is, the buildings were not crushed or pulverized, nor were they heated to the point where they vaporized. Mostly, they were turned to dust in mid air, or *dustified*.[25]

"The implications of this fact are monumental. The fact that the buildings were mostly turned to dust in mid air proves that a technology that can cause such a thing to happen must exist. Pursuing the operator of this technology or those who directed its usage does not change the fact that this technology exists. But let us look at another implication.

"The evidence of what happened on 9/11 is evidence of a technology that can do the things that were done. It is also evidence that a technology capable of providing enormous quantities of free (or very cheap) clean energy must exist, and can free us from being slaves to the energy industry. For many years we've been told that 'free energy is just around the corner.' The evidence of what happened on 9/11 shows that it's already here, but that it has been used for evil purposes. But the technology used on 9/11 need not be used for evil purposes. It could instead be used to provide free energy to the world. Here the word 'free' is used in the sense of 'liberation' – from extortion, blackmail, and slavery. Hence the subtitle of the book *Where Did the Towers Go?* is *Evidence of Directed Free-Energy Technology on 9/11.*[26]

"Many people view 9/11 as a false-flag event, yet it was unlike any other. The events of 9/11 cannot be viewed as a car wreck that happened twelve years ago with the wrong party being blamed. Yes, 9/11 has been used as an excuse to start wars, take away the rights of the people, and even to dismantle the U.S. Constitution. But it was even more. 9/11 was an attack on human consciousness that affected the entire planet.

"The Foreword to this book was written by Dr. Eric Larsen and begins, 'The book you hold in your hands is the most important book of the twenty-first century.' If you were to read the book, you would know why. But there is still more to learn from this."

I am most grateful for such an amazing summary of this gargantuan issue. I hope it will encourage you to get a copy of Dr. Wood's book *Where Did the Towers Go? Evidence of Directed Free-Energy Technology on 9/11*, which is available from Amazon.

It is hard to conceive of a deception so monstrous that it would change the world for years, if not forever. It would provide President George W. Bush with the excuse to declare an attack on the U.S. – without naming any country in particular – and claiming that NATO members were bound by their treaty to come to America's aid. Thus ended the innocence of that worthy alliance that had been dedicated to maintaining the peace.

The Arabs, who were merely bit players in this tragedy of tragedies, were vilified by the American press. The condemnation was so compelling that a very significant proportion of Americans were ready to "nuke them," according to a poll I saw. Defense measures were tightened everywhere. Airport security screening was dramatically tightened at considerable cost to the U.S. and many other countries who were subject to much collateral damage.

In this category, the most profoundly worrisome was the attack on civil rights. New legislation allowed arrest and confinement without warrant. Hundreds of years of hard won victories against the arbitrary rule of tyrants went down the tube in one infamous day that crowned and confirmed the cult of deceit, and disinformation, that had become endemic since World War II.

Iraq – And the War of Lies

Most friendly observers could understand why a strike on the Taliban might have been justified – despite pleas for mercy, and reminders that it had been an ally of the U.S. in the Cold War – because it appeared to be essential, if only for domestic political reasons, to retaliate for harboring Osama bin Laden. This despite a Taliban offer to turn bin Laden over if the U.S. could provide evidence of his complicity – an offer that was rejected out of hand.

The war against Iraq, however, was quite a different matter. Iraq was not harboring al-Qaeda operations, and it posed no imminent threat to the United States – the essential condition for a pre-emptive strike. None of this really seemed to matter. Iraq had been on the Defense Department's hit list for years, and the final decision to attack made within weeks of the September 11 tragedy.

Advance knowledge of the strike was voiced by Israeli Prime Minister Benjamin Netanyahu and published in the *World Tribune* in December 2001. "They have decided (on Iraq)," he told the annual Herzliya Conference on Israeli strategy. "It will not be in the long-term future." Netanyahu said Bush had decided that Iraq would be the U.S. next target in the U.S. war on terrorism."[27]

My first inkling occurred some months before any public announcement. I just happened to be listening to the radio and heard President George W. Bush use the term "weapons of mass destruction" eight or nine times in the course of three or four minutes.

"Oh, oh," I said to myself, "something's up; that is brainwashing."

It would be impossible to count the number of times that same quotation was used by the president and his advisers in the weeks that followed. It didn't take long for everyone to get the point. Saddam Hussein and his Iraqi regime were the possessors of "weapons of mass destruction," and these posed a threat to the United States. Ultimately, the majority in the U.S. and many others, especially in the English-speaking world, were convinced.

It didn't really matter. The die was cast. The decision to attack Iraq had been made in the Pentagon years earlier at the time the PNAC had been written. So the Bush administration, which inherited the responsibility for implementing the plan, had to grasp at any available straw to justify an action so blatantly in contempt of international law. The one they chose turned out to be the short straw – the loser.

The war was launched. American forces marched towards Baghdad virtually unopposed. Later, President Bush declared that the war had been won. There was some fleeting embarrassment when no weapons of mass destruction could be found, but with little more than a flick of an eyelash the rationale for the war was reformed. When insurgents in Iraq, and others from outside, refused to lay down their arms, the Iraqi conflict became an integral part of the global war on terrorism.

The war on terrorism, however, was lost the minute the first bombs rained down on Baghdad. Within a matter of a few weeks, the small band of terrorists in the Arab world was being reinforced by literally thousands of young Muslims outraged by this further demonstration of American insensitivity toward them, their beliefs, and their sovereignty. Instead of dousing the flicker of international terrorism, the Iraqi war was the equivalent of pouring on gallons of explosive high octane fuel. One doesn't resolve conflict by stoking the fires of hate. On the contrary, conflicts are resolved when the two parties meet face-to-face, make an all-out effort to understand each other's point of view, and reach a resolution.

Even though the war on Iraq was one of the greatest strategic blunders in American history, with immeasurable negative benefits for the vast majority of the American people, it achieved exactly what its planners had in mind. The long-term and widespread war on terrorism provided the justification for military expenditures and operations far in excess of what the military-industrial complex might have achieved in an environment free from so much deliberately induced hatred.

As military operations in the East wind down, however, one has to be increasingly concerned about the next of Dr. Wernher von Braun's list of three largely trumped up targets. It is, of course, the extraterrestrials and their highly advanced technology. Already there are faint hints of future mischief originating in that sphere of ignorance and misinformation.

The Third "Enemy" Will Be The Extraterrestrials

– Dr. Wernher von Braun

The more I think about it, the greater my conviction is that an alleged threat of an extraterrestrial attack would be the perfect foil to frustrate the hopes and dreams of the peacemakers. Knowledge is power, and the MIC, or Cabal, as is the more inclusive and accurate description, knows a very great deal about the extraterrestrials, their technology, and their agendas which, most definitely, may not be all the same. The average person, on the other hand, may know little or nothing, and that includes most politicians of all stripes.

I found adequate assurance for that conclusion in early 2013, when I was one of 40 witnesses that ufologist Stephen Bassett, President of Paradigm Research Group, had assembled for a Citizen Hearing on Disclosure held at the Washington Press Club. His novel idea was to establish a simulated Congressional hearing on the subject of UFOs and related matters. Stephen recruited five former congressmen and women and one former U.S. senator to participate: Congressmen Roscoe Bartlett, Merrill Cook, Congresswomen Darlene Hooley, Carolyn Kilpatrick, Lynn Woolsey and Senator Mike Gravel.

This group was asked to listen to testimony, under oath, and interrogate the witnesses to elaborate on their testimony. When we began Monday morning, April 29, 2013, all six members of the panel were skeptics who didn't really believe that UFOs were real. When we completed the exercise at 6:00 p.m. Friday evening, May 3rd, they were all convinced by the information presented by former pilots, air traffic controllers, military personnel, and some of the best informed ufologists in the U.S., Canada, the U.K., Italy, China and Peru.

What was so amazing was not that they all changed their minds when faced with such overwhelming evidence, but that it took five days of concentrated briefing to persuade the last holdout. Remember that this was not just a panel recruited at random. They were all experienced politicians who had been part of a system that had allocated hundreds of billions of dollars for "Special Projects," usually referred to as "Black Ops," the nature of which they were obviously unaware.

Any reader, especially American readers, who find themselves similarly uninformed, might wish to fulfill your responsibility as a citizen by going to www.paradigmresearchgroup.org and watch the proceedings until you, too, are convinced of the reality of UFOs and the ET presence. Then you will be better prepared for the next step, which is to demand full disclosure of what has been achieved by the trillions of your tax dollars that have been spent without your knowledge or consent.

Once you have mastered Ufology 101, as they say, you will want to know what some of your brightest and best-trained scientists and engineers have accomplished since 1950. Is it true that the U.S. has back-engineered the saucers that crashed at Roswell and elsewhere to the point that those ships have been replicated either largely or totally? One of Dr. Stephen Greer's Disclosure Hearing witnesses, says they (the U.S.) have flying saucers that look so much like those of the Visitors that you can't tell them apart by just looking at them. That could be consistent with the statement by Ben

Rich, former CEO of Lockheed's Skunk Works, where many Black Ops have been developed, who said: "We (the U.S.) now have the technology to take ET home."[28]

This all means that the time is fast approaching when the final phase of the trilogy will be a real possibility. The propaganda build-up would be a breeze. Perhaps a scary movie, an increase in UFO sightings, a controlled leak or two, and then a mock attack by U.S. manufactured saucers probably augmented by those of their extra-terrestrial collaborators.

The aim would be to create panic and alarm on a scale that would convince us that we had to accept martial law and abrogate the last vestiges of our civil rights. This plan would be the fulfill-ment of the words of Henry Kissinger recorded in Chapter 1, that are worth repeating here. "Today, Americans would be outraged if UN troops entered Los Angeles to restore order; tomorrow, they will be grateful. This is especially true if they were told there was an outside threat from beyond, whether real or promulgated, that threatened our very existence. It is then that all people of the world will plead with world leaders to deliver them from this evil. The one thing that every man fears is the unknown. When presented with this scenario, individual rights will be willingly relinquished for the guarantee of their well-being granted to then by their world government."[29]

If all this sounds far-fetched, remember that nothing could be more far-fetched than 9/11 which was accepted, at least at first, as a genuine attack by enemies of the United States. At first blush, an attack by flying saucers would appear just as authentic. Fortunately, in this case, to be forewarned is to be prepared with the simplest pos-sible defense. Just ignore the whole show knowing that it is just one more monstrous deception that should be regarded as "Strike three, you are out," for the Cabal and the New World Order pretenders.

Chapter Eleven

GLOBAL WARMING –
A RECIPE FOR DISASTER

*The great enemy of the truth is very often not the lie – deliberate, contrived
and dishonest – but the myth, persistent, persuasive, and unrealistic.*

– John F. Kennedy

Since I published *Light at the End of the Tunnel* in 2010, I have
become more active on the UFO circuit, and have made guest
appearances on myriad radio and Internet shows. I have tried
to emphasize, to the extent that my hosts would allow, that there are
three great problems for humankind. The number one in importance
is global warming because the future habitability of the planet is in
jeopardy. The second in importance is the international banking and
financial system. It is second in importance but number one in urgency because without revolutionary change, nation states will lack the
fiscal flexibility to finance the changeover from fossil fuels to exotic
clean energy sources. Number three is the extraterrestrial presence
and technology. Its potential for good or ill is boundless, including
the knowledge of the energy sources essential for our survival.

The feedback has been enormous. I get hundreds of e-mails
from all over the globe, but primarily from the United States. All
too often my American cousins will say something along the following lines: "Hellyer (or Paul), I agree with every single word you
said except for that nonsense about global warming. That is just
a hoax. What we are seeing is just a natural cycle. So you should
check your facts on that one."

This kind of response fills me with foreboding. Far too many Americans, citizens of the most powerful country on Earth, believe that global warming doesn't belong on the action priority list. When I respectfully disagree, the response usually registers the degree to which they have been misled by the popular press, influenced by a well-financed and politically powerful oil lobby.

As a result of reading "Enemy of the Planet" by Paul Krugman, I was particularly incensed. "Lee Raymond, the former chief executive officer of Exxon Mobil, was paid $686 million over 13 years. But that's not a reason to single him out for special excoriation. Executive compensation is out of control in corporate America as a whole, and unlike other grossly overpaid business leaders, Raymond can at least claim to have made money for his stockholders. There's a better reason to excoriate Raymond: For the sake of his company's bottom line, and perhaps his own personal enrichment, he turned Exxon Mobil into an enemy of the planet."[1]

Though the company denies the allegations – naturally – Al Gore agrees with the critics. In an article headlined "Public Misled," Gore says:

> There has been an organized campaign, financed to the tune of about $10 million (U.S.) a year from some of the largest carbon polluters, to create the impression that there is disagreement in the scientific community (about global warming). In actuality, there is very little disagreement. This is one of the strongest of scientific consensus views in the history of science, he said. We live in a world where what used to be called propaganda now has a major role to play in shaping public opinion.[2]

The propaganda continues. In March 2009, Andrew C. Revkin wrote that 600 self-professed climate skeptics were meeting in a Times Square hotel to challenge the widely-held scientific and political consensus that human beings <u>are</u> over-heating the planet. The sponsoring organization, according to the article that appeared in the *New York Times*, was the Heartland Institute.

A later article by Andrew Revkin headed "On Climate Issue, Industry Ignored Its Scientists," states that:

For more than a decade the Global Climate Coalition, a group representing industries with profits tied to fossil fuels, led an aggressive lobbying and public relations campaign against the idea that emissions of heat-trapping gases could lead to global warming …

Environmentalists have long maintained that industry knew early on that the scientific evidence supported a human influence on rising temperatures, but that the evidence was ignored for the sake of companies' fight against curbs on greenhouse gas emissions. Some environmentalists have compared the tactic to that once used by tobacco companies, which for decades insisted that the science linking cigarette smoking to lung cancer was uncertain. By questioning the science on global warming, these environmentalists say, groups like the Global Climate Coalition were able to sow enough doubt to blunt public concern about a consequential issue and delay government action.

George Monbiot, a British environmental activist and writer, said that by promoting doubt, the industry had taken advantage of news media norms requiring neutral coverage of issues, just as the tobacco industry once had. "They didn't have to win the argument to succeed," Mr. Monbiot said, "only to cause as much confusion as possible."[3]

This "Let's take a chance and see what happens," attitude really bugs me. It reminds me of a time many years ago when I was bitten by a bat. I went to the doctor for advice. He said there was a probability that the bat did not have rabies, but on the other hand it might have. "How many people who have contracted rabies have lived?" I asked. "None yet," was his reply. Needless to say I was not wildly enthusiastic about playing Russian roulette with my life, so I took the shots.

An example that is more relevant is the failure to heed the warning that increasing intensity of ultraviolet radiation from the sun will certainly result in more skin cancer for those who allow themselves to get burned. Young people, in particular, pay no heed because the unhappy consequences may be decades away. This same generation routinely ignores the warning that listening to a lot of rock music is very likely to cause significant loss of hearing at an early age. Why worry, because all that is somewhere in the distant future.

James Lovelock is a maverick to some, but his views are increasingly gaining credence in respectable circles. He has been proclaiming his Gaia Theory for a generation. This states that the Earth is a living, self-regulating system and that by filling its atmosphere with CO_2 (carbon dioxide emissions) we have destroyed the balance and overheated the planet. We are in the phase when the thermometer suddenly shoots up.[4]

"Crackpot or visionary, the fact is that more and more people are paying attention to Lovelock, and that he, himself, supports the Intergovernmental Panel on Climate Change (IPCC) – the influential group who shared the Nobel Peace Prize with former American vice president Al Gore for their campaigns on global warming."[5]

The scientist who had the greatest impact on my knowledge and understanding of the issue is Dr. James E. Hansen, a member of the National Academy of Sciences, an adjunct professor in the Department of Earth and Environmental Sciences at Columbia University and at Columbia's Earth Institute, and director of the NASA Goddard Institute for Space Studies. My wife Sandra and I were listening to him being interviewed on the radio a few years ago and found him to be both interesting and convincing. Sandra bought one of his books, *Storms of my Grandchildren*,[6] and gave it to me for my birthday.

It was not a light read because it was pure science. But it was compelling for me because he raised and dealt with all alternative reasons for global warming, such as its being a natural cycle, and firmly established the fact that we Earthlings are responsible for the phenomenon and that it is within our power to do something about it. It is a brave stand that has resulted in censure and attracted criticism from the naysayers, who have their own agenda. It is the high price paid by pioneers.

On the other hand, many admire Hansen. I agree with the following plug from Bill McKibben, coordinator of 350.org and author of *The End of Nature*:

> Jim Hansen is the planet's great hero. He offered us the warning we needed twenty years ago, and has worked with enormous courage ever since to try and make sure we heeded it.

We'll know before long if that effort bears fruit – if it does, literally no one deserves more credit than Dr. Hansen.[7]

Bravo! But I am astonished to learn that the warning came twenty years ago and that so little action has resulted. Is there no one capable of reading the tea leaves when the evidence is so obvious to anyone keeping records of rising temperatures? It is also obvious that the storms Dr. Hansen predicted for his grandchildren are already happening, all over the world! So many have been reported from one country after another, and the consequences have been so horrendous, that I started to keep a file on them for the first time in my long life.

More solid evidence of the widespread nature of global warming came like a lightning strike to anyone who could read when they opened the Toronto *Globe and Mail* newspaper on July 29, 2010. The headline read SIGNS OF WARMING EARTH 'UNMISTAKABLE.' Each of the past three decades has been the hottest on record, according to a new report that offers stunning evidence for climate change. The study was the most extensive ever done on global warming.

Indeed the facts assembled by the U.S. National Oceanic and Atmospheric Administration (NOAA) in a report co-edited by researchers in the United States, Canada, Britain and Australia, based on data from 10 climate indicators measured by 160 research groups in 48 countries, are ominous.

SEA LEVEL RISING

For the past 15 years, sea levels have been rising a little more than one-eighth of an inch per year.

SNOW COVER DECLINING

Snow cover in the Arctic showed a continuation of relatively shorter snow seasons.

AIR TEMPERATURE RISING

Average surface temperatures in the last three decades have been progressively warmer than all earlier decades.

OCEAN TEMPERATURE RISING
Warming has been noted as far as 6,000 feet below the surface, but most of the heat is accumulating in the oceans' near-surface layers.

SEA ICE DECLINING
The summer sea ice cover was the third-lowest recorded since 1979.

HUMIDITY RISING
Humidity from the tropical Pacific contributed to unusually low temperatures in northern and central Mexico as the humid air mixed with cold fronts.

SEA AIR TEMPERATURE RISING
A warmer climate means higher sea levels, humidity and temperatures in the air and ocean.

GLACIERS DECLINING
Early data shows that 2009 will likely be the 19th consecutive year glaciers have lost mass.

OCEAN HEAT RISING
Studies show oceans absorb most of the extra heat added from the build-up of heat-trapping gases.

LAND AIR TEMPERATURE RISING
The surface air temperature record is compiled from weather stations around the world. Analyses show an upward trend across the globe.

While the facts speak loud and clear they are all the more dramatic when presented in graph form in bright red ink!

— • —

An encouraging sign that the facts are being increasingly recognized and accepted was underlined by the following headline of an article in the *Toronto Star* of August 8, 2012, "Skeptical climate scientist warms up into a believer." In an article written by staff reporter Michael Woods, about Richard A. Muller, a physics professor at the University of California, Berkeley, we read about his self-proclaimed total turnaround.

"Call me a converted skeptic," Muller wrote in a July 28 *New York Times* article. "Three years ago," he said, "he doubted whether global warming ever existed. Last year, following an intensive research effort involving a dozen scientists, I concluded that global warming was real and that the prior estimates of the rate of warming were correct.

I'm now going a step further: Humans are almost entirely the cause."[8]

One of the most dramatic illustrations I have seen was a full double-page spread in the Toronto *Globe and Mail* in its weekend paper of Saturday, March 16, 2013. Folio:

Climate Science. Title: "The incredible shrinking summer ice cover." This was followed by schematic illustrations of the Arctic ice cover in 1982, 2002 and 2012.

For 1982, the icecap extended from one side of the double page to the other – 7.5 million square km.

In 2002, the icecap extended about three quarters of the way across representing 5.36 million square km.

In 2012, the icecap extended just under half way – 3.41 million square km.

The bottom line on the page reads: "Scientists now say the Arctic will become ice free during the summer some time between 2015 and 2030. The year 2030 = 0"

The lead of the article was: "Why is Arctic sea ice vanishing even faster than climate models predict?" This was followed by: "A world-leading research centre in Manitoba is trying to find answers." The whole article is worth reading because the information is fundamental to the solution of our No. 1 problem.[9]

I read the article with horror and foreboding as my mind reflected on the concern of people who live in Bangladesh, the Philippines and other low-lying areas worldwide. What does the future hold for them? Do they even have a future? The polar bears and Arctic birds, too, will have lost their habitat.

– • –

I can't resist the temptation to include a little of my own empirical evidence. I realize that is a no-no in the middle of a scientific debate, but I was encouraged by a quotation from my friend, Dr. Judy Wood, "Empirical evidence is the truth that theory must mimic." So this is some of the truth that I have observed over the course of many decades.

In 1981, when my late wife Ellen and I moved back to Toronto from Ottawa, we bought a nice condominium apartment overlooking the bay in downtown Toronto. Although I hate recessions and depressions because I know they are not necessary, I was the beneficiary of Fed Chairman Paul Volcker's disastrous experiment in trying to crack a nut with a bulldozer, and bought our new place for cost.

On that February day when we signed the offer, the bay was covered with ice more than a foot thick, and the resident Canada geese had a hole only about six feet across, to splash in and out of. On the south side of the bay, close to the Toronto Islands, ice-boats were sailing full speed from horizon to horizon.

For many years in winter it was pleasant to watch people skating and ice-boating with grace and speed while steering clear of the cracks made by ice-breakers opening a path for the ferry boats crossing to and from Wards Island to pick up and deliver the permanent residents who live there all year round. There were two or three years when the ice-breakers couldn't navigate for a day or two until better conditions prevailed.

In more recent years, however, the scene has changed. The ice has often been unsafe for skating or walking as well as sail boating; these have become a rarity. The ferries have been able to act as their own ice-breakers most of the time without help. Finally, in the winter of 2012, I don't remember the ice being much more than half-an-inch thick and usually it was gone by early afternoon if the sun was shining. (As I write, 2013/14 is proving to be an exception.)

One other observation is the occurrence of unprecedented rain storms in various parts of the country and in several urban areas that have always seemed immune to such disasters. Something similar might have occurred long ago, but I and most of my friends, who are also members of the "old-timers" club, have no recollection of anything like it.

My final story goes back to August 2012. Sandra and I took several members of my family on the wondrous "Alaska Trip" which had been on my "bucket list" for a long time. We flew to Anchorage and then sailed south from Whittier along the coast to Vancouver, with stops at Skagway, Juneau and Ketchikan.

We were blessed with good weather, and the several shore trips accentuated the glorious scenery that has to be seen to be fully appreciated. The only bad news was that every glacier we saw, with the exception of three, was receding. It was the handwriting on the wall to see glaciers losing mass and creeping inexorably back up the valleys where they had been born.

– • –

The Clincher

As I mentioned earlier James Lovelock supports the Intergovernmental Panel on Climate Change (IPCC) as do many others who rate global warming as number one on the world's problem list. Its report of March 31, 2014, is the most alarming of the series to date. A report by Justin Gillis that appeared in the *New York Times* is as follows:

Panel's Warning on Climate Risk: Worst Is Yet to Come

YOKOHAMA, Japan – Climate change is already having sweeping effects on every continent and throughout the world's oceans, scientists reported on Monday, and they warned that the problem was likely to grow substantially worse unless emissions are brought under control.

The report by the Intergovernmental Panel on Climate Change, a United Nations group that periodically summarizes climate science, concluded that ice caps are melting, sea ice in the Arctic is collapsing, water supplies are coming under stress, heat waves and heavy rains are intensifying, coral reefs are dying, and fish and many other creatures are migrating toward the poles or in some cases going extinct.

The oceans are rising at a pace that threatens coastal communities and are becoming more acidic as they absorb some of the carbon dioxide given off by cars and power plants, which is killing some creatures or stunting their growth, the report found.

Organic matter frozen in Arctic soils before civilization began is now melting, allowing it to decay into greenhouse gases that will cause further warming, the scientists said. And the worst is yet to come, the scientists said in the second of three reports that are expected to carry considerable weight next year as nations try to agree on a new global climate treaty.

In particular, the report emphasized that the world's food supply is at considerable risk – a threat that could have serious consequences for the poorest nations."[10]

A little more than two weeks later, *The Economist* reported the political aspects of the IPCC report as follows:

Another Week, Another Report

Options for limiting climate change are narrowing.

The Intergovernmental Panel on Climate Change (IPCC), a gathering of scientists who advise governments, describes itself as 'policy-relevant and yet policy-neutral.' Its latest report, the third in six months, ignores that fine distinction. Pressure from governments forced it to strip out of its deliberations a table showing the link between greenhouse gases and national income, presumably because this made clear that middle-income countries such as Canada are the biggest contributors to new emissions. It also got rid of references to historical contributions, which show that rich countries bear a disproportionate responsibility. That seems more like policy-based evidence than evidence-based policy and bodes ill for talks on a new climate-change treaty, planned to take place in Paris next year.[11]

The science is clear, despite a handful of skeptics who hold fast to their prejudice. My problem is not the skeptics, who act as if they must be living on another planet; it is with the politicians who mouth the same old platitudes but plan to do nothing.

The Canadian government's reaction to the IPCC report of September 2013, was to blame our slow motion on previous governments and to blast the official opposition. Certainly their actions back up their seeming indifference to global warming and, to be fair, the same charge could be made against the U.S. government, as well. A few random clippings from my files of the last two years indicate we are living in a dream world.

Headline: "Canada won't budge on environment, Peter Kent insists."

We are taking our obligations seriously," he said. "But we are balancing our obligation and engagement on climate change with sensitivities to the realities of Canada's still-recovering economy, job creation and job growth, and we will continue on that course.[12]

Headline: "BP's punishment unlikely to deter drilling."

The $4.5-billion (U.S) settlement slapped on BP for its catastrophic Gulf of Mexico oil well spill in 2010 won't drastically change the way the oil business works, industry watchers agree.

Not everyone thinks that's a good thing.

Eleven workers died when the Deepwater Horizon well blew. An estimated 172 million gallons of crude spewed into the Gulf before the well was capped.

But the size of the settlement, which includes criminal charges against company officials, won't stop the search for oil, said David Detomasi of Queen's School of Business, who follows the oil industry.

Not if the oil price justifies," he said in an interview.

At the end of the day, if the project has the right sort of return and can be done with existing technologies commensurate with the company's operating practices, they'll do it, he said.[13]

Headline: Feds bow to Alberta on carbon rules."

Ottawa will allow Alberta to use its own greenhouse-gas rules – rather than federal regulations being drafted – to corral the soaring carbon emissions of the oil sands, as the Conservative government moves to assure the energy industry that it will not take steps to slow the sector's growth.

Industry and government sources say the federal regulations being drafted will essentially mimic one of the most controversial parts of Alberta's greenhouse-gas regulations, placing limits on the emissions from each barrel of oil, but not on the sector – an approach that would clear the way for the oil sands to double production.[14]

Headline: "Imperial Oil aims for Arctic depths."

Major energy companies led by Imperial Oil Ltd. have applied to drill for crude in the Beaufort Sea, targeting an area that could require operations in the deepest water yet for the industry in the Canadian Arctic.

Imperial, Exxon Mobil Corp. and BP PLC filed a project description with regulators this month as a first step in the proposed drilling on two jointly held licences about 175 kilometres northwest of Tuktoyaktuk, NWT.

This would certainly be the farthest offshore, and deepest, that Imperial has ever drilled in the Beaufort." Imperial spokesman Pius Rolheiser said in an interview.

It is too early to estimate what it might cost to drill wells on the ocean floor blocks, known as Ajurak and Pokak, where water depths can reach 1,500 metres, Mr. Rolheiser said. Early indications are that the partners would use a floating drill ship, according to the document.

Under the current schedule, drilling could start before the end of this decade. Imperial and Exxon each have 25 per cent of the venture, and BP the remainder.[15]

Headline: "N.W.T.: The latest fracking frontier."

Nobody can say with any certainty exactly how much oil is embedded in dense rock buried thousands of metres underneath frozen tundra in the central Mackenzie Valley.

But John Hogg, vice-president of exploration and operations at Calgary-based MGM Energy Corp., figures the so-called Canol shale in the Northwest Territories could hold "billions and billions of barrels" of light, sweet crude.

"If it all works the way we think it will, we think this play is as viable as any of the major plays in Canada or North America," he said. "I would put it up against any one of them and say it's as good as, if not better than, most of them."[16]

Headline: "Canada to emerge as the fourth-fastest growing oil player in the world: IEA."

Canadian oil sands production could 'easily' surge by an additional one million barrels per day if key pipeline projects are approved, according to the International Energy Agency.

The IEA's latest annual report, published Tuesday, expects Canada's oil production to rise to 5.7 million barrels per day by 2030, but believes some oil sands development may hinge on market access.

"While the [Canadian] resources are unquestionably large enough to support such an expansion, achieving it is contingent on the construction of major new pipelines to enable the crude to be exported to Asia and the United States," the Paris-based agency said.[17]

Headline: "Canada sees risk in U.S. oil boom."

The United States is on track to become the world's biggest oil producer by the end of the decade, a stunning turn of fortune that threatens to stifle the growth prospects of Canada's oil exporters.

America's rising oil output is "nothing short of spectacular" and will exceed that of Saudi Arabia or Russia by 2020, the International Energy Agency said in a report that starkly illustrates why the Canadian industry – and the federal and Alberta governments – are determined to build pipelines that would serve Asian markets.

The U.S. currently imports about 10 million barrels per day of crude, and Canada accounts for nearly 30 per cent of that total. But oil companies are using new technologies to extract vast amounts of crude from the U.S. Midwest. The IEA forecasts the Americans will be producing 11.1 million barrels per day by 2020, up from 8.1 million last year.

At the same time, the IEA expects American demand for petroleum products to decline significantly. The double-edged forecast has the potential to cause upheaval in the oil patch in Western Canada, which drew $40-billion in investment last year and is a major driver of economic growth and jobs in the country.

Nearly all Canadian oil is exported to the U.S., and Natural Resources Minister Joe Oliver said the IEA report 'dramatically emphasizes' the need for Canada to find new markets.[18]

Headline: "Exxon-Mobil moves ahead with massive East Coast oil field."

Exxon-Mobil Corp. is giving the green light to its $14-billion (U.S.) project to pump oil from the massive Hebron oil field off Canada's East Coast, which will launch a major new source of production for Canada later this decade – a new wave of resource revenue for Newfoundland and Labrador.

The announcement marks the formal end of a feud which former premier Danny Williams escalated in 2006, when he demanded the province receive a 4.9 per-cent stake in the project. Newfoundland eventually got its way, but further sparring followed over benefits such as whether all of the platform would be built in the province, thus creating jobs on the East Coast.

However, the dispute was settled in October when the U.S. company agreed to build much of the platform in the province, and offered Newfoundland $150-million to offset the portion that will be built elsewhere.[19]

Disconnect

Have you noticed something fundamentally wrong here? Scientists have been spending years taking readings and assembling statistics that say loud and clear that the future habitability of the planet for millions of people is in crisis mode. If anything, their plan seems significantly watered down because they don't know the extent to which we can do better. The politicians pay lip service to the "problem" for a day or two while the IPCC report is in the news – not even headline news – and then it's back to business as usual.

The headlines indicate widespread plans for drilling in the Gulf of Mexico, the Beaufort Sea, the Atlantic Ocean off Newfoundland, expansion of the tar sands development in Northern Alberta and fracking everywhere. The latter despite any proof that it will not degrade drinking water that is far more valuable than gas and oil that isn't needed, and whose availability will be another strike against survival.

It is my opinion, shared by many friends and colleagues, that allowing any of these projects that are designed to produce hydrocarbons for decades into the future is a crime against both present and future generations of Earthlings. One can understand greedy corporations who don't care about the environment making such plans; but it is incomprehensible that politicians, who have the final say, turn a blind eye at best, or actively aid and encourage new development at worst.

It seems that most politicians have contracted a disease called "votavision." This widespread malady restricts the vision to the date of the next election.

Where Are the G20 Leaders in All of This?

The G20 leaders are sleepwalking along the road to hell on Earth. Surely they took note of typhoon Haiyan that wreaked indescribable death and disaster on many of the Philippine islands in November 2013. And surely, they must have at least wondered if it wasn't a climate disaster, a disaster fueled by our collective use of coal, oil, and gas that continues to pour billions of tons of carbon dioxide into our atmosphere, disrupting our climate and loading the dice for extreme storms like Haiyan.

The warning is not new. When I published *Light* in 2010, it contained the following:

A subject that should be close to America's heart is *BREED-ING PERFECT STORMS: A Canadian researcher has demonstrated how global warming has widened the spawning grounds for hurricanes by hundreds of square kilometres since 1970, explaining for the first time why recent storm seasons have shattered one record after another.* "Canadian researcher, Robert Scott, is the first to offer a physical explanation – backed up by statistics and measurements spanning decades – linking the Earth's warming to increased hurricane activity and intensity. Hurricanes are not entirely natural disasters. Humanity has had a discernible impact on hurricanes, Scott, a 40-year-old oceanographer at the University of Texas, said in an interview."[20]

The sky-high cost of global warming witnessed following Hurricane Katrina in 2005, is just the tip of the global cost iceberg.

A lead editorial in the Toronto *Globe and Mail* had this to say about conclusions concerning the financial cost of global warming reached by Sir Nicholas Stern, the World Bank's former chief economist:

> A comprehensive study by Britain's top government economist has helped to fill that gap. It provides some hard truths about the enormous costs to the global economy if governments worldwide fail to take drastic measures to tackle the problem. It also provides an important counterweight to those who argue that such action would carry too high a price tag and pose too big an economic risk for an uncertain result.
>
> In fact, Stern argues that the opposite is true. It is doing too little too late that would have by far the more devastating impact on the global economy. He says that a weak global response to climate change in the next few decades could cause economic and social disruptions on a scale similar to those triggered by the world wars and the Great Depression, but at a far higher cost than all of them combined. He calculates that the cost in lost output could reach $7-trillion. What's worse, it will be hard, if not impossible, to reverse such changes.[21]

Even Secretary of Defense Chuck Hagel is now sounding an alarm on the subject of global warming. A report by Jane Taber in the Toronto *Globe and Mail* of November 23, 2013, titled "U.S. sounds alarm over melting Arctic," began as follows:

U.S. Defense Secretary Chuck Hagel is concerned about climate change and the melting Arctic, an unexpected worry for the man who controls the most lethal arsenal of weapons in the world.

The senior Obama administration official was speaking in Halifax on Friday, using his keynote address to the Halifax International Security Forum to deliver a strong message about climate change, and to launch his department's eight-point Arctic strategy, which includes ensuring security of the region, protecting its environment and working together in the area with other nations.

Climate change, Mr. Hagel said, does not directly cause conflict 'but it can significantly add to the challenges of global instability, hunger, poverty and conflict.' He added that food and water shortages, pandemic disease, disputes over refugees and resources and more severe natural disasters "all place additional burdens on economies, society and institutions around the world."[22]

It's Time for Realists to Yell "Fire" at the Top of Their Voices

Sound the alarm! Our global home is ablaze, and our political firefighters are arguing about jurisdiction over Arctic waters, because of the oil that lies beneath them, the routes of new pipelines to carry oil to world markets, and new licences for fracking. It is all irrelevant! When you get a call saying your house is on fire, you don't just carry on what you are doing. You move p.d.q.! I know; I had the experience when I was attending an opera school rehearsal in 1946.

Not one more permit should be granted for drilling in the oceans of the world. No new oil sands projects should be approved. The same is true of fracking. The practice should end – at once! The energy is not needed, and the long-term consequences are unknown. I keep thinking of thalidomide and Agent Orange. In both cases the "experts" said they were safe, and in both cases their assurance was incorrect, leading to very unhappy consequences. The near universal use of fossil fuels must end, as fast as they can be replaced.

When I published *"Light"* I suggested that we had ten years to make the changeover to clean energy in order to have any reasonable hope of arresting global warming before it is too late. I have recently reduced my estimate to seven years. We have, perhaps, seven years to replace the power source in every car, truck, tractor, airplane and house on planet Earth. Is this possible? Yes! The new technology is known; financing is possible if we switch from a cyclical system to a steady one; the manpower and physical capacity is available to be tapped. The biggest challenge is the political will to act decisively and immediately.

New Breakthrough Energy

For decades rumours have circulated about the development of new exotic energy sources that have been kept secret from us by the same people who have so successfully kept the extraterrestrial presence and technology under wraps. The Cabal, which includes the oil cartel, appears to have taken extraordinary measures not only to obtain control of the new technology but to "discourage" anyone who claims to have been able to replicate it. A number of laboratories have been ransacked or have seen prototypes removed. This appears to be an indication of how valuable the developments may be.

Evidence that the Black Operations had been involved in developing new energy sources was provided by Dr. Michael Wolf who worked in Area 51 and its satellite, Area S4, and who allegedly had one of the highest security clearance of anyone in the United States. In an extensive interview with Chris Stoner, Dr. Wolf said:

> Satellite government scientists have successfully created zero point energy and cold fusion. There needs to be a smooth transition into these new sciences. Otherwise the world economy could be wrecked.[23]

The transition could have been much smoother if the new sciences had been made public years ago when Dr. Wolf first spoke of them. Now, it has to be a crash program, a mobilization comparable to that of World War II when nearly every factory producing consumer goods was converted to manufacturing armaments of some kind. Today we must do exactly the reverse! The factories producing armaments must be converted to the manufacture of clean energy boxes to power our vehicles and homes. And, as someone who has been studying economics all my life, may I say that the world economy doesn't need to be wrecked! To the contrary, millions of new jobs will be created worldwide just as happened at the outbreak of World War II.

Early confirmation that these developments were well known in other realms, came as a result of a U.S. Defense Intelligence Agency (DIA) program referred to as Operation Crystal Knight, or what has since been called Project Serpo, in which it is claimed that 12 astronauts left Earth in July 1965 and were taken aboard an alien spaceship to the planet Serpo in the binary star system Zeta Reticuli, as part of an exchange program.

The team commander's account of their first reaction to the new planet included the following, as recorded:

> They were quartered in four huts that appeared to be adobe-like, and all their gear was stored in an underground facility. The temperature was 107°F and the buildings all had lights and electricity generated by a small box. They were able to plug their electrical devices into the box, and they all worked.[24]

Fifteen days before these words were written, Toronto was subjected to a terrible ice storm. Three hundred thousand households were suddenly without power as ice-loaded tree branches came crashing down on hydro lines. It took extra crews a week to restore service to homes and businesses, many of which were obliged to celebrate the Christmas holidays in the freezing dark. And it was not just Toronto that was affected. Many other areas, including several U.S. states, suffered equally.

Little did the unhappy people realize that their suffering could have been avoided, had technology that has been known for decades been made available in an orderly fashion. The fact that it has been deliberately withheld is just one more crime against humanity that appears to belong on the Cabal's list.

Now, the world is in crisis on the weather front, as on many others. Time, as we know it, is running out. Political weasel words won't keep you warm when you are freezing in the dark. Only knowledge that will fuel the engine of action can save us.

Will the changeover from carbon-based fuels to clean energy disrupt the economy? Of course it will, in exactly the same way that motorized cars disrupted the carriage business, or, more relevant to the experience of my generation, in the same way that the mobilization required to win World War II was disruptive. First the decision had to be made, and then the administrative and innovative genius of the people went into action to make victory possible. This time, too, there is no other option!

Chapter Twelve

FULL DISCLOSURE

"For we wrestle not against flesh and blood, but against principalities, against powers, against the rulers of the darkness of this world, against spiritual wickedness in high places."

– Ephesians 6:12

When I first said in September 2005 that "UFOs are as real as airplanes flying overhead,"[1] it was because I felt strongly that there were major policy issues flowing from that new (for me at least) knowledge that should be debated openly and honestly. American taxpayers had a right to know what they had been paying for, but were unaware of. Was it directly related to "national security," as alleged? Or were there other much broader considerations than cannot be described in one single category?

As my knowledge has increased in the intervening years my concern has grown exponentially. Even allowing for the fact that official confirmation is virtually impossible, information from apparently reliable witnesses, and a few brave whistleblowers, is more than adequate to set off alarm bells. The veil must be lifted from 60 years of above top secret wheeling and dealing so that Americans in particular, and the world in general, have access to the facts that may directly impact their dreams and hopes for the future.

Before peeking under a small corner of that veil, however, I would like to respond, albeit inadequately, to a few of the questions most often asked by those of us who are seeking for the truth.

The first is probably, "where do the Visitors come from and what are some of the species?" Various places. They include Zeta Reticuli, the Pleiades, Orion, Andromeda, Mars, and Venus. The species include the Short Greys as they are called, Tall Greys, Nordic Blondes, Oranges, Tall Whites, Semitics and Reptilians, each with their own distinct characteristics. These are just a small sample for illustrative purposes.

The late Dr. Michael Wolf, who served as a scientific consultant to the American President and NSC on ET related matters, and who specialized in gathering information on the different ET races, provided the following information in an interview with Chris Stoner in July 2000.

The first U.S. crash/retrieval of an ET aircraft occurred during 1941 in the ocean west of San Diego. Retrieved by the navy, dead Zeta Reticulans, alias the 'Greys,' were found inside. Craft and bodies were taken to the Foreign Technology Section at Wright-Patterson Airforce base in Dayton, Ohio, and studied by the Retfours Special Studies Group. After dismantling the craft, parts were sent to S4 and Indian Springs in Nevada. This craft crashed due to the recently invented pulse radar being tested on the nearby Tinian island, located three miles south/south west of Saipan. The U.S. navy has held a leadership position in UFO matters since.

The Roswell crash during July 1947 did happen, and the account in Colonel Corso's book '*The Day after Roswell*' is accurate. Dr. Wolf had, in his possession, the official satellite government ET crash/retrieval list and while others occurred between 1941 and '47 he was not willing to offer examples.

Two craft crashed at Roswell after colliding with each other during an electrical storm. One contained 'Greys,' the other 'Orange' ETs – both named due to the color of their skin. The 'Orange' types come from the Andromeda star system. The Santilli autopsy film is genuine – Dr. Wolf had seen other similar footage – and is an autopsy of an 'Orange' ET. There were two different autopsies being carried out on two different ET beings during the same period – hence the confusion.

The autopsy on the 'Orange' ET revealed that it had a very large head; big dark eyes with no irises or whites; six digits on hands and feet; the brain has four lobes; is more developed and connected with no corpus callosum; different optic orbs and nerves; and a sponge like digestive system. Dr. Wolf said he had met one alive.

There are different types of 'Grey's. He worked alongside highly evolved ones which had, contrary to present opinion, personalities and even a sense of humor. Dr. Wolf never met a 'Grey' whom he disliked. To him they were family. These 'Greys' enjoyed hugging and kissing humans. This upset some of his colleagues. One nicknamed them 'kissey facey'. Their smooth and soft bodies feel like dolphin skin to touch. He communicated with these ETs through telepathy. Dr. Wolf became especially friendly with one called Kolta. A picture of this 'Grey' is on the front cover of his book, *The Catchers of Heaven* – an actual photograph taken by an admiral friend.

There is active trading between the 'Greys' and 'Oranges'. Dr. Wolf said, 'Trading has a different meaning for ETs. They share knowledge like technology and philosophy and send their people to each other's planet to learn the culture.'

He had conversed with human looking ETs from the Pleiades and Altair star systems – nicknamed the Nordics and Semitics. Dr. Wolf explained they are very spiritual people and act more as galactic counselors. A photograph of a Pleiadian friend called Sa Ra adorns the back cover of his book, *Catchers of Heaven* published in July 1996 after 15 years to persuade his bosses to allow him to publish, and even then it had to be fictionalized and include three different denials at the beginning concerning the authenticity.[2]

One of the crashes between 1941and 1947 that Dr. Wolf did not mention occurred near San Antonio, New Mexico, in August 1945. Ufologist Paola Harris relates the story in her book *Exopolitics: Stargate to a New Reality*,[3] after interviewing two eye witnesses Jose Padilla and Rene Boca who were aged 9 and 7 at the time. According to their recollection the visitors were of the Praying Mantis type.

When Apollo astronaut Ed Mitchell and I both guessed that the number of species was somewhere between 2 and 12 when we first met in July 2006, we underestimated the reality. Higher figures like 30, 70, and even several hundred have been mentioned. It is difficult to believe the high numbers, but I don't dismiss them out of hand because much of what I now know would have stretched my credibility just a few years ago. The numbers themselves are no longer of great interest to me. It is more important to concentrate on the principal players, and their possible agendas.

One additional question from the skeptics is how did they get here when, as Einstein proved, nothing can travel faster than light. One of my inside sources opened the window on that one for me when he said: "Gravity travels faster than light." Evidence of a kind of physics we are not taught in school was provided by an exchange program, when in July 1965 twelve courageous U.S. astronauts boarded an Eben (Grey) craft on an exchange visit to the planet Serpo. The trip took 10 months to reach its destination 37 light years distant.[4]

I am not a physicist, so the whole subject of space travel is light years beyond my comprehension. Still, I am convinced that it is real, and that there are explanations for people who understand them. The following from Dr. Michael Wolf relates to what are called "wormholes."

> The author states that in a *hyperspacial environment,* using a ship-board generation of amplified gravity waves, it isn't speed that increases, it is the *relative time-space,* when acted upon by a force such as gravity waves, which reduces itself within the *hyperspace field* generated around the hull of the craft where space-time becomes 'warped.' An Einstein-Rosen bridge 'wormhole' created by a gravity-exerting craft in space is but one example.
>
> The 'Star Trek' scenario may be based on an actual reality! *Artificially created gravity waves* can theoretically reduce time to near zero and acceleration to near infinity. Einstein only had a problem with gravity in his unified field theory, as it did not seem to fit, although he did come to the conclusion that gravity and acceleration were somehow connected. With such travel it is not space itself which is physically traversed, since space folds in on itself as gravity waves act upon time.
>
> The author refers to the work of Theodore Kaluza, who used a *fifth dimension* algebraically to equate Einstein's four-dimensional gravity with Maxwell's electromagnetism, and this extending of space-time to five dimensions instead of four was a foundation for further relational *unification* theoretical development. The author also speaks of quantum mathematical theories and calculations that allow for as many as *12 dimensions*; however he warns that one must be careful as the normal laws of "human log-

ic" seem to break down the closer one delves into the sub-atomic
or quantum levels of reality.[5]

There are also something known as Stargates and one of them
is allegedly located in Egypt for use by ancient celestial navigators.
These subjects are interesting for people who love science. But for
me there are far more urgent and important questions that have to
be posed and answered. They relate primarily to governmental-ET
relations and interaction and the agendas of both.

United States – ET Relations

It is alleged that the first agreement between the U.S. and ETs
was signed by President Truman with the Greys, which would
seem logical because they would have followed the Nazi scientists
who entered the U.S. under Operation Paperclip. It is also suggested that some Greys had lived in underground caverns in the U.S.
southwest for a long time, and operated one or more bases from
which they could service their space vehicles.

President Truman established a group of 12, which became
known as the MJ-12, to take charge of the ET file and be responsible for interaction with the aliens, retrieval of crashed vehicles and,
most important of all, the back-engineering of the alien technology
recovered from Roswell and elsewhere. The group was given extraordinary powers and mandated to operate in total secrecy, including the fact of its own existence.

In subsequent years the original TOP SECRET/MAGIC EYES
ONLY was leaked to one or two ufologists who have gone to great
lengths to establish their authenticity. The manuals include handling
of crashed vehicles, of dead EBEs (Extraterrestrial Biological Entities), etc. The text is published at the back of Ryan S. Wood's book
Majic Eyes Only: Earth's Encounters with Extraterrestrial Technology.[6]
Dr. Michael Wolf, who was associated with the MJ-12, confirmed its
existence and said that it now has 36 members.[7] Another source suggested that the enlarged group is an international board of directors.

The contact pace picked up on February 20, 1954 when President Dwight D. Eisenhower met with an extraterrestrial con-

tingent at Edwards Air Force Base in California, then called Muroc Air Base.[8]

The visitors offered their assistance in the development of incredible new technology. All we (the U.S.) had to do in return was to 'beat our swords into plowshares,' that is, give up our nuclear weapons. Apparently the top generals at the Pentagon believed this to be some sort of ruse that would leave us defenseless in very dangerous times. So we had to say 'no thanks.' It seems evident now that the president and his advisors had their conclusions confirmed, at that point, that one or more of the extraterrestrial groups that had reached Earth were hostile and that we had to assume a defensive posture against a possible interplanetary war. After all, Eisenhower, as supreme commander of the Allied forces in Europe, had undoubtedly been privy to the information about extraterrestrial involvement in World War II. That defensive posture, of course, required ultra-secrecy, just as in wartime. That basically sealed the deal as regards disclosure. From that point on, all negotiations with extraterrestrials of every stripe was deemed too sensitive for public consumption, and the curtain of secrecy descended for the foreseeable future.[9]

Whether this was the right decision or not we will never know. The alternative was to accept the offer at face value, and rely on the Galactic Federation of Light, an alliance of advanced, spiritually oriented civilizations in this galaxy and beyond to protect us from the potential marauders.

It was also in the fifties that the 'space brothers' made their appearance. Those highly civilized, extraordinary spiritual, humanlike visitors from nearby planets and distant stars called directly on those whom they believed to be most open to contact, thus circumventing the official secrecy and suppression machine. They arrived in glistening, silent saucers, and all came with a message of peace, love, and brotherhood. George Adamski, Howard Menger, and George Van Tassel were some of the major 'contactees.' Giant Rock in the California desert became the mecca that called sirenlike to the believers and non-believers alike. Apparently, the space brothers had taken the secrecy problem into their own hands, since most of the contactees wrote books and appeared on radio and television shows. Their message slowly permeated the mass consciousness as reports of these contacts reached the public.[10]

This brief look back to an era when nearly all the Visitors wanted to help us is excerpted from *The Secret History of Extraterrestrials* by Len Kasten, a virtual goldmine of information about the whole story of contact and interaction between Earthlings and Star Visitors as some of my friends like to call them. I highly recommend that you read it for a much clearer picture than is possible here.

As I said earlier, I think General Eisenhower felt betrayed by some of his advisors and that was the reason he issued his classic warning about the military-industrial complex. He could not have imagined the development in the years following his death. The military-industrial complex operated on three levels – in the air, on the ground, and underground. It is the latter, and some of the things that have been going on there, that are most desperately in need of disclosure and discussion.

Have you heard of Area 51, I am often asked? Yes, of course. Dr. Wolf described this underground base, built with the help of the EBEs, as a sprawling city the size of Rhode Island, which continues to grow and has a sister base called S4, some 12 miles away, and another named Indian Springs. It employs hundreds of civilian and military personnel on a number of Special Projects usually referred to as Black Ops. They are very highly classified – as high as Ultra 4 which is allegedly higher than the U.S. president is cleared for.

There are other underground bases including Area 29 for which Ryan Wood arranged a briefing for his father, Dr. Robert Wood, and me by intelligence officers who had previously worked there.

These all pale in cosmic geo-political importance when compared to the Dulce base, located near the small town of Dulce, New Mexico. It was built at immense cost to U.S. taxpayers to accommodate what were purported to be joint ventures with the Greys in areas such as cloning, cross-breeding, and other procedures similar to those carried out by the Germans in the 1930s but more diverse and, as it turned out, more distasteful.

The structure was entirely underground and comprised at least seven levels, with each level requiring a higher security clearance than the one above it. Level 1 contained the garage for street maintenance. Level 2 was the garage for trains, shuttles, tunnel-boring machines, and disc maintenance. It was the lower levels, however, which were out of bounds to almost everyone, where activities took place that finally persuaded decent American patriots that what was taking place there was morally repugnant and something had to be done about it.

U.S. guards were not even allowed to talk to one another. But one of them became suspicious in an area where alleged mentally deficient persons were kept in cages. Moved by a plaintive look from one of the "inmates," he risked his job and maybe even his life by surreptitious contact to find out the man's name. On a hunch he checked out the U.S. "missing persons" list and found out that the man was indeed on the list. This incident was probably the beginning of what was to follow.

It was determined that there were large numbers of abductees being held hostage against their will, including female hostages. The whole scene was one that violated both U.S. law and moral law. It appears to be mere happenstance that something was eventually done about it.

The turning point came when National Security advisor Dr. Zbigniew Brzezinski met with President Jimmy Carter on June 14, 1977, with a number of other 'intelligence operatives and leaders,' to bring the President up to speed on a number of top secret programs, including Project Aquarius, and the work done at Dulce, Area 51, and other secret bases. Brzezinski, a member of the power elite that backed the 'Grey' cause, never guessed that the President would be so shocked that he would turn to trusted military advisors in the military intelligence community for options of how to stop what had been going on.

The National Security Agency (NSA) had been secretly fighting the alien cause, and the humans that worked for or with the aliens, since it was established in the mid-1950s. Project Aquarius was originally established in 1953, by order of President Eisenhower, under control of NSC and MJ-12. In 1966, the Project's name had been changed from Project Gleem to Project Aquarius, and portions of it went into DEEP

COVER, hidden even from the CIA and the NSC. At that point, the NSA had opened 'Department X' (to identify and study all alien or enemy operations that could be a threat to the United States or the Human Race in general), and 'Department Z' (to 'react' and 'neutralize' any sort of threat to the United States or the Human Race.)

Under secret Presidential Order, signed by President Jimmy Carter, the NSA's Department Z, the newly established DELTA FORCE, and a specially hand-picked group of Air Force SOC, Navy SEAL, and Army Rangers were organized for a mission so secret that not even command officers were told what it was about until the night of the attack. The only 'Attack Team' leaders who knew what this would be about were the men involved in the NSA Department Z, who had been involved with fighting aliens for years. The commanding officer of the attack was none other than Captain Mark Richards, the son of the infamous 'Dutchman,' Major Ellis Lloyd Richards, who had been the commander of International Security (IS) since Admiral Chester W. Nimitz died in 1966."[11]

I had read an abbreviated account of the battle that was almost beyond the imagination of the most skilled science fiction writer. Many hostages were liberated and the casualties on both sides were high. The patriots prevailed with the help of some other alien species, but there were few survivors to verify the story. The facility must have been shut down for a while and there are conflicting stories of whether or not it has been restored and rehabilitated.

One of the few survivors of the "Dulce War" was Phil Schneider, a government geologist and structural engineer who carried a level three security clearance, and had 17 years experience working in the U.S. government Black Project underground bases at Area 51, Dulce and Los Alamos. I have heard Schneider lectures on YouTube but they were difficult to transcribe so some of the quotes are taken from that source and others from the Dulce book.

Deep Underground Military Bases and the Black Budget

I love the country I am living in, more than I love my life, but I would not be standing before you now, risking my life, if

I did not believe it was so. The first part of this talk is going to concern deep underground military bases and the black budget. The Black Budget is a secretive budget that garners 25% of the gross national product of the United States. The Black Budget currently consumes $1.25 trillion per [2] years. At least this amount is used in black programs, like those concerned with deep underground military bases. Presently, there are 129 deep underground military bases in the United States.

I have been building these 129 bases day and night, unceasingly, since the early 1940s. Some of them were built even earlier than that. These bases are basically large cities underground connected by high-speed magneto-leviton trains that have speeds up to Mach 2. Several books have been written about this activity. Al Bielek has my only copy of one of them. Richard Sauder, a Ph.D. architect, has risked his life by talking about this. He worked with a number of government agencies on deep underground military bases. In around where you live, in Idaho, there are 11 of them.

The average depth of these bases is over a mile, and they again are basically whole cities underground. They all are between 2.66 and 4.25 cubic miles in size. They have laser drilling machines that can drill a tunnel 7 miles long in one day. The Black Projects sidestep the authority of Congress, which as we know is illegal. Right now, the New World Order is depending on these bases. If I had known at the time I was working on them that the NWO was involved, I would not have done it.

I was lied to rather extensively.[12]

Schneider's Worries about Government Factions, Railroad Cars and Shackle Contracts

Now, I am very worried about the activity of the 'federal' government. They have lied to the public, stonewalled senators, and have refused to tell the truth in regard to alien matters. I can go on and on. I can tell you that I am rather disgruntled. Recently, I knew someone who lived near where I live in Portland, Oregon. He worked at Gunderson Steel Fabrication, where they make railroad cars. Now, I knew this fellow for the better part of 30 years, and he was kind of a quiet type. He came to see me one day, excited, and he told me 'they're building prisoner cars.' He was nervous. Gunderson, he said, had a contract with the federal government to build 10,720 full length railroad cars, each with 143 pairs of shackles."[13]

If I were an American I would certainly want to know if I was one of the more than a million and a half people on some secret list to be transported to a concentration camp somewhere!

Star Wars and Apparent Alien Threat

Still, 68% of the military budget is directly or indirectly affected by the Black Budget. Star Wars relies heavily upon stealth weaponry. By the way, none of the stealth program would have been available if we had not taken apart crashed alien disks. None of it.

Some of you might ask what the 'space shuttle' is 'shuttling,' large ingots of special metals that are milled in space and cannot be produced on the surface of the earth. They need the near vacuum of outer space to produce them.

We are not even being told anything close to the truth. I believe our government officials have sold us down the drain – lock, stock and barrel. Up until several weeks ago, I was employed by the U.S. government with a Ryolite-38 clearance factor – one of the highest in the world. I believe the Star Wars program is there solely to act as a buffer to prevent alien attack – it has nothing to do with the 'Cold War,' which was only a ploy to garner money from all the people – for what?[14]

Some Statistics on the Black Helicopter Presence

The black helicopters. There are over 64,000 black helicopters in the United States. For every hour that goes by, there is one being built. Is this the proper use of our money? What does the federal government need 64,000 tactical helicopters for, if they are not trying to enslave us? I doubt if the entire military needs 64,000 worldwide with Lidar and computer-enhanced imaging radar. They can see you walking from room to room when they fly over your house. They see objects in the house from the air with a variation of 1 inch to 30,000 miles. That's how accurate that is. Now, I worked in the federal government for a long time, and I know exactly how they handle their business.[15]

Government Earthquake Device

The federal government has now invented an earthquake device. I am a geologist, and I know what I am talking about. With the Kobe earthquake in Japan, there was no pulse wave as in a normal earthquake. None. In 1989, there was an earthquake in San Francisco. There was no pulse wave with that one either. It is a Tesla device that is being used for evil purposes. The Black Budget programs have subverted science as we know it.[16]

Phil Schneider was a true patriot who became deeply concerned about what was really going on in the shadows of government. He handed in his extreme high security pass and started to speak the truth publicly. What he revealed is more than enough to demand immediate full disclosure. Seven months after giving one of the lectures quoted here he was found strangled. The "official" cause of death was "suicide." The NWO deals harshly with whistleblowers.

* * *

As discussed earlier, there were allegedly one or two agreements between the U.S. government and the Greys. The first signed by President Truman and a possible second by MJ-12. In exchange for advanced technology the aliens would be allowed to abduct a specified number of people, and mutilate a certain number of cattle in order to use the blood and certain body parts in the preparation of a food. A list of the abductees was to be kept and, apparently, there was a timetable for disclosure of the U.S.-alien interface.

> The U.S. government was not initially aware of the far-reaching consequences of their 'deal.' They were led to believe that the abductions were essentially benign, and since they figured that they would probably go on anyway, whether they agreed or not, they merely insisted that a current list of abductees be submitted, on a periodic basis, to MJ-12 and the National Security Council. Does this sound incredible? An actual list of abductees sent to the National Security Council?[17]
>
> During the period between 1979 and 1983 it became increasingly obvious to MJ-12 that things were not going as planned.

It became known that many more people [in the thousands] were being abducted than were listed on the official abduction lists.

By 1984, MJ-12 must have been in stark terror at the mistake they had made in dealing with the EBEs. They had subtly promoted 'Close Encounters of the Third Kind' and 'E.T.' to get the public used to 'odd looking' aliens that were compassionate, benevolent and very much our 'space brothers.' MJ-12 'sold' the EBEs to the public, and were now faced with the fact that quite the opposite was true. In addition, a plan was formulated in 1968 to make the public aware of the existence of aliens on earth over the next 20 years, to be culminated with several documentaries to be released during 1985-1987 period of time. The discovery of the 'grand deception' put the entire plans, hopes and dreams of MJ-12 into utter confusion and panic.

Meeting at the 'Country Club,' a remote lodge with private golf course, comfortable sleeping and working quarters, and its own private airstrip built by and exclusively for the members of MJ-12, it was a factional fight of what to do now. Part of MJ-12 wanted to confess the whole scheme and shambles it had become to the public, beg their forgiveness and ask for their support. The other part [the majority] of MJ-12 argued that there was no way they could do that, that the situation was untenable and there was no use in exciting the public with the 'horrible truth' and that the best plan was to continue the development of a weapon that could be used against the EBEs under the guise of 'SDI,' the Strategic Defense Initiative, which had nothing whatsoever to do with a defense for inbound Russian nuclear missiles.[18]

This responsibility was assigned to Dr. Edward Teller, 'father' of the H-bomb who personally worked in the test tunnels of the Nevada Test Site, driving his workers and associates in the words of one, "like a man possessed." And well he should have, for Dr. Teller was a <u>member of MJ-12</u> along with Dr. Kissinger, Admiral Bobby Inman, and possibly Admiral John Poindexter, to name a few of the then current members.[19]

* * *

According to Brandon, and the Dulce book, there are basically three alien networks at work on earth:

- The Anti-Grey Nordic [Federation] factions,

- the Anti-Nordic Grey [Empire] factions and

- the Nordic-Grey collaborators, which would also include those Terran intelligence agencies and occult lodges who are involved in the collaboration for whatever motive.

Even within the collaboration, there is a great deal of struggle over whether the humanoid or reptiloid agendas should have the upper hand. Within the collaboration itself 'specie-sism' [akin to racism] exists at certain levels, so in spite of the species prejudices the collaboration continues nevertheless because of a 'marriage of convenience.' In other words the Greys want to take over the planet and impose a slave society to ultimately serve their empire, but they need the Illuminati's international economic connections to do so; and the Illuminati wants the same thing but they realize that they need the alien mind-control and abduction technology to accomplish their goals.

So, then, it is more of a love-hate relationship. They collaborate in order to set up a planetary government; however both the humanoids and reptiloids are constantly plotting for the time when the world government arrives so that once it is established they can move in and take full control and expel the necessary collaborators – the humans doing away with the Greys or the Greys doing away with the humans or whatever the case may be. For instance the Illuminati might negotiate with the Greys while at the same time develop SDI weapons to potentially use against them.

On the other hand the Greys may continue negotiating with the humans while at the same time implanting micro-electronic mind control devices in the human agents with whom they negotiate in order to ensure that they remain under alien control once the planet succumbs to the New World Order. So a one world government will not bring peace to the planet, it will merely be a matter of fighting for control of one super government rather than for many smaller ones.

What many do not realize is that there appears to be a third element behind this agenda, a 'race' of paraphysical entities that some might refer to as the "Luciferians' or the 'Poltergeists' – who are often described by abductees who have encountered them, as being in the appearance of quasi-physical etheric or energy beings who have often been seen overseeing and directing the actions of the humanoid-reptiloid collaborators.

Although it might sound simplistic to imply that this cosmic battle is essentially being fought between the Nordic bases near Death Valley and the Grey bases near Archuleta Mesa, the true fact of the matter is that when we are dealing with multi-leveled subterranean systems the 'border zones' are a little more complex than on the surface, where we have obvious horizontal borders between countries. In 'inner-planetary' warfare the 'battle lines' are horizontal, vertical and in some cases inter-dimensional.

The battle would be one that is being waged above, below and within our society, even though the outward manifestations of that 'war' might not be immediately seen for what they are, unless one is aware of the real conflict behind the scenes. There are also indications that at least certain factions of the NSA-MJ-12-CIA-AVIARY agencies have 'defected' from the neo-Nazi New World Order agenda of 'joint interaction' with the Reptiloids/Greys, and are now at war with the same."[20]

If all this seems too complicated for words, it is. Linda Moulton-Howe, one of America's best-informed ufologists, calls it, "A house of mirrors with a quicksand floor."

Meanwhile, in addition to the network of underground bases, the supersonic underground transportation system that interconnects many of them, the rail cars with manacles, the flying saucers of diverse origins, and other developments that rival the most imaginative science fiction, there are some inexplicable actions in full public view that demand explanation.

A Global Research article entitled "Urban Warfare Training and the Militarization of America," by Bill Van Auken, sums up the situation with such clarity that I am taking the liberty of including it verbatim.

This week's deployment of Blackhawk helicopters in Chicago is only the latest in a series of 'urban warfare training' exercises that have become a familiar feature of American life.

As elsewhere, this exercise was sprung unannounced on a startled civilian population. Conducted in secrecy, apparently with the collusion of local police and elected officials, Democrats and Republicans alike, the ostensible purpose of these exercises is to give U.S. troops experience in what Pentagon doctrine refers to as 'Military Operations on Urban Terrain.'

Such operations are unquestionably of central importance to the U.S. military. Over the past decade, its primary mission, as evidenced in Afghanistan and Iraq, has been the invasion and occupation of relatively powerless countries and the subjugation of their resisting populations, often in house-to-house fighting in urban centers.

The Army operates a 1,000 acre Urban Training Center in south-central Indiana that boasts over 1,500 "training structures" designed to simulate houses, schools, hospitals and factories. The center's web site states that it "can be tailored to replicate both foreign and domestic scenarios."

What does flying Blackhawks low over Chicago apartment buildings or rolling armored military convoys through the streets of St. Louis accomplish that cannot be achieved through the sprawling training center's simulations? Last year alone, there were at least seven such exercises, including in Los Angeles, Chicago, Miami, Tampa, St. Louis, Minneapolis and Creeds, Virginia.

The most obvious answer is that these exercises accustom troops to operating in U.S. cities, while desensitizing the American people to the domestic deployment of U.S. military might.

Preparations for such deployments are already far advanced. Over the past decade, under the pretext of prosecuting a "global war on terror," Washington has enacted a raft of repressive legislation and created a vast new bureaucracy of state control under the Department of Homeland Security. Under the Obama administration, the White House has claimed the power to throw enemies of the state into indefinite military detention or even assassinate them on U.S. soil by means of drone strikes, while radically expanding electronic spying on the American population.

Part of this process has been the ceaseless growth of the power of the U.S. military and its increasing intervention into domestic affairs. In 2002, the creation of the U.S. Northern Command for the first time dedicated a military command to operations within the U.S. itself.

Just last May, the Pentagon announced the implementation of new rules of engagement for U.S. military forces operating on American soil to provide "support" to "civilian law enforcement authorities, including responses to civil disturbances."

The document declares sweeping and unprecedented military powers under a section entitled "Emergency Authority." It asserts the authority of a "federal military commander" in 'extraordinary emergency situations where prior authorization by the president is impossible and duly constituted local authorities are unable to control the situation, to engage temporarily in activities that are necessary to quell large-scale, unexpected civil disturbances.' In other words, the Pentagon brass claims the unilateral authority to impose martial law.

These powers are not being asserted for the purpose of defending the U.S. population against terrorism or to counter some hypothetical emergency. The U.S. military command is quite conscious of where the danger lies.

In a recent article, a senior instructor at the Fort Leavenworth Command and General Staff College and former director of the Army's School of Advanced Military Studies, laid out a telling scenario for a situation in which the military could intervene.

"The Great Recession of the early twenty-first century lasts far longer than anyone anticipated. After a change in control of the White House and Congress in 2012, the governing party cuts off all funding that had been dedicated to boosting the economy or toward relief. The United States economy shows signs of reawakening, but the middle and lower-middle classes have yet to experience much in the way of job growth or pay raises. Unemployment continues to hover perilously close to double digits ..."

In other words, the Pentagon sees these conditions – which differ little from what exists in the U.S. today – producing social upheavals that can be quelled only by means of military force.

What is being upended, behind the scenes with virtually no media coverage, much less public debate, are constitutional principles dating back centuries that bar the use of the military in civilian law enforcement. In the Declaration of Independence itself, the indictment justifying revolution against King George included the charge that he had 'affected to render the Military independent of and superior to the Civil power.'

Side by side with the rising domestic power of the military, the supposedly civilian police have been militarized. An article published by the *Wall Street Journal* last weekend [August 2013] entitled "The Rise of the Warrior Cop" graphically described this process:

"Driven by martial rhetoric and the availability of military-style equipment – from bayonets and M-16 rifles to armored personnel carriers – American police forces have often adopted a mind-set previously reserved for the battlefield. The war on drugs and, more recently, post-9/11 antiterrorism efforts have created a new figure on the U.S. scene: the warrior cop – armed to the teeth, ready to deal harshly with targeted wrongdoers, and a growing threat to familiar American liberties."

The article describes the vast proliferation of SWAT (Special Weapons and Tactics) units to virtually every town in America, fueled by some $35 billion in grants from the Department of Homeland Security, "with much of the money going to purchase military gear such as armored personnel carriers."

This armed force was on full display in April when what amounted to a state of siege was imposed on the city of Boston, ostensibly to capture one teenage suspect. The entire population of a major American city was locked in their homes as combat-equipped police, virtually indistinguishable from troops, occupied the streets and conducted house-to-house searches.

Underlying this unprecedented militarization of U.S. society are two parallel processes. The immense widening of the social chasm separating the billionaires and multi-billionaires who control economic and political life from American working people, the great majority of the population, is fundamentally incompatible with democracy and requires other forms of rule.

At the same time, the turn to militarism as the principal instrument of U.S. foreign policy has vastly increased the power of the military within the U.S. apparatus.

Both America's ruling oligarchy and the Pentagon command recognize that profound social polarization and deepening economic crisis must give rise to social upheavals. They are preparing accordingly."[21]

* * *

What is this? Do America's super rich and powerful plan to use police and military forces to beat an increasingly disillusioned working class into submission? Do they intend to do this without even attempting to discuss the deep-seated cause of the dissatisfaction as a precursor to positive action necessary to alleviate it, and renew hope in the America of their dreams?

There are so many questions relating to all aspects of contemporary American life, power and politics it is absolutely essential that the *Truth Embargo* that was clamped down with ferocious intensity more than half-a-century ago be lifted at once! *Then Full Disclosure can begin.*

FULL DISCLOSURE

There has been so much information withheld from the public for such a long period of time that it will be difficult to know where to begin. Certainly the crashes of UFOs in the 1940s and the frantic efforts to replicate the aliens' technology would be one appropriate launching place. This deep river will lead to many tributaries including the loss of governmental and congressional control of such an enormously important file.

Appropriate commissions will have to be established including one in the Congress which should be intrigued and perhaps dismayed to learn the means by which its constitutional rights and responsibilities have been so substantially eroded. Screening staff to ensure that it is innocent of any possible conflict of interest will be the fundamental step in moving ahead.

A few of the thousands of questions that should be asked might include where and how many alien vehicles have been recovered by

United States armed forces? Where were they stored? When did back-engineering begin? What has been the relationship between the several armed forces and private industry in this endeavor? What costs have been incurred and what techniques were employed to keep both the public and the Congress in the dark?

Do the Germans still have a military base in Antarctica? If not, when was it removed, and by whom? What agreements have been signed between the U.S. government or any of its agencies with any of the alien species? Are they still operative after actions that might have justified abrogation? Is the Dulce base back in operation after the alleged war to capture it? Is it still a joint U.S.-Grey operation?

The number of questions is legion, but they are all important. It may be necessary to repeal or suspend the National Security Act of 1947 so that witnesses will be free to speak truthfully. It may also be necessary to grant a general amnesty to the many civilians and members of the armed forces who have broken numerous laws in the course of what they were led to believe was their duty.

This idea was raised with Jim Sparks in a frank interview with a number of extraterrestrials and is related in his book *The Keepers: An Alien Message for the Human Race*,[22] and in mine, thanks to his permission. They admitted that serious crimes had been committed in the name of maintaining secrecy, but not by them. They urged amnesty in the interests of disclosure. While a total amnesty may be appropriate for most misdemeanors, it may be considered inappropriate in cases of murder, or complicity in mass murder like 9/11, where lack of some punishment could not be justified.

* * *

2014 – The Year of Decision for Humankind

At the end of Chapter 9, "Visitors from Starry Realms" I related the story of Charlie Paz Wells and his brother who had been in direct contact with several species from afar. Here are some key points from their story.

> The extraterrestrials explained that there are more than 80 different civilizations interacting within our solar system, all of which have gone through an evolutionary process. Now there

is peace in the universe and they want to keep it that way. Earth and human beings are going through their own evolutionary process and are unstable. Humans risk destroying themselves and their planet. Humanity is not in balance with the universe, and the universal laws that control it. The extraterrestrials explained that they want to help us realize we are not alone, and that there is a better way of living and evolving that is sustainable. But before they give us the tools and technology to continue our evolution, they need to be assured that whatever they do for us will be for the benefit of ALL humanity. Not just those in power who will use it to further their own agendas.[23]

They were told, in 1974, that in 30 + 10 years we would reach our year of decision, our watershed, when we would have to change our ways dramatically or it would be too late to reverse the trend and we would be subject to great calamities.[24] I, for one, have taken their warning seriously. Some good things have begun to happen and I list a few of them in the Postscript to this book. But we have a very long way to go and time is of the essence. The lists of essentials both in my previous book, *Light at the End of the Tunnel: A Survival Plan for the Human Species*, and the list in later chapters of this book have been largely ignored.

Global warming has not yet been taken seriously by world leaders! And their priorities of wanting to spend more for weapons of death at the expense of a fairer, more just world of peaceful pursuits, and their antiquated pre-occupation with empire building just won't wash. We are writing our own history day-by-day and the result, so far, is not good!

Chapter Thirteen

THE TWO AMERICAS

"And ye should know the truth, and the truth shall make you free."

– John 8:32

There are two quotations that should be read as fire alarms to Americans and all humankind. The first is contained in a story told by Dr. Stephen Greer, one of America's best ufologists. President Clinton responded to a question by White House reporter Sarah McClendon about why he didn't do something about UFO disclosure. Clinton replied, "Sarah, there's a government inside the government and I don't control it."[1] Excuse me, doesn't the commander-in-chief and the person who allegedly has his finger on the nuclear trigger have a right to know what subordinates are doing?

Senator Daniel K. Inouye who in 1987 chaired the Senate Select Committee on Secret Military Assistance to Iran and the Nicaraguan Opposition, which held public hearings on the Iran-Contra affair, summarizes here the cover-up of the U.S. shadow government involvement by saying: "There exists a shadowy government with its own air force, its own navy, its own fundraising mechanism, and the ability to pursue its own ideas of the national interest, free from all checks and balances, and free from the law itself."[2]

This is most revealing! An air force and navy with its own fundraising mechanism operating outside the law? How does this square with America's campaign to "sell" its brand of democracy to Third World countries?

President Obama spoke about Inouye during a memorial service at the Washington National Cathedral on December 21,

2012, saying the Hawaii senator had been one of his "earliest political inspirations." The president said the late senator had served the country with "fundamental integrity." That is correct. But it appears that the Cabal, which has been running the U.S. for more than half-a-century, exerted pressure on the senator to the extent that in later hearings, following the one where he had so eloquently summed up the reality of post-World War II U.S., he had cautioned witnesses wanting to speak about these subjects to be quiet because "it was classified material."

This decades old "truth embargo" is definitely not justified in the name of "national security." It appeared to be the consensus of witnesses at the Citizen Hearing on Disclosure, which as you may recall was held at the National Press Club in Washington in May 2013, that the cover-up had little if anything to do with national security. Instead it could be summed up in two words – power and greed. It is not the interests of the Republic that are threatened by lifting the veil of secrecy. It is the continued dominance of the tiny group of elite bankers, corporate tycoons, intelligence collectors and high-ranking military officers, who have been calling the shots under the guise of "national security," that would be ended by disclosure of the facts and the reinstatement of the rule of law.

How long has the current lawlessness and contempt for democracy been dominant? It appears to have begun under the presidency of Dwight Eisenhower, if not before. On the final day of the Citizen Hearing on Disclosure we were shown a film entitled "Deathbed Testimony" about UFOs given by an anonymous alleged former CIA official in an interview with UFO author and historian Richard Dolan, on March 5, 2013. The following is a report filed by Alexandra Bruce, publisher, ForbiddenKnowledgeTV.com

> Facing impending kidney failure, this individual felt compelled to disclose secret information he feels is too important to keep secret. In the video he claims to have served in the U.S. Army, worked for the CIA, and worked on the U.S. Air Force's Project Blue Book – one of the USAF's official studies of UFOs. And he refers to the project as 'partially a fraud.' Asking for clarification, Dolan states, 'You're saying some of the

Blue Book cases were completely fictitious?' The anonymous man responds, 'Yes.'

'Anonymous' alleges that, after an invasion threat from President Dwight Eisenhower, he and his superior at the CIA were allowed inside the secretive Area 51 in Nevada to gather intelligence and report back to the president.

[Alexandra Bruce Note: President Eisenhower realized that he had been left 'out of the loop' of the Black Projects' ongoing activities between various members of ET races and their UFO technologies at the 'remote detachment of Edwards Air Force Base ... located in the southern portion of Nevada in the western United States, 83 miles (133 km) north-northwest of Las Vegas.' A.k.a. Area 51.

Eisenhower became so angry that he threatened those in charge of Area 51 that he would call in the 1st Army from Colorado Springs to invade the base, if they did not allow two of his trusted CIA associates, including the narrator of this story, to visit.]

There, 'Anonymous' describes seeing several alien spacecraft, including the craft that crashed in Roswell, New Mexico. Then, he and his superior were taken to the S-4 facility southwest of Area 51 where they observed live extraterrestrials.

This testimony will be included in an upcoming documentary titled 'Truth Embargo.' "[3]

I have complete confidence in Richard Dolan, a good friend who did the interview. In addition, one of my prime anonymous sources watched the video, checked it out, and confirmed that the information it contained had been known for some time by government insiders.

Although General Eisenhower, by threatening the use of force, was given a glimpse of what was going on in some of those highly guarded secret areas, he obviously was not able to do anything about it. He must have been sold down the river by one or more of his trusted advisers. As a result, apart from a general warning to the American people that they should beware the military-industrial complex, a heads-up that has been ignored by both the Congress and succeeding presidents, no action was taken to end the insubordination of those he warned against. Consequently a wall of secrecy far more important than the Berlin Wall was erected by the pirates who had their own idea of what was best for America and, ultimately, the world and its place in the cosmos.

One can understand the paranoia of the U.S. military in the early post-World War II era when it was confronted by alien technology light years more advanced than its own. The concern must have been magnified by uncertainty about how many of the Nazi scientists the Soviets had been able to recruit following the allied victory in Europe, and whether or not they, too, had made contact with the extraterrestrials. In a situation of so many unknowns a slice of the military, in lock step with their industrial and ET collaborators, decided to take the law in their own hands. They have never looked back.

President Harry Truman was probably the last president who could count on the truth from his advisors. Eisenhower had to threaten the use of force to gain access to part of the truth. Subsequent presidents have all had to live double lives where they were theoretically in control but actually powerless to use their constitutional authority. Each was given a briefing on the ET presence and technology but only to the extent the overlords trusted them to stifle the truth and play dumb on the subject. Any deviation would result in a single term, or worse. In addition, curious congressmen and senators were bluntly told to butt out.

That raises the 64-trillion dollar question. If neither the president nor the Congress have been allowed to exercise their constitutional responsibilities, and literally trillions of dollars of U.S. taxpayers money has been spent with neither congressional review nor public audit, who has really been in charge? The answer is: The "Cabal," as I call it.

The Cabal

The Cabal is impossible to describe with precision because it is an amorphous conglomeration of different persons and groups whose interests may not be identical, but who have enough in common that they are willing to submit to a common plan or discipline in the belief that they will share in the ultimate benefits. In broad strokes they may represent the New World Order gang, who believe in an unelected world government of bankers and elite persons. But it is impossible to understand either the depth or breadth of their vast power without looking at some component parts.

At or near the top of the pyramid you will find the Three Sisters that I referred to earlier in the text. They are the Bilderbergers, The Council on Foreign Relations and the Trilateral Commission. These groups have been responsible for picking and then helping finance presidential candidates for both the Republican and Democratic parties since World War II. Consequently their influence in the White House is a given.

But the direct and indirect influence doesn't end there. It extends to the intelligence community, the CIA, the FBI, the NSA, etc. as well as the military "Junta," that part of the military that is obliquely, though definitely, controlled by the Cabal, rather than the president. If this group has back-engineered spaceships, as well as powerful lasers and particle guns capable of virtually disintegrating solid matter, there is little doubt where the ultimate power of the military lies. The Cabal is in control. So its threat of installing a New World Order (dictatorship) is not one that can be dismissed lightly. It has to be faced head on with the utmost seriousness.

While one hesitates to name names, it is essential to know some of the principal proponents of the NWO and examine any evidence they might have to support such a proposal as being in the public interest. The first name that comes to mind is that of David Rockefeller, head of the Rockefeller clan. He is a member of each of the Three Sisters and, probably, the most powerful man in the international banking cartel, and the international banking system which is integral to the Cabal.

Ellen Hodgson Brown, author of the incredibly revealing book *Web of Debt*, alleges that Rockefeller took over as webmaster after World War II presumably succeeding the famous Rothschild dynasty which had dominated international banking for the previous two centuries. So it is important to know what Rockefeller thinks. The following quote, that he denies but that I believe is authentic because it corresponds exactly with events in the real world, sums it up.

We are grateful to the Washington Post, the New York Times, Time magazine and other great publications, whose directors have attended our meetings and respected their promises of discretion for almost forty years. It would have been impossible for us to develop our plan for the world if we had been subjected to the lights of publicity during those years. But, the world is more sophisticated and prepared to march towards a world government. The supranational sovereignty of an intellectual elite and world bankers is surely preferable to the national auto-determination practiced in past centuries.[4]

There you have it! In a one paragraph "thank you" to attendees at the close of a meeting of Bilderbergers at Baden Baden in Germany, David Rockefeller sums up what the New World Order is all about – the substitution of elite rule for democracy. Even a casual reading of U.S. history for the last half-century is sufficient to convince any fair-minded observer that Rockefeller has already succeeded in substituting elite rule for democracy in his native America. He and his associates have been calling the shots so it is fair to assess the results. Has this been good for the United States, or not? Let's apply the old axiom of "The test of the pudding is in the eating."

It would be rude of me to compile a list of tests but recently Steve Bassett, CEO of Paradigm Research Group, who organized the uniquely successful Citizen Hearing on Disclosure at the National Press Club in Washington in May 2013, sent a list he had compiled to everyone on his mailing list. I asked for permission to reprint it verbatim and he generously agreed. It is titled "Ending the Truth Embargo: Disclosure and the State of the Union."

COMMENTARY: In the past I have steadfastly avoided straying too far from the core issues of the ET truth embargo and government abuse of secrecy. I am going to make an exception with this commentary. At the end of this non-partisan essay you will find out why.

The recent debacle in Washington, DC over the budget and debt ceiling is only one of many indicators the body politic is suffering from multiple organ failure. Nations, empires, kingdoms – they die the same way people do. No society is perfect, no person is perfectly healthy. Both can withstand the odd dysfunction (illness). When the illness spreads and becomes multiple organ failure the person (society) dies or is enfeebled.

It happened to the Sun-never-sets-on-the-British Empire. The Soviet Union was able to sustain multiple system dysfunction well past its shelf life by sheer force of raw suppression, but inevitably blew up into fifteen republics (mercifully without too much violence). And, of course, there is the famous and extensively studied collapse of the Roman Empire. What took several hundred years in the time of Rome now can be accomplished in a few decades.

That said, it still takes years to achieve the state of affairs in which the U.S. now finds itself. Time enough for too many citizens to not see the process of failure unfold. Not anymore. Eventually the suffering person realizes they are terminally ill. The American people, thanks in large part to the power of the internet, are now quite aware their vaunted society is coming apart at the seams. Let's review.

• The two-party political system by virtue of bad law, bad judicial decisions and pure greed for money and power has frozen into a block of ice. ('Some say the world will end in fire …'). New ideas are strangled in their crib. New political parties are throttled. Independent candidates crippled.

• The American education system is slowly imploding with U.S. students collectively falling further behind other nations in every category.

• The American health care system, while satisfactory for the very wealthy, is collectively one of the worst in the developed, industrialized world. It is helping to destroy the middle class – the primary engine of social stability. Health issues are the leading cause of personal bankruptcy.

• The massive U.S. military spending – not long ago greater than all other nations in the world combined – guarantees that fiscal balance and adequate funding in support of the human condition will not be possible.

• Along with war spending, massive entitlement commitments made without any effort to control that war spending going back to 1960 now place the nation in immediate debt of $17 trillion dollars with an almost incomprehensible long term exposure of $80 to $100 trillion in unfunded liabilities.

• Economic recovery after the 2008/2009 greatest train robbery is a temporary illusion created by an enormous "printing" of $trillions of new money that will eventually lead to inflation.

• The investment and standard banking industries have bought politicians to pass laws that have allowed a massive shift of wealth to the upper class and stripping the middle class of pensions, jobs, home values, and home ownership. Virtually no one is held criminally accountable for this. Eventual fines are trivial.

• Behind the confiscation of middle class assets by the investment banking abuses is the exposure to derivatives (casino debt). Some experts claim this exposure is over $200 trillion. If you're counting, that's over $300 trillion in risk exposure for the U.S. society.

• Voting systems in the U.S. are an antiquated joke with voter turnout one of the lowest in the developed world. This is made worse by a venal policy of one of the political parties to suppress voter turnout in every way possible that would undermine the other political party.

• The very infrastructure of the nation – roads, bridges, dams, waterways, power grids, sewers – are falling apart with little funds to fix. $2.5 trillion of investment is needed by 2020. Half-baked efforts and illusionary promises are put forward that few believe sufficient.

• American international influence, trust levels and esteem are declining under a plethora of terrible policies, brutal war measures and outright stupidity.

• American political institutions, particularly the U.S. Congress, have fallen to record levels of disapproval, and distrust in government has polarized the nation making common sense policies next to impossible.

• The U.S. dollar, the cornerstone of American financial power, is being circled by a number of nations quite willing to replace or diminish it for their own benefit. The U.S. literally submits to this process with profoundly destructive financial decisions year after year. Loss of reserve currency status all or in part would trigger significant inflation.

• American manufacturing jobs are disappearing by being shoved offshore or replaced by low paying service jobs at minimum wage.

• The gap with the rich and poor grows and the American middle class is diminished. This is recipe for violence and disorder in the most heavily armed nation in the world.

• The criminal system is antiquated, extraordinarily expensive and hamstrung by absurd laws which have created the highest level of incarceration in the world.

• Perhaps well-intentioned legislative and judicial blunders resulted in the granting of "personhood" status to corporations leading to a destructive shift of power away from actual persons (citizens) and a wholesale corruption of the election process in the United States at all levels.

• A fossil fuel based energy industry has bought politicians in order to get away with monopolizing energy production, fixing prices, misrepresenting both held and potential reserves, not building new refineries and pushing exploitation of more dangerous extraction modalities such as tar sands, shale and fracking. In other words, utilize every trick to drive the price of energy higher at the nation's expense. Meanwhile, government and corporate entities have been buying up and suppressing competing energy patents, intimidating inventors and confiscating competing technology under national security imprimatur. All this while fossil fuels are contaminating U.S. air, rivers, soils and ground water and bringing premature death to millions.

• The food industry is being taken over by a consortium of companies led by Monsanto that intend to own a re-engineered food and seed supply designed to force the use of their own pesticides in mass quantities. Few things are more representative of the concept of system failure than the losses in the honey bee population (Colony Collapse Disorder). Growing evidence connects CCD to the actions of companies like Monsanto, easily the most dangerous corporation in the world today. The environmental impact will be devastating. The government does nothing. Huge corporate spending thwarts citizen activism.

• Lastly, a secret empire was built to service the $10+ trillion (in adjusted dollars) Cold War (acknowledged) and address the presence of extraterrestrials (non-human intelligence) engaging the planet (not acknowledged). This "empire" has become a world unto itself with a low opinion (perhaps justifiable) of politicians meaning senators, congresspersons, the president and their staff. Just yesterday the White House indicated the NSA had not informed the president about the surveillance of foreign heads of state's phone calls. This empire is vast, out of control and in dire need of overhaul and reform.

Read enough? It's a partial list, but the point is made.

Why am I telling you this?

The children, grandchildren and great grandchildren of the baby boomers are more likely to inherit a greatly diminished rather than a viable society moving forward unless something very powerful, very profound intervenes to short circuit the multitude of current trends leading to the emasculation of America.

What could possibly be sufficiently powerful to alter the worldview of political institutions, corporations, and 300+ million people overnight, and open the door to multi-system reform? The usual candidate is a war equal to the magnitude of distress. The last version of that scenario was WWII. Sadly any war worthy of the present dilemma would destroy the world itself. What does that leave?

Disclosure. Every day the citizens of Earth are denied the truth they are not alone in the galaxy as sentient life, that a vast new world awaits them when that truth is out in the open – a world where once again all things are possible – is one more day closer to the end of the American Dream – the 21st century nightmare study after study projects.

Disclosure will be the most profound event in human history. It is inevitable, but will it be soon enough? All who have a basic understanding of this have a decision to make. Stand up and support the Disclosure advocacy movement or stand down and hope for the best.[5]

Stephen Bassett's summary underlines some of the weak spots in the U.S. system of government. The February 17-23, 2014 edition of *Bloomberg Businessweek* highlighted another, the disparity between rich and poor in America. The cover was a picture of Nate Smith, 21, of Philadelphia, a baggage handler who works 40 hours a week, and covers the weekend shift. For handling more than a thousand bags a day he earns $7.25 an hour. Three pages later there were pictures of five other people in various jobs – four earn $8.00 and one is paid $9.00 an hour.

A few pages later an article by Peter Coy begins, "Get beyond the political noise, and there's a strong case for a 40 percent boost in the minimum wage." If one reads his well documented objectivity one can conclude that it makes the case for a much higher minimum – something in the $14-$15 range. For anyone who thinks that sounds high, Coy points out that the $5.00 an hour Henry Ford paid his auto workers would be $14.71 today, adjusted for inflation. An even more compelling number is the $22.27 an hour that would be a "living wage" for a single parent with two children in Pascagoula, Mississippi.[6]

When President Obama said no one working full-time in the world's richest nation should be poor there are many who would agree. But the Cabal running the United States and much of the Western world dissents. It has been slowly but inexorably destroying the middle class in America and, by extension, around the world. It has been exporting the middle class manufacturing jobs in order to benefit from cheap labor and medieval working conditions.

This puts downward pressure on wages and working conditions in the U.S. Right to work legislation is destroying workers rights to bargain collectively. Public service jobs are being privatized to avoid paying benefits in health and old age. It appears that the bankers and elite industrialists and militarists have declared war on the poor.

The irony of the situation is often lost. Workers rights to negotiate better living standards are increasingly denied. This is generally true for most of the people who do the real work and produce the real wealth, while globalization enables the rich and powerful to set their own rules and rewards. The oil producers have their union. In many industries the number of producers is so small they can use their market power to set prices. Even the banana distributors appear to know a good thing when they see it. Meanwhile the low wages for the masses and the high levels of unemployment are threatening the system under which the elite become rich.

The exploitation is by no means limited to American workers. Most of the jobs that have been outsourced offer neither living wages nor safe working conditions. When the Rana Plaza collapsed in a suburb of Dhaka in Bangladesh in 2013, 1,129 workers died and more than 2,500 were injured, maimed or paralyzed.[7] The Cabal sponsored trade agreements make it impossible for importing countries to demand fair wages and working conditions in the exporting countries.

Another *Toronto Star* article on the same subject was titled "Tannery Boys: The Rana Plaza tragedy has put Bangladesh's garment factories under the microscope. In many ways the leather industry, where young workers are dying slowly, makes the sweatshops look good." Zakir Hussain is a cricket addict who coughs as he speaks. "I can't run as fast between wickets as I used to. I get tired quickly now … and my eyes burn sometimes. Hussain works at a leather tannery in Dhaka for 12 hours a day, seven days a week. In the five months he has been working, he has lost about 12 pounds and much of his stamina. He also lives in the tannery. Should he stay in the job, he is expected to live only another 35 years."[8] The New World Order's brand of globalization has set the "fairness" clock back 100 years.

The Eurozone is Not Exempt

An article by *BBC News* – "In graphics: Eurozone crisis" April 25, 2013, tells the story. The charts, GDP, employment, deficits and debt as percentage of GDP are too detailed for inclusion here even though, as the introduction suggests, if there is any need to understand why global final demand is shrinking, these will help. Instead, I will just quote a few of the highlights that paint the unhappy picture.

Spain and Ireland, which enjoyed property booms and rapid debt-fueled growth before 2008, have failed to recover. The latest data shows them back in recession this year. While Portugal and Italy did not experience huge dips in 2009, their GDP growth was very weak for much of the previous decade. For Portugal, this made the big infrastructure projects it was pursuing difficult to afford, while for Italy it made the government's enormous debt load harder to bear. Lastly, the economy of Greece seems to have been driven into freefall by the government's austerity measures, and the collapse in confidence in the country's future.[9]

The unemployment rate has been rising significantly in the three countries that have needed bailouts – Greece, Portugal, and the Republic of Ireland. It has also risen sharply in Spain reaching 25% in 2013 although Spain has a long history of unusually high unemployment. Contrast their fates with Germany, where unemployment has fallen to its lowest level since the country was unified more than two decades ago. Many countries have seen unemployment rise as austerity measures, following the financial crisis, have led to cuts in government spending, which has involved public sector job losses.[10]

European countries overburdened by debt, and dependent on their creditors to keep re-lending it the money, risk a sudden loss of confidence, resulting in a refusal by creditors to continue lending. Or, more likely, a demand for usurious interest rates and game playing with the market for their bonds. These practices are exacerbated inside the eurozone by the fact that the European Central Bank is banned by treaty from bailing out governments.

This restriction, in my opinion, was not an accident. It was a coldly calculated move on the part of the banking cartel, which is the apex of the Cabal, to make the eurozone countries completely dependent on the private banks for either life or growth. It is a case of total dependency and a terrible curse that will have to be removed before the world can move forward.

The Militarization of America

The expenditure of substantial sums on the military during the cold war era can be justified as a legitimate reaction to possible uncertainty about Soviet capabilities, despite doubts anyone might entertain on that score. That rationale lost any validity it might have enjoyed when the Berlin Wall came down and most of the Soviet Empire was disbanded. So the U.S. refusal to cash in on the peace dividend, and share it with the world was inexplicable in the absence of any military threat to its security. So a continued high priority on abnormally high military budgets had to be a signal that something was going on that the public was not aware of. There was!

It went far beyond the military-industrial complex inbred greed for more money and higher profits. The shadow government was already firmly in control, although it maintained a façade of representative government to hoodwink voters and help justify military operations in defense of democratic principles. The shadow government has been as difficult to define as any shadow would be but comprises the banking cartel, the oil cartel, the large multinational corporations that are controlled directly or indirectly by the banking fraternity, the intelligence community including the CIA, FBI and NSA, and a formidable slice of the U.S. military.

Its objective is an unelected world government brought into being by deliberately reducing millions of ordinary people to relative poverty and hopelessness and then compelling their compliance by unprecedented police and military might. It is difficult bordering on impossible to peg the ideology of the "bankers and elite" groups involved. The Council on Foreign Relations that has played a pivotal role for more than 60 years was founded by a communist. The post-World War II Nazi influence, stoked by Operation Paperclip and probably encouraged by other Nazi underground groups, has been significant. It really doesn't matter because far-left dictatorships and far-right dictatorships end up at the same point. The dictators, their families and their collaborators live in opulence while the people who provide the real goods and services are treated as slaves of the system.

The gargantuan transfer of power that has already occurred, and the much greater one that is in the planning stage, requires a voracious intelligence apparatus to stifle opposition, maintain secrecy and anticipate points of resistance. This is endemic to police states and dictatorships either embryonic or full-blown. The CIA has played a key role. A child of wartime necessity, it was modeled on the British MI6 and the Soviet KGB. A cynic might conclude that it adopted all of the most questionable traits of both organizations.

On this base it is necessary to add the Earth-shattering developments of the post-World War II period. In his new encyclopedic book entitled *UFOs for the 21ˢᵗ Century Mind*, the widely known ufologist Richard M. Dolan quotes from the work of Joseph P. Farrell on the subject of German experiments on flying saucers near the end of the war, and the dispersal of Nazi intelligence units in the post-war era. Dolan noted the lack of supporting documentation for some of the alleged experiments with flying saucers, but added that this fact was not reason enough to ignore the research that had been recorded.

"Still," said Dolan, "Farrell's work bears close scrutiny, as he makes a strong case that, at the very least, the fundamentals of the Nazis' fringe research continued on after the war, especially in Argentina but perhaps elsewhere, with substantial cooperation from within the U.S. First, the massive Nazi intelligence group led by Reinhard Gehlen was brought into the Anglo-American fold organizationally intact, and run essentially by the same people after the war as during it – and with a great amount of independence. Secondly, not only did the importation of so many Nazis into the CIA via Project Paperclip fundamentally undermine the nature and purpose of that organization, but many Paperclip Nazis who went elsewhere (such as into the U.S. rocket program in the south-west) also exhibited a striking level of independence from U.S. military authority. (Remember that President Eisenhower had to threaten to use the army in order to find out what they were doing in Area 51 and elsewhere.) These Nazis, Farrell suggested, were a 'classic Trojan Horse operation.'

"Thirdly, these U.S.-based Nazis were in all likelihood collaborating with Nazis elsewhere in the world, most importantly Argentina but probably other places, too. 'Our Nazis,' he wrote 'may not really have been 'ours' after all.'[11] Argentina under Juan Peron provided them with a secure home and infrastructure in return for Nazi gold and whatever other ample resources they brought with them."[12]

For whatever reason the CIA took a hard right turn, and abandoned whatever remained of what once might have been regarded as American values. A book entitled *Dirty Wars: The World is a Battlefield*[13] by Jeremy Scahill chronicles the slippery slope into competing intelligence agencies, CIA prisons, rendition, the depersonalizing of killing through drone attacks, and the evasion of Congressional oversight of operations by the creation of secretive military units reporting directly to the Pentagon or the president.

A review of Scahill's *Dirty Wars* by Frank Bayerl that appeared in the *Canadian Centre for Policy Alternatives Monitor*, November 2013, beautifully condenses the message that everyone, everywhere should read.

> Scahill begins by explaining how Dick Cheney, as Defense Secretary, began during the administration of George Bush Sr. to lay plans for privatizing as much of the military as possible as a way of creating another barrier to civilian oversight and strengthening the hand of the Executive branch. When George W. Bush became President, Cheney, as Vice-President, lost no time in carrying out these plans. He was aided by the new administration's decision that Iraq had to be attacked and Saddam Hussein destroyed.
>
> In declaring a global war on terror, the Bush administration redirected the purpose of the CIA. 'Rather than having the agency serve as the President's premier fact-checking and intelligence resource, the CIA's new job would be to reinforce predetermined policy,' Scahill states. One of the president's key new tools would be the use of covert action. Under the National Security Act, such action first requires a 'finding' that it is in accord with law and the U.S. Constitution. The Act also explicitly prohibits assassination. But on Sept. 17, 2001, Bush

created a secret program code named Greystone that essentially declared all covert actions to be pre-authorized and legal. They would no longer need direct presidential approval on a case-by-case basis. 'I had never in my experience,' said a CIA attorney, 'seen a presidential authorization as far-reaching and aggressive in scope. It was simply extraordinary.'

Central to all secretive U.S. military operations in the war on terror is the Joint Special Operations Command (JSOC). Formed in 1980, it was unique in reporting directly to the president. It was, the author says, intended to be his small, private army and, under Donald Rumsfeld, gradually took over covert operations from the CIA. Scahill cites a 1992 Predator drone strike in Yemen as a seminal moment in the war on terror. It killed Ahmed Hijazi, said to be an al-Qaeda agent, but also a U.S. citizen, and it was the first such attack outside Afghanistan.

This operation would constitute a precedent for President Obama's targeted killing in 2011 of Anwar Awlaki, which constitutes an ongoing narrative thread throughout this book.

Anwar Awlaki was the American-born son of a Yemeni immigrant who studied in the U.S. on a Fulbright scholarship before returning to teach in Yemen, where he eventually became an Imam and a very popular speaker. His preaching before 2001 was non-political and showed no sign of any affinity for radical Islamist doctrines, and, after 9/11, he was frequently sought out by the media as a spokesman for 'moderate' Muslims. He was interrogated by the FBI, however, simply because several known Muslim radicals had attended his services.

To simplify a very convoluted tale, Awlaki, feeling harassed by the FBI, returned to Yemen, was imprisoned for several months at the behest of the U.S. government, and gradually became radicalized to the extent of justifying terror attacks on U.S. citizens and interests. This made him a prime target in the U.S. war on terror, and he was finally hunted down and killed in Yemen in 2011. He was the second American citizen to be so targeted, raising serious questions about the illegitimate use of state power.

The Obama administration's targeted killings came as a great surprise to many of his supporters. As Scahill puts it, 'Obama sent a clear message that he intended to keep intact many of the aggressive counterterrorism policies of the Bush era. Among these were targeted killings, warrantless wiretapping, the use of secret prisons, a crackdown on habeas corpus rights for prisoners, indefinite detention, CIA rendition flights, drone bombings, the deployment of mercenaries in U.S. wars, and reliance on 'State Secrets Privilege.'"[14]

These ignoble policies herald the death and burial of The Rule of Law, a pinnacle of human achievement that millions of Americans and Allied forces fought and died for in World Wars I and II.

Of course the FBI deserves its share of "credit" in helping to develop the "Secrecy Industry" to the point where it is one of the nation's major industries. Sadly, it is an integral part of the National Security State that the U.S. has become. The FBI has been and continues to be a major player in the transformation of America. I would dearly love to develop the subject here but I will leave that to others as I must get on with the role of the National Security Agency and the rest of the incredible story.

The National Security Agency

The fictional Big Brother has become flesh and blood and grown to maturity in half-a-century. Today, no one, anywhere, can escape the silent eye of universal surveillance by an organization with powers that no one on the planet should have. And I, for one, deeply resent the fact that every word I say or write can be recorded without my knowledge or permission.

An article entitled "No Morsel Too Small for Spy Agency" by Scott Shane that appeared in the *New York Times International Weekly* on November 10, 2013, provides an interesting glimpse of how the system works.

> When Ban Ki-moon, the United Nations secretary general, sat down with President Obama at the White House in April to discuss Syrian chemical weapons, Israeli-Palestinian peace talks and climate change, it was a cordial, routine exchange.
>
> The National Security Agency nonetheless went to work in advance and intercepted Mr. Ban's talking points for the meeting, a feat the agency later reported as an 'operational

highlight' in a weekly internal brag sheet. It is hard to imagine what edge this could have given Mr. Obama in a friendly chat, if he even saw the N.S.A.'s modest scoop.

But it was emblematic of an agency that for decades has operated on the principle that any eavesdropping that can be done on a foreign target of any conceivable interest should be done.

From thousands of classified documents, the National Security Agency emerges as an electronic omnivore of staggering capabilities, eavesdropping and hacking its way around the world to strip governments and other targets of their secrets. It spies routinely on friends as well as foes; the agency's official mission list includes using its surveillance powers to achieve 'diplomatic advantage' over such allies as France and Germany and 'economic advantage' over Japan and Brazil, among other countries.[15]

It was the revelation that the NSA had been routinely spying on world leaders that has caused the biggest backlash. I felt ashamed for my country when it was revealed that we had allowed the NSA to spy on the G20 leaders from Canadian soil when that august body met in Toronto in 2010. It is little comfort to learn that the practice is routine. No wonder there was such a strong reaction that President Obama had to do something. So he tried to calm the storm by ordering the NSA to stop eavesdropping on foreign leaders. I laughed when I heard him say that because even if the order were obeyed, which could be open to doubt, it wouldn't make any difference when he didn't include the leaders' chiefs of staff and other close advisers who would be privy to the leaders' thoughts and plans.

Although the carte blanche snooping of the NSA is coming under increasing scrutiny by the public and anyone old fashioned enough to still believe in the rule of law, it retains the support of both the courts and the administration. An article titled "NSA phone surveillance is lawful, judge rules" by Michael S. Schmidt that appeared in the Toronto *Globe and Mail* of December 28, 2013 tells the story.

A federal judge in New York on Friday ruled that the National Security Agency's program that is systematically keeping phone records of all Americans is lawful, creating a conflict among lower courts and increasing the likelihood that the issue will be resolved by the Supreme Court.

In the ruling, Justice William Pauley, of the U.S. District Court for the Southern District of New York, granted a motion filed by the federal government to dismiss a challenge to the program brought by the American Civil Liberties Union, which had tried to halt the program.

Justice Pauley said protections under the Fourth Amendment do not apply to records held by third parties, such as phone companies. 'This blunt tool only works because it collects everything,' Justice Pauley said in the ruling. 'While robust discussions are under way across the nation, in Congress and at the White House, the question for this court is whether the government's bulk telephony metadata program is lawful. This court finds it is.'

A spokesman for the Justice Department said, 'We are pleased the court found the NSA's bulk telephony metadata collection program to be lawful.' He declined to comment further.[16]

Wow! One wonders the nature of the law school that the judge attended. His ruling, and the opinion of the spokesman for the Justice Department who was pleased with the ruling, raises questions concerning the extent to which that department has been infiltrated by the NWO gang who revere neither the U.S. Constitution nor the Rule of Law.

This concern was underlined by an article titled "Secret U.S. court put Web firms in a bind," by Claire Cain Miller that appeared in the *New York Times*.

In a secret court in Washington, Yahoo's top lawyers made their case. The government had sought help in spying on certain foreign users, without a warrant, and Yahoo had refused, saying the broad requests were unconstitutional.

The judges disagreed. That left Yahoo a choice: Hand over the data or break the law. So Yahoo became part of the National Security Agency's secret Internet surveillance program, Prism, according to leaked N.S.A. documents, as did seven other Internet companies.[17]

Needless to say the NSA's massive eavesdropping and hacking programs have upset activists at home and diplomats abroad. It is as if the U.S. Constitution's Fourth Amendment, which prohibits unreasonable searches and seizures never existed. Worse, there is no intervention protocol other than common decency to protect the rights of foreigners.

An interesting sidebar is the distinct possibility that no one is exempt including the President of the United States. Michael Hayden, the former chief of the National Security Agency, was overheard saying that President Barack Obama's 2008 Blackberry had been modified to block foreign eavesdropping.[18] If I were a betting man I would bet two to one that it was not modified to prevent NSA eavesdropping on the president so that his every thought would be available to NWO headquarters.

When one estimates the massive scale and near universal domestic and international reach of the NSA's networks it leads to the inevitable conclusion that the NSA is the nerve center of the New World Order project. It provides the intelligence necessary to influence appointments and influence policy decisions consistent with the plan. The vast data stored for future reference will be invaluable when the day comes for the demise of the nation state, and the installation of the new world dictatorship by whatever name you want to call it.

Does this sound far-fetched? Just reflect a minute on the events of September 11, 2001. Nothing could be more far-fetched than 9/11. In retrospect it qualifies as the most despicable deception in modern history. Yet who among us was not taken in by the press reports and the official version of what happened. Not even the great Houdini could have pulled off such a magnificent illusion.

The Fallout from 9/11

The fallout from 9/11 is probably unequalled in the annals of deception. Race has been set against race, religion against religion, and culture against culture. Muslims have been harassed both verbally and physically. In some cases their property has been desecrated with graffiti. They have been made to feel isolated and vulnerable in an unfriendly environment.

The 9/11 incident was the catalyst that the neo-cons needed to launch an illegal war on Iraq. The irony was that none of the alleged hijackers came from Iraq. But that didn't seem to matter. The Pentagon's Plan for a New American Century had targeted Iraq as its first priority on the list of Middle East wars, so that's where the so-called war on terror began.

President Bush's declaration of a war on terror was used to engage NATO countries to come to the defense of America. It was a dreadful precedent, and one that was quite inconsistent with the purpose of the Alliance which was to come to the aid of one that was subject to armed aggression.

Another questionable result flowing from 9/11 was the dramatic increase in defense expenditures. These went from a high of $281 billion in 2000 to an even higher $721 billion in 2001. Who would benefit from this? Not U.S. taxpayers for sure. It would only benefit the Military-Industrial Intelligence Complex which would see the dollars pouring into their enterprises. In 2012 the U.S. budget was $645.7 billion boasting 41% of the world's total. Military spending by NATO members accounted for 58% of the global total.[19]

This can be compared to $59.9 billion for Russia and $102.4 billion for China.[20] The wide discrepancy raises questions of who is setting the priorities in the U.S. when it has neither perceived nor real enemies that present a military challenge. Its principal challenge is from Muslim extremists with primitive weapons who became extremists after 9/11 when the U.S. started dropping bombs on Baghdad.

These are all incredibly important developments, but even more significant is the erosion of human rights and freedoms resulting from the perceived war against terrorism. They have been so extreme in total that one wonders how it has been possible. The technique has been the old salami theory – you just cut one slice at a time. So, in no particular order:

- You tighten border security and screening, which sounds reasonable.

- You establish a Department of Homeland Security, with extraordinary power.

- Then you ignore the Geneva Convention.

- Guantanamo base is used to circumvent the rule of law.

- Torture is sanctioned.

- Habeas Corpus is suspended.

- The Fourth Amendment is ignored.

- The Patriot Act – a law unto itself.

The process goes on and on. One slice after another of the rights and freedoms of citizens is taken away and, like another slice of salami, it is neither noticed nor missed except by a few activists who receive scant attention in the mainline press. Eventually there is nothing left of the salami but the string. The long list of human rights that have been won at inestimable cost in human lives is gone, and centuries of what was called progress has disappeared.

This is all very sad for people who have loved America, including me. I attended school in California in 1940-41 and considered the U.S. a really great and wonderful country. I sang the Star Spangled Banner with the enthusiasm of a patriot. But I couldn't sing it now because it is no longer "The Land of the Free."

My disappointment today is by no means unique. A happenstance discovery of a copy of *Vanity Fair*, January 2012, reflects almost exactly what I have been saying and writing.

One Nation, Under Arms

The private papers of the late George F. Kennan, Cold War architect and diplomat *extraordinaire*, reveal his anguish over the way his famous 1947 warning against Soviet expansionism helped transform the America he loved into one he no longer recognized: a national-security state. A half-century after a similarly historic warning – President Dwight D. Eisenhower's speech about the dangers of a powerful 'military-industrial complex,' Todd S. Purdum shows how completely Kennan's and Eisenhower's worst fears have been realized, warping almost every aspect of society, deflecting attention from urgent problems, and splitting the country into two classes.

By 1961 the problem that Eisenhower had identified was well advanced. Already, the United States was spending more on military security than the net income of all American corporations combined. In the years since, the trend has warped virtually every aspect of national life, with consequences that are quite radical in their cumulative effect on the economy, on the vast machinery of official secrecy, on the country's sense of itself, and on the very nature of national government in Washington. And yet the degree to which America has changed is noticed by almost no one – not in any visceral way.

The transformation has taken hold too gradually and over too long a period. Almost no one alive today has a mature, firsthand memory of a country that used to be very different – that was not a superpower; that did not shroud the workings of its government in secrecy; that did not use ends-justify-the-means logic to erode rights and liberties; that did not undertake protracted wars on the president's say-so; that had not forgotten how to invest in urgent needs at home; that did not trumpet its greatness even as its shortcomings became more obvious. An American today who is 25 or 50 or even 75 – such a person has lived entirely in the America we have become.[21]

A subsequent headline reads "The Degree To Which America Has Changed Is Noticed By Almost No One. The Transformation Has Taken Hold Too Gradually."[22]

I can attest to that. When the Department of Homeland Security was given power to seize cell phones from anyone, anywhere within 100 miles of the border, and without the necessity for "reasonable suspicion" of the person involved, I was appalled! So I wrote to a U.S. cousin in Florida to bring the regulation to his attention and see if he was not similarly appalled. His reply, to my total shock and amazement, was opposite to mine. He thought the requirement was okay if it pertained to security.

I would strongly recommend that all Americans look up this issue of *Vanity Fair* (January 2012) and read the article so they will be able to understand the deep concern felt by people of my vintage who have seen both pictures – the "before" and "after."

The Fourth Estate

The press used to boast that its function was to expose greed and corruption wherever it was found and act as protectors of those who are too busy earning a living to fight for honesty and fairness. Sometimes they still do, but mostly on the small issues at the neglect of the really big ones including global warming, a corrupt banking and financial system and the extraterrestrial presence and technology. In effect, anything that is really critical to the future of humankind and our survival as a species is largely ignored.

A closed meeting of the Bilderbergers provides a clue to the problem. A look at lists of the persons attending the meetings of that secret organization discloses the names of many more of the elite top executives of newspapers around the world. And remember that the CIA boasts of hiring 200 reporters to write stories supporting the party line, in addition to the collaboration of one person in each of the major news media to screen stories before they appear. How else would they have avoided being exposed as major drug runners to raise funds to support their Black Ops for years while the U.S. official policy is a war on drugs, and American jails are heavily populated with offenders.

A very critical view of the U.S. press appeared in an article by Lisa O'Carroll in the *Guardian* under the title "Seymour Hersh on Obama, NSA And The 'Pathetic' American Media."

> Seymour Hersh has got some extreme ideas on how to fix journalism – close down the news bureaus of NBC and ABC, sack 90% of editors in publishing and get back to the fundamental job of journalists which, he says, is to be an outsider.
>
> It doesn't take much to fire up Hersh, the investigative journalist who has been the nemesis of U.S. presidents since the 1960s, and who was once described by the Republican party as "The closest thing American journalism has to a terrorist."
>
> He is angry about the timidity of journalists in America, their failure to challenge the White House and be an unpopular messenger of truth.[23]

Hersh might uncover a great story if "he followed the money" and found the extent to which the major media are controlled directly or indirectly by the Cabal. He might become apoplectic, as many concerned people are, if he knew the extent to which that same Cabal plan to use the Trans Pacific Partnership (the TPP) that President Obama is trying to "fast track" through Congress to stifle the last remaining vehicle of free speech. A petition circulated by the Stop the Trans Pacific Partnership reads as follows:

> The Trans Pacific Partnership includes provisions that would lead to extreme Internet censorship and undermine democracy and national sovereignty. I demand that my government oppose this agreement and refuse to sign.[24]

The stakes couldn't be higher. Even if Hersh did the story on media control, who would print it? If the major media aren't willing to let their good investigative reporters go after the great stories of the century – the legitimacy of the official 9/11 report, a banking and financial system that has introduced near universal slavery through its system of creating all money as debt that has to be paid with interest, and the trillions of taxpayers dollars used for Black Ops, including space vehicles, there is not much more than a hope in Hades that they would be willing to expose who actually controls them.

So, there are two Americas, the hypothetical one of pre-cold war days when the U.S. was a quite wonderful place to live and a model to be admired, if not emulated, and the 21st century police state that is planning diabolic things for at least some of its citizens with consequences so explosive and unpredictable that they must not be allowed to happen!

In a book that I wrote about 15 years ago, I said that the U.S. had lost its moral compass.

Now it seems self-apparent that in the early post-World War II years America sold its soul in exchange for space technology, including killing machines previously unheard of except in science fiction. Tragically, the future of the human species, as well as our relationship with our diverse extraterrestrial neighbors, seems to be at play on the cosmic chessboard.

The end game was ably stated by David Rockefeller in his *Memoirs*.

> Some even believe we are part of a secret Cabal working against the best interests of the United States, characterizing my family and me as 'internationalists' and of conspiring with others around the world to build a more integrated global political and economic structure, one world, if you will. If that's the charge, I stand guilty, and I am proud of it.[25]

I would respectfully disagree! The 60-year dash down the road to rule by "bankers and elite" has not produced a better world. On the contrary! It has created a world of increasing misery, uncertainly and hopelessness. After World War II many patriots swore "never again." Yet the tell-tale ingredients seem to be re-appearing before our very eyes. When it comes to the life and death issues we humans are slow learners, and tend to repeat our worst mistakes. So what do we need?

We need a full stop of just about every policy trend initiated by the NWO since the 1960s. First, then, a "full stop" to facilitate a 180-degree U turn. As we used to say in the army, "about ta."

Chapter Fourteen

An Action Plan For The Redemption Of America and Humankind

"The World Cannot be Changed Without Changing our Thinking."

– Albert Einstein

The President of the United States

I was one of the majority of Canadians who were positively delighted when Barack Obama won the presidential election on November 4, 2008. He was not only handsome and extremely erudite, he was upbeat and radiated hope. I thought that he would prove once and for all that there was no such thing as a superior race and that all of God's children should be treated with equal reverence and respect.

I made a special effort to get a draft of the book I was writing into his hands before the day of his inauguration. It contained a chapter on monetary reform that, if implemented, might have provided him with a legacy in a class with Abraham Lincoln. Regretfully his "gatekeepers" made sure that didn't happen. Subsequent efforts proved to be equally futile.

When I picked up my morning paper I saw the newly elected president surrounded by his financial and economic advisers. After scanning the photo quickly I said to myself, "Oh, oh, it's game over." His advisers were the same old gang who were responsible for the economic mess the neophyte president had inherited from George

W. Bush. They routinely rotate from one party to another and from one branch of the international banking cartel to another. I knew at once that any policies they would recommend would not result in early relief from the dreadful recession. So the president would be unable to earn brownie points in the number one area of public concern.

I thought at once of Lewis Lapham, editor of *Harper's* magazine and his description of the two governments in the U.S. – the permanent and the provisional. The permanent government is the secular oligarchy that comprises the Fortune 500 companies and all their attendant lobbyists, the big media and entertainment syndicates, the civil and military services, the larger research universities and law firms.[1]

That pretty well sums it all up in a way that conforms with my sense of the real politic. The big transnational corporations with their lobbyists, public relations firms and lawyers, the international banks with their close ties to both the Fed and the Treasury Department, not to mention the IMF and the World Bank, the close, almost incestuous relationship between the Bretton Woods institutions and the State Department, the information conglomerates that blur the lines between the manufacture of news, and culture and its dissemination. These are all parts of the permanent government that hold the reins of real power. It is a power camouflaged by the antics of the politicians comprising the provisional government.

If you add up the power of all the institutions mentioned in the last two paragraphs, it spells "Cabal." Remember the admission of President Clinton at the outset of the previous chapter that there is a government within the government that he didn't control. So the president is not in control. Then who is? Certainly not the Congress that has been in a deep sleep for decades. It has approved hundreds of billions that were spent on Black Ops that it was not even aware of. This was in direct violation of the principle of representative government. Congressmen and women have a solemn duty to review all expenditures of taxpayers' money and, in effect, certify that they are in the public interest. But for decades this has not been done. So the Congress is not in control.

So if neither the president nor the Congress is in control, who is? Only the shadow knows. But one thing is clear to anyone who takes the time to examine the evidence. The present trend lines are leading to events that will be totally disastrous for the United States and the world – events of such magnitude that they defy description. Therefore the president and the Congress are duty bound to reclaim their constitutional power and, in the case of the president, to renounce those powers that no man on Earth should have.

On the positive side the first and most urgent requirement for the president is to initiate the creation of enough money to stimulate the economy, end the cutbacks, and renew hope for the unemployed both young and old. This should be accompanied by very large increases in minimum wages both federal and state. The short-term goal should be "living wages" that offer everyone the self respect, dignity and comfort they deserve. They are the ones who produce the real essential wealth, as opposed to armaments and machines of war which are, in the end, a total write off.

On other occasions I have suggested that the minimum wage scale could be somewhat lower for students 18 years of age and younger, and for seniors who receive pension income. But there are several objectives intertwined. There must be useful jobs for people who want to work. Wage levels have to be high enough to start closing the enormous gap, albeit ever so slightly, between the rich and poor. Finally, and most important, as I have stressed in earlier chapters, the total dependence on bank-created virtual "credit" money must end! The omnipotent banking cartel which has captured billions of people, and reduced them to the level of debt slaves, must be converted from master of all it surveys to just another service provider.

To start the ball rolling the president may have to resort to the legislative anomaly of minting trillion dollar platinum coins. This would simply be an expedient until a proper Bank of the United States is chartered, and the Fed expropriated and wound up. The U.S. should begin with 2 trillion as its appropriate share of a worldwide 10-12 trillion initial stimulation package, designed to end the Great Recession and renew hope everywhere.

It is true that when the platinum coin experiment was discussed in 2013, both Treasury Secretary Timothy Geitner and Fed chairman Ben Bernanke said they would not cooperate. What would you expect? They were both loyal members of the cartel and, as such, representatives of the power structure that must be ended. If the new incumbents adopted a similar stance, as is quite likely based on their resumes, the remedy is to fire them, by whatever means are necessary. No two individuals, no matter how important they may think they are, can be permitted to stand in the way of a long, long overdue restoration of the world economy.

1. The ability of individuals to either directly or indirectly maintain the status quo in the face of essential reforms raises a fundamental and near universal problem. There have been so many of the top jobs filled by nominees recommended by the Cabal for such a long time it would be a miracle if they did not constitute a majority. As stated earlier, no president since Harry Truman could be reasonably assured that his advisors were loyal to the Republic as opposed to the New World Order. Sorting things out at this stage may be a near impossible task, but some attempt must be made, and without a McCarthy-type witch-hunt.

2. A Supplementary Oath of Office.
Perhaps the easiest approach with a reasonable chance of success would be to require everyone on the federal government payroll, including members of the armed forces and intelligence agencies, as well as everyone working for a company with a contract with any branch or agency of the federal government, to swear a supplementary oath to uphold the Constitution of the United States and renounce any allegiance to a New World Order dedicated to a supranational unelected government. I am not competent to draft such an oath; that is a task for experts in the field.

Anyone currently supporting the idea of a NWO totalitarian government of bankers and elite persons who renounce that allegiance should be allowed to keep their jobs. If, however, by their subsequent actions they show that they have sworn falsely, the prescribed penalty should be several years in a federal prison. Persons who cannot in conscience swear the oath should be allowed to resign their positions and follow their own "non-sensitive" pursuits.

The program should begin with the President of the United States who, surely, would be willing, even anxious to take such an oath. Once taken, his first act should be to remove his entire coterie of financial and economic advisors, and replace them with people who really understand the current impossible banking system and what we have to do to develop one that works consistently and well.

A few names in this category include people like professors Michael Hudson and L. Randall Wray of the University of Missouri-Kansas City, or someone they would recommend. Other suggestions include Ellen Brown, author of *Web of Debt* or Bill Still, author of *The Money Masters*.

This is an absolutely essential first step toward a full employment, recession proof economy that will ultimately free the masses from their slavery to debt!

3. The President should issue an Executive Order for the immediate release of all patents concerning clean alternative energy including and especially cold fusion and zero- point energy. The latter is the free energy that exists everywhere in the cosmos. Its potential has been known for decades but the applications have been kept secret by persons and organizations more interested in their own pocket books than they are in preserving planet Earth for the peaceful enjoyment of their children and grandchildren.

The secret technology should be made available to all countries of the world, free from royalties or other charges, as a kind of reparation for 9/11 and the incalculable damage resulting from the misrepresentation of the alleged perpetrators. If holders of patents or other proprietary rights can prove a legitimate loss of their private investment, the U.S. government can compensate them for reasonable out-of-pocket expenses. But there can be no holding back of technology essential to the preservation of our Earthly home.

4. The President should withdraw his support for the proposed Trans Pacific Partnership due to its close association with the plan for a NWO and give back to the Congress its

power over trade matters.

5. The President should begin at once to reactivate the rule of law and reinstate constitutional provisions. The list is long and includes the reinstatement of habeas corpus and due process. The rules for the CIA should be re-written to include no more assassinations, and no more use of drones for that purpose. The use of drones is an abomination. It is as if the Ten Commandments found in the Jewish and Christian Bibles had never been written. In addition to the general prohibition on assassinations, the use of drones often results in the death of innocents which compounds the felony. To top off the objections, it is bad strategy. For every alleged terrorist killed by a drone ten times as many new ones are created.

6. The President should never again act as an arms salesman as he appears to have been during a trip to India in 2011. It is a sad day for the world when presidents and prime ministers add that responsibility to their job description on behalf of the military-industrial complex or its foreign equivalent.

The Congress

For several decades the United States Congress has become increasingly disinterested in its role as watchdog of the taxpayers' money, and protector of the public interest. Sadly this charge applies equally to many parliaments including that of my own country. There appears to be too much time spent on trivial and unimportant issues, including partisan bickering, and not nearly enough on the huge global issues that affect us all. Legislatures give the impression that they are little more than rubber stamps for laws promoted and supported by the all-powerful banking and corporate interests that provide the "ammunition" for electoral warfare.

The resulting cynicism is so deeply embedded that it could lead to despair. Then one is reminded of Winston Churchill's claim that, "It has been said that democracy is the worst form of government except all the others that have been tried." When we begin to reflect on the "others," including the one in Germany under Hitler, and that of the Soviet Union under Stalin, we have to conclude that even incompetent democracies are superior to the alternative. But, as my grandfather used to say, "The biggest room in the world is the room for improvement," and there is a long list of positive actions available that could restore faith in democracy and the process under which it operates.

A few suggestions follow:

1. The Congress should create a law that would make it a criminal offense for any bank or financial institution, its directors and officers, to make a financial donation to any person holding political office or candidate for political office, subject to severe sanctions for offenders, including automatic disqualification from holding political office for recipients. As global warming is at the top of the priority list of issues it would be a good idea to include oil companies, distributors, etc.

In view of the fact that running for office in the U.S. has become so frightfully expensive it would be a revolutionary improvement to devise some means of public financing to break the stranglehold of the Cabal. It would not be easy because politicians know and like the present system. But it would be most desirable and it could be done if politics were to evolve to a higher level. It is no longer acceptable to rely on the "devil you know." Meanwhile, there are other profound reforms that must be undertaken.

2. The Congress must initiate the inquiry into the extraterrestrial presence and technology. It, too, must be a bipartisan effort without waiting for a presidential initiative. In would be far too dangerous for a solo effort as several former presidents could attest, but the Congress has both the authority and the solemn responsibility to get the truth into the public domain both for their own education and that of taxpayers.

The Citizen Hearing on Disclosure held in Washington in May 2013, where five former Congressmen and women and one former U.S. senator listened to evidence under oath from 40 witnesses for five days, was most revealing. At the outset, all six were skeptics. They didn't know that UFOs were real. They didn't know that the U.S. government, with some assistance from ETs, had been back-engineering their technology for 60 years. They didn't know that they had approved expenditures of vast sums of money for projects that they were unaware

251

of. After five days, and many hours of evidence, they were all convinced. But they were all retired. It is long since time that current members of the Congress were aware of what has occurred and how this affects their plans and priorities.

3. The Congress should initiate audits of each of the armed forces and all intelligence agencies or contractors, and all research establishments associated with national security and related matters. I read not too long ago where one agency said it would be ready for an audit in 2017. Such chutzpah! Any organization spending taxpayers' dollars should be prepared for audit at any time with or without notice. Furthermore, audits are an essential element of Congressional control of public spending at the federal level, and it is the solemn duty of elected representatives to be able to account for every penny spent.

Did anyone ever find the $2.3 trillion that former Defense Secretary Donald Rumsfeld said was unaccounted for? A proper search might prove to be an important piece of the disclosure puzzle.[2]

4. As part of the about turn in how the world works and a massive change in direction from preparing for war to building a permanent peace, Congress should forthwith reduce appropriations for the defense services and all intelligence agencies by 10% across the board. This would be leadership by example. The same 10% flat line reduction should continue for four additional years, at which time they can be reassessed.

Meanwhile other nations can be encouraged to make proportional reductions. Even if they failed to respond positively, the U.S. would still be the No. 1 spender on arms and armaments after reducing their expenditures by half.

Another issue for negotiation should be the reduction in arms sales. It was disappointing to see President Obama promoting arms sales to India.[3] The U.S. should lead the band in the opposite direction. It is the easy access to guns and ammunition that facilitates conflict in many countries, especially some of the under-developed ones who can least afford it.

In addition to an era of relative peace, which is priceless, the jobs and commercial activity lost from cuts in both arms procurement and sales to others can more than be made up in the conversion from a fossil fuel economy to clean energy, and the re-building of urban infrastructure and facilities of many different kinds. So beating our swords into ploughshares will not only save lives, it can be a key element in saving our Earthly home.

5.   Critical to this transition is financing. The U.S., like most other countries, has lost much of its financial flexibility from carrying too much debt. That problem will be exacerbated when the U.S. ceases to be the near-universal reserve currency for the world, which China and other creditors will increasingly demand.

So Congress must pass legislation to establish a 100% publicly-owned Bank of the United States (BUS) to act as its central bank in charge of the money creation process. It can be modeled on the Bank of Canada Act which is a good precedent. To provide the flexibility essential to facilitate a certain amount of government-created money (GCM) (this book recommends 34% GCM once the system has been reformed and stabilized as a recession-proof one) the Act will have to include a clause authorizing the BUS to accept non-transferable, non-convertible, non-redeemable shares in the United States as collateral against which new money can be created. As Thomas Edison said, "If the nation can issue a dollar bond it can issue a dollar bill." The difference is that one has to be repaid with interest to private lenders and the other does not.

Not only is a certain amount of GCM the only way that economic growth can be stimulated without piling on more debt, it allows for a tiny bit of income redistribution without inflaming the ire of the rich who are not willing to pay high taxes for that purpose, notwithstanding such a grand chasm between the incomes of the poor and the well to do.

Concurrently with the introduction of a new Bank of the United States, the Federal Reserve System will have to be expropriated and wound up. Congress should be ruthless in determining the level of compensation to the private owners. Nearly all of the appreciation has been at direct cost to the taxpayers whose currency has been diluted. Ending the Fed will be the final chapter in righting a hundred year old wrong. Letting a handful of the richest American and foreign bankers on Earth take over the right of the people to create their own money was one of the biggest mistakes ever made by anyone, anywhere, at any time. The cost has been incalculable!

Since the 2008 bank-created meltdown the Fed has created trillions of dollars for the aid and comfort of the bankers. They have done well! Yet the economy still languishes, and millions of people are looking for work. Killing the dragon Fed will remove an albatross from the neck of the body politic.

One additional benefit will be the re-introduction of United States Notes and the phasing out of Federal Reserve Notes. That will provide a great opportunity to smoke out illegal hoards either domestic or foreign.

The benefit of reclaiming their sovereign right to create money will be a big boon for Americans – and the world. It is also an opportunity to learn how the money system works, and the extent to which taxpayers have been duped for over a hundred years.

6. Another project that Congress should initiate and promote is a massive tree-planting program. One of the major concerns of the Star Visitors is our careless and callous attitude toward the environment. And a principal element of this concern is the continual destruction of the rain forests that form such an integral element of the Earth's ecology. Yet despite all the warnings about global warming, the vast majority of Earthlings continue to allow one of our most precious environmental assets to be destroyed. We have even allowed the World Bank to finance projects to convert rain forests into pasture to satisfy our passion for red meat.

An article in the *New York Times* of November 11, 2009, by Thomas L. Friedman underlines the almost incomprehensible immensity of the problem. "Imagine if you took all the cars, trucks, planes, trains and ships in the world and added up their exhaust every year. The amount of carbon dioxide they collectively emit into the atmosphere is actually less than the carbon emissions every year that result from the chopping down and clearing of tropical forests in places like Brazil, Indonesia and the Congo. We are now losing a tropical forest the size of New York State every year and the carbon that releases into the atmosphere now accounts for roughly 17 percent of all global emissions contributing to climate change."[4]

The sacrilege has to stop. This is part of the message that abductee Jim Sparks was given. Jim was so impressed that he started a foundation to raise money to save a slice of the rain forests. Three cheers for him and his initiative, and those of others. These need to be supplemented by a massive program that will stop, totally, any further deliberate destruction, and provide the economic alternatives for those whose livelihood may be negatively affected by the change in policy.

The United States should take the lead, but it should recruit a consortium of the major economic powers to pledge the money necessary to make it happen. It doesn't matter how much it might cost in dollar terms, the cost of not doing anything is ten times higher, and could soon be irreversible. So immediate action is required! The plan should be even more comprehensive than just the rain forests. Some poor Africans are forced to cut down any tree in sight because they can't afford any other fuel for cooking and warmth. The plan must include subsidized clean energy fuel sources that provide an economically acceptable alternative to tree harvesting.

These two steps should be implemented at once, but there is a complementary long-term initiative that must follow in train. The whole world must embark on the most extensive reforestation in history. No country should be exempt. And those that literally cannot afford the small cost of growing the seedlings should be included, but subsidized by the well-to-do countries to the extent required to make the plan work quickly and efficiently. Some years down the pike the extent of the reforestation required can be assessed in light of the progress being made toward stabilizing the planet's ecology.

The G20

When the much-touted G20 met in Toronto June 26-27, 2010 security was so tight that those of us in the downtown area, where I live, felt like caged animals. I needed a new security pass just to get into my office. The sacrifice might have been worth it if our esteemed leaders had accomplished anything worthwhile. But if news reports reflected the discussions, the leaders spent almost all of their time trying to rescue a corrupt and outdated banking system that was responsible for the Great Recession – the number one problem on their agenda. Canada's *Maclean's* magazine summed up their accomplishment in its headline of June 28, 2010 which read: "Billion Dollar Photo Op."

If the meager news of subsequent meetings was the least bit reliable, little has been accomplished in the intervening years, despite billions more in costs charged to hapless taxpayers. A new plan adopted at their meeting held in Saint Petersburg on September 5-6, 2013 received muted applause, but by my assessment, it is little more than useless, and can be summed up in four words – too little, too late! The following agenda provides the G20 with a golden opportunity to help rescue the human species from impending disaster and thereby justify its existence.

End the Great Recession

1. The first and most urgent project is to end the Great Recession, create jobs for millions of idle workers and restore hope for a meaningful future. That entails apportioning the 10-12 trillion dollars of government-created, debt-free money for the first round of stimulus. Precision is neither possible nor necessary at this stage because the shortfall in purchasing power is so enormous. A few months after the bulk of the money has been spent into circulation, and the effect can be measured, it will be easier to estimate the aggregate amounts appropriate to each situation for the second round.

Simultaneously the whole system of reserves will have to be changed. The capital adequacy system, under which the banks have control, must be phased out and replaced by a cash reserve system which gives governments the control that is both their right and their responsibility. It is a power that must not be delegated by any country that even pretends to be a democracy. That said, the rate of conversion to a radically new recession-proof system might be about seven years, as recommended in Chapter Seven.

The eurozone countries have a unique problem. They will have to amend their treaties to give the European Central Bank the power to accept shares in member countries as collateral for the debt-free cash created. There is no real impediment other than its lack of political will in the face of incredible lobbying on the part of the private bankers, who helped engineer the creation of the existing system that has reduced much of Europe to penury and economic impotence.

Support Full Disclosure

2. Adopt the principle of full disclosure of the ET presence and technology and hold public hearings on all related matters. Russia, China, France, Germany and Brazil all have stories to tell, as well as some of the smaller players including Canada, Spain, Peru, etc. In most of these countries it is unlikely that a general amnesty will be required as secrecy has not been as ruthlessly enforced as in the U.S., where just about every law in the book has been broken. In any event, all measures necessary to reveal the truth should be adopted.

A Massive Tree Planting Campaign

3. The G20 should formally adopt the massive worldwide tree planting rain forest conservation plans described earlier in this chapter.

A Seven-Year Transformation to Clean Energy

4. Adopt a 7-year plan to replace the power source in every car, truck, tractor, airplane and home on Earth. Insist that the U.S. make the technology available universally, so that each country can adopt its own approach to achieving the goal.

Write Off Third World Debt

5. Write off Third World debt so poor countries can begin their long journey. Much of the existing debt qualifies as "odious."[5] The World Bank, the IMF, private foreign banks and the Wall Street banks have all been major contributors to what has become an impossible situation.

The World Bank and private international banks lent far too much money to poor countries, often for projects that did not generate enough income to repay principal and interest. Paul Volcker and the Federal Reserve made a bad situation impossible when interest rates were raised to intolerable 18% levels. The debt compounded. Then the IMF, and later the World Bank, exacerbated the situation by providing new loans so the poor countries could pay the interest on what they already owed, and the international banks could remain solvent. Sure, some of the Third World leaders borrowed the easy money with the fervor of kids in a candy store. But the lenders were equally, if not more, culpable. So the wealthy Western world, in particular, must be held responsible for a bad situation it could have prevented.

Wind Up the International Monetary Fund

6. Wind up the International Monetary Fund (IMF), write off all the money it is owed, and declare null and void all the conditions it has imposed on borrowing countries. The IMF was never intended to act as a fire brigade to rescue international banks when they make bad loans. Its original function was to provide temporary assistance to countries in trouble as a result of fixed exchange rates after World War II. But when fixed exchange rates proved to be impractical, and one country after another abandoned the idea, and went off the gold standard, the IMF lost its raison d'être, and should have been wound up. But bureaucracies once born, refuse to die.

Paul Volcker, as Fed chairman, gave the IMF a new lease on life. When his high interest rate policy of 1981-82 made it impossible for several South American countries to pay the interest on their debt to the big New York banks, which made them all technically insolvent, Volcker cajoled the banks into making new loans to enable the debtors to service their debt until he could get the IMF to ride to the rescue with taxpayers' money.

The system of transferring responsibility for bad debts from the lenders to taxpayers worked so smoothly that it became standard practice. The Cabal then persuaded the IMF to impose conditions on borrowers that would make it possible for foreign financial interests to pillage their assets, while the IMF imposed its version of austerity. This usually resulted in riots that became known as the "IMF riot."

The misery it has caused can't end too soon!

A Tobin Tax

7. Impose a significant Tobin Tax to provide the relief required for the world's refugees. The Tobin Tax, named after the economist James Tobin, is another idea whose time has come. The idea is to tax every exchange of one country's currency for another. The purpose of the tax is to slow down short-term speculation in currencies. For a number of years about two trillion a day has been involved.[6] The imposition of a small cost – it was originally to be 1% – even a levy of, say, 0.25%, might be enough to make the gamblers pause before making their overnight bets.

While the rationale for a tax of this kind is primarily to create greater stability in financial markets – a worthy cause as we have learned to our total dismay – a secondary benefit would be a steady stream of income that could be earmarked for the U.N. High Commissioner for Refugees at a time when the need for support has never been greater.

Global forced displacement hits record high. UNHCR Global Trends report finds 65.3 million people, or one person in 113, were displaced from their homes by conflict and persecution in 2015. The report, entitled "Global Trends," noted that on average, 24 people were forced to flee each minute in 2015, four times more than a decade earlier.[7]

A World Bank and A World Dollar

A solution, that would put the U.S. dollar, the euro, the renminbi, the yen and all other currencies on an equal footing, is a new world bank with a new world dollar. It could be called "The Universal," or "Uni," for short. It would be the currency of travelers' checks and of central bank reserves. It would be, in effect, the universal world currency in which all international transactions were denominated.

The new world bank – unlike the Fed or the BIS – must be publicly owned, by the people of the world, under a formula that would prevent undue influence from any country or region. Its assets would comprise very large deposits of all world currencies and gold. Each would be convertible into any other at market prices, as the bank would be the *de facto* bank of international settlements, replacing the highly secretive existing Bank for International Settlements (BIS), with its shadowy past and Nazi connections, that is an accessory to the system that had been running the world into the ground.

There is considerable urgency in this area. The Chinese are dissatisfied with the long-standing American monopoly and the early establishment of a universally backed world currency, would forestall a lot of jockeying for position. It would effectively end the diplomatic, financial and sometimes shooting wars over possession of the endless supply of golden eggs.

Roll the World Trade Organization Back to a General Agreement on Trade and Tariffs

The World Trade Organization itself was not intended to help the poor. It was designed to enhance and consolidate the power of the elite at the expense of the poor nations and poor people. It, too, has transferred far too much sovereignty from nation states to unelected, unaccountable bureaucrats working under rules actually written by, or at the behest of, the chief executive officers of multinational corporations.

The concept of a rules-based system is great in theory. It sounds very reasonable. But surely not just one set of rules applying to all countries equally?

The World Boxing Federation has fifteen classes including flyweight, lightweight, middleweight and heavyweight. I would guess that the world's many different countries could be classified in as many as fifteen different categories. Certainly not just one! The WTO rules were written by or on behalf of the heavyweights for the benefit of heavyweights. The result is a trade regime under which everyone else is going to be clobbered.

The second objection is, as I said, the loss of democracy. The WTO exercises *de facto* executive, judicial and legislative powers equivalent to that of a world government. These powers were transferred to it without the advice or consent of the peoples affected. Apologists for the WTO say that consent was granted when people elected the governments which did the deal. But that is a cop-out. The governments neither told their electors what was involved, nor asked their opinion about it. Needless to say this was deliberate policy on the part of governments attempting to serve two masters.

The only satisfactory remedy is to abolish the WTO and go back to the General Agreement on Tariffs and Trade (GATT) from which it sprang. From there we can build a trade regime which preserves the essential powers of nation states, recognizes the different needs of countries based on size, population and state of development, and provides the flexibility for cooperative rather than coercive relationships. For want of a better description I call them the "Marquess of Queensberry" Rules of Trade.

The Marquess of Queensberry Rules for Trade and Investment

– Fair trade, not "free trade." There is no such thing as genuine free trade, as Canada has found in its relationship with the U.S.

– Every country should have the right to protect some of its infant industries. If it doesn't, they will never grow to adulthood.

– Every country has the right to determine the conditions under which direct foreign investment is welcome.

– Every country has the right to impose controls on the movement of short-term capital in cases of emergency.

– Every country has the right to determine the limits of foreign ownership in each area of economic activity.

– Every nation state should have the right to decide what trade concessions it will put on the table in exchange for others as was the case under the GATT.

– Every country should have control over its own banking system.

261

– Every country has the right to use and should use its own central bank to assist in the financing of essential services and to keep the economy operating at or near its potential at all times.

– Rich countries should be encouraged to license the use of their technology by poor countries at modest cost.

– Every country should be obligated to cooperate with other countries in the protection of the oceans, their species, the ozone layer and in all ways essential to protect the Earth's ecosystem for the benefit of future generations.

– Every country should be encouraged to maintain some control of its own food supply, to the extent practical, and not become dependent on patented seeds and products.

– Every country should be encouraged to pass a law amending corporate charters in a way that would require directors to consider the interests of all stakeholders, and not just those of shareholders when making decisions.

– Every country should have the right, and should be encouraged, to develop and maintain a significant degree of self-sufficiency in the production of goods and services for the use and enjoyment of its own people. The objective should be to reduce its vulnerability to the vagaries of decisions made by people far away who think of foreigners in terms of economic digits, rather than as human beings.

Some may say that I am proposing a return to a "protectionist" world. Let me put it another way. I am proposing a system where the rights and interests of billions of people are protected from the predators – so the rich barons do not have unrestricted license to poach on other people's estates.

The New World Order is a gigantic hoax. It is not interested in trade. Its plan is centralized ownership and control as a means to facilitate a world government under its control. Its brand of globalization is a greed-driven monster legitimized by academic abstractions far removed from the real world and real people.

Fundamentalist economics is a numbers game, in which people are digits. They are counted, sorted, exploited when useful, and abandoned when surplus. It would be numerically inefficient to treat them otherwise. The system I am proposing is one where human beings are entitled to a status greater than inanimate objects – one where they will have some control over their own lives and destiny. Such a system would be closer to the model of nature, where babies and children are protected until they reach maturity and can compete on their own. Even then, there are physical and intellectual differences between adults that must be taken into account.

What I am proposing is the transformation of a system that is immoral and inefficient, into one that is fundamentally moral and much more efficient – a system where everyone, everywhere, can hope for better things to come.

Massively Reduce Defense Expenditures and Atomic Weapons Worldwide

While the United States can afford to reduce defense expenditures by 50% unilaterally without compromising its security, it is only fair in a world that can only survive by shifting to a new paradigm, that all countries shift their priorities from defense and war-making capability to peace and international cooperation. A combination of a positive banking system, and major reductions in arms expenditures, will provide each country with the financial flexibility necessary to subsidize the transformation to clean energy, with enough left over to increase expenditures on a wide range of initiatives to improve the quality of life for its citizens.

Then there is the question of reducing nuclear stockpiles. In a sane world none of these weapons can be used under any circumstances! Ever! The risk for the planet is too great and the extraterrestrial consequences too alarming. So it is ridiculous for the U.S. to still have missiles on alert in silos in the Midwest. All it can possibly justify is a few submarine missile carriers – just enough to guarantee the "mutually assured destruction (MAD)" that should deter even a madman from launching an attack.

Consequently I fully support a recommendation of the 2006 Weapons of Mass Destruction Commission, i.e. number 19 under "Nuclear Weapons."

"Russia and the United States, followed by other states possessing nuclear weapons, should publish their aggregate holdings of nuclear weapons on active and reserve status as a baseline for future disarmament efforts. They should also agree to include specific provisions in future disarmament agreements relating to transparency, irreversibility, verification and the physical destruction of nuclear warheads."[8]

That is a very modest beginning. It should be followed by an immediate reduction of stockpiles to the absolute minimum consistent with mutually assured deterrence and as a protection against cheating.

Any nation refusing to cooperate should be subject to severe sanctions like a 10% tariff on all its exports to be increased each year of non-compliance. The existence of atomic weapons is a threat to the viability of the planet itself, and any person or nation that even contemplates circumstances under which they might be used should be the subject of universal condemnation.

A similar but greatly accelerated plan should apply to biological and chemical weapons.

Reorganize and Streamline the United Nations Organization

This suggestion is not new and much work has already been done in anticipation of a more streamlined United Nations. Agreement for action, however, is still pending. So change, especially where there are so many disparate interests involved, does take time.

Probably the most important reform is in reference to the Security Council, and the single country veto. Obviously this has to be replaced with some sort of majority decision-making formula. It is not my task to suggest what the formula should be, but a decision should require a substantial majority, as opposed to unanimity. Giving each of the big powers an absolute veto is as unrealistic as giving every shareholder of a large, publicly traded company the right to overrule management. The principle, which is a recipe for stalemate, is wrong. The majority must rule having in mind, as always, the interests of those who are opposed for one reason or another.

The principle of a United Nations to carry out many of its existing functions, and perhaps some new ones, is sound. In any streamlining, however, it has to be kept in mind that some of its original proponents were less than altruistic toward the plan. The Council on Foreign Relations saw the new organization as a cover for a new kind of colonialism, one that provided the advantages of colonial rule without the corresponding responsibilities.

The U.N. has not always worked to the Council's liking. On more than one occasion it has exercised its independence to the annoyance of the United States. Sometimes the Congress has been sufficiently irritated that it has held back part of the U.S. share of funding in a not too subtle effort to get its way. This, of course, is contrary to the spirit of community that was envisaged by most of the founders.

One new area of U.N. involvement should be in establishing diplomatic relations and channels of communication with visitors from other planets and galactic federations. The U.N. is the obvious choice for negotiations rather than any single nation. It is a development that may be stoutly resisted by that small group of Americans who have enjoyed privileged access to much alien technology, and have used some of it in ways that might not meet the approval of either American or world citizens.

Again we will have to ask the Congress of the United States to take the high road under a new policy of cooperation, rather than confrontation, and insist that valuable technology be made available for the benefit of humankind, and that the existing Cabal surrender its power to make life and death decisions concerning our treatment of, and relations with, our cosmic cousins.

In recent years I have been impressed by the wonderful humanitarian aid being provided by the United Nations Children's Fund (UNICEF), United Nations Human Rights Council (UNHRC) and other U.N. agencies. Also, U.N. leadership in promoting important treaties for the benefit of all humankind is precisely the kind of initiative one would expect and hope for from such a body. To be even more effective, some major powers should be prepared to drop their opposition to proposals that their military view as impediments to their war-making capabilities, such as land mines and cluster bombs. The war-making capabilities, as well as the reliance on military force, should be phased out of all plans for the future!

A Limit on Executive Salaries

In the early '90s CEO salaries were about forty times the average salary of their employees. Since then they have escalated to 237 times (one report says 433) on average – ratios that cannot be justified by any economic or moral standard.

Inevitably it will be argued that big bonuses are warranted as a reward for extraordinary corporate results. It is an argument for which there is a counter argument. Doing a good job is what CEOs are paid for, and their principal satisfaction should be in a job well done. Rewarding short-term results has often resulted in short-term planning at the expense of a longer-term vision. Equally perverse, the culture of exorbitant rewards has become so all pervasive that it extends even to mediocre results and separation agreements.

This example of greed and avarice is totally unacceptable. How can you ask union leaders to accept increases of 2% or less, let alone reductions in pay to make companies more competitive, when executives are given double or triple digit increases?

Executive compensation including salary, bonuses, stock options and retirement benefits should be limited to fifty times the average for their employees and any excess should be subject to a 100% excess profit tax, in order to end the abuse of privilege.

These are Not Top of the Head Suggestions

This agenda is not one that was dreamed up to fill space in a new book. It is not an academic treatise written by a professor unfamiliar with the real world in which most of us have to live. It is a carefully crafted package based on 65 years experience in politics and business including farming, manufacturing, retailing, construction, land development, tourism and publishing in addition to community affairs. My obsession with banking and macroeconomics spans this entire period, and has its roots in the Great Depression of the 1930s of which I was a child. I saw poverty in its rawest form! So I have confidence in the Action Plan which is a synthesis of all that I have learned.

At the same time, I am a realist. I know very well that none of the long list of radical reforms proposed to restore rights and freedoms lost and then move on toward a new paradigm of universal peace, prosperity and, above all, justice, is just going to happen on its own. Our politicians are too complacent and comfortable to want to take significant risks for the benefit of voters not yet born. They lack the incentive to free the slaves from their shackles of hopelessness.

Yet it must happen! Changes must occur! Failure is not an option! The Cabal controls big money, big business and a huge military-industrial complex. What it lacks, in the final analysis, is people power. It is the young people, who have the most at stake, who should lead this greatest revolution of heart and mind. Judging from the amount of mail I have been getting from teenagers, they are ahead of the curve and restless for action. They should be joined by the veterans of all wars, who must lament the erosion of hard-won rights and freedoms, and by activists, reformers, truth seekers and seekers of the light. They can take heart from the lives of people like Martin Luther King and Mahatma Gandhi who won seemingly impossible battles against formidable foes by peaceful means. My prayer is that you will enjoy Godspeed in your immortal struggle.

Mahatma Gandhi, 1948

POSTSCRIPT

SPIRITUALITY IS THE MISSING LINK

"A small body of determined spirits fired by an unquenchable faith in their mission can alter the course of history."

– Mahatma Gandhi

Spirituality is the missing link, not only to our past, however vague and uncertain that may be, but to our future as we strive to evolve to new dimensions more in keeping with those of our Galactic neighbors. Those that we know about, and there are inevitably more that we don't know about, are more advanced than we are both intellectually and physically. Some are also more advanced spiritually, though there appears to be a few notable exceptions.

The Venusians, as reported by an early contactee, Howard Menger, in his book *From Outer Space*, are very spiritual. They serve and adore "The Infinite Father." This is the same God many Earthlings worship whether He is known by that name or as Allah, the Great Spirit, the Creator, or the Forever. As an aside I did not know until I was in my 80s that Allah is my God. To be up front, my God is the God of Abraham, Isaac, Ishmael and Jacob. My role model is Jesus, the Nazarene.

Three of the five great religions began with Abraham. They are Judaism, Islam and Christianity and each is deeply rooted in Hebrew history. Toronto researcher Barry Brown in a book he is writing titled *Humanity: The World Before Religion, War & Inequality,* has discovered some aspects of that history that are certainly new to me, and most of my friends and acquaintances.

He quotes Aristotle as saying that the Jewish people are descended from the Brahman priests of Ancient India. This claim is supported by Indian swastikas in 2,000-year old synagogues in Israel. Brown claims Noah came from India and the story of the flood refers to the end of the Indus Valley Civilization which had given birth to the world's first "modern" society based on "equality between people and the sexes, no war or war weapons, open trade, the separation of 'church and state,' urban planning and democracy."

Brown reminds us that the Bible says the Garden of Eden was in a land called Havilah (Genesis 2:10-11) and that Jewish tradition says Havilah was India and the Pison River. "War," he claims, "is only about 6,000 years old and the fall of Eden is a fragmented memory of the Kurukshetra War (c. 3067 BC), and the word Hebrew means 'wanderers from the East' and refers to the people who left the Indus after its decline and migrated as newly homeless people into Mesopotamia."[1]

Yahweh was the God of the Hebrew Abraham who was chosen to leave Mesopotamia in search of a land of promise that he and his heirs would occupy. But it was not to be a smooth or untroubled path. The children of Israel were destined to detour to Egypt from where God chose the prophet Moses to lead the liberation of His chosen people. Moses was also the conduit through whom God established the laws that were to govern the Israelites. The first and most important was "Thou shall love the Lord thy God and Him only shall Thou Serve." Another was "Thou shall love your neighbors as yourself."

It is a supreme irony that these two most important laws, repeated by Jesus as being the sum total of the law and the Prophets, are the ones that are most consistently ignored. In *Light at the End of the Tunnel*, one chapter was headed "Mammon Rules the World." The further we get away from World War II, the more we have become worshippers of the near universal god, money.

C.S. Lewis says that the root sin is pride and all the others flow from the narcissism of prideful people. No matter what one of our religions teaches, the teachings do not get lived out because we find a way to be the controller of the religion and use it to justify all manner of evil acts rather than being willing to submit to the teachings God is seeking us to understand through all religions.

The second root is a corollary of this one. It is the feelings of insecurity that are not dealt with because we do not understand and experience God's love in our lives that drive us to need to control others in whatever way it becomes necessary for us to feel safe and secure.

Too many people will cheat, steal or short-change their fellow beings to accumulate money. Corruption is rampant in the extreme, and it almost always involves treating others as we would not wish to be treated. Power and wealth are the new deities as we continue the slide down the slippery slope to moral chaos. I have already listed many reforms that cry out for attention, but only changed individuals can make them happen.

Meanwhile there are three areas in need of special attention by persons of goodwill. There must be a just settlement of the Israeli-Palestinian standoff. The Sunni and Shia Muslims must settle their differences and stop killing each other. And, finally, the Christian doctrine of exclusivity must be abandoned in favor of a doctrine of inclusivity.

A Just Israeli-Palestinian Peace Agreement

> *He has shown you, O man, what is good*
> *And what does the Lord require of you*
> *But to do justly,*
> *To love mercy,*
> *And to walk humbly with your God?*

– Micah 6:8[2]

If there is one certainty in world politics it is this: there will be no peace on Earth until there is a just settlement of the Israeli-Palestinian conflict. Consequently, a just resolution — and

I emphasize the word just — should be at the top of the list of priority considerations for any U.S. administration and all concerned world leaders.

It seems apparent to an outside observer that Israeli strategy, at least since the 1967 war, has been one of gradual encroachment on those areas that remained in Palestinian hands after the United Nations awarded Israel the lion's share of the land at the time the state came into existence in 1948.

The implementation of this strategy has resulted in a policy of constant and sometimes cruel harassment of those Palestinians living in the occupied territories and Gaza. One suspects that this may have been an unspoken attempt to make life so difficult for the Palestinians that many more of them would abandon their lands, and find refuge or start a new life elsewhere.

On balance the strategy has not worked, nor will it, ever. Palestinians have dug in their heels and fought back in a desperate effort to regain autonomy over the small area that the U.N. had left under their ownership. The root of the conflict can be found in a fundamental disagreement over who really owns the land — on both sides of the Israeli border.

I decided to read *Whose Promised Land: Israel or Palestine?*[3] by Colin Chapman, as additional background to that which I knew from the Bible. At the end I thought that both sides may have an equal claim to all the land but on very different premises. The Palestinian claim is based on hundreds of years of possession. The Israeli claim is based on the Bible and a covenant God made with Abraham. At this point in history there is no acceptable solution other than to share the land in two adjoining autonomous states. I would like to quote a few paragraphs from a piece written by my Messianic Jewish Zionist friend Gavriel Gefen, who takes the path of love and compassion that is also, in my opinion, the practical approach of live and let live.

> We are told that God promised Abraham to give his physical children the land that extends from the river of Egypt to the Euphrates River. Egypt is where Africa meets the Arabian subcontinent. The Euphrates flows through southern Turkey and

passes through Iraq to the Persian Gulf. This vast territory is the heart and the bulk of the Middle East. Who lives there today? Exactly the descendants of Abraham — the children of Ishmael and Isaac, and the children of Esau and Jacob. It is just as we were told it would be.

Tragically, the three great Abrahamic faiths of Judaism, Christianity, and Islam have all developed religious traditions that interpret the Abrahamic covenant exclusively, leaving out the other children in one way or another. Judaism sees in the Hebrew Scriptures that Isaac and Jacob inherited the promises of the covenant, and assumes that it is to the necessary exclusion of the other brothers. Christianity interprets the covenant as now being spiritual and belonging exclusively to the Church. Islam holds that Ishmael received the inheritance.

Some Jewish and Christian fundamentalists embrace a joint Judeo-Christian worldview that excludes Muslim descendants of Abraham. They have visions of a Greater Israel that would encompass all of the territory between the Euphrates and Egypt. This is complete insanity. What do they plan to do with the millions of people already there? Drive them out? Rule over them? Kill them all? It is madness.

Each time the Israeli government enters into serious negotiations with Palestinian leaders, Jewish and Christian fundamentalists accuse Israel of "dividing God's land." Dividing it with whom? With her Abrahamic brothers who are also heirs of the same father? How is that "dividing God's land"? It isn't. It is rightfully seeking how to share a common heritage.[4]

Gavriel's words reflect great wisdom. That is because they flow from a God of love, a God of mercy, a God of justice as revealed by Micah, Zechariah, and the other prophets. It is the fundamentalists in all camps who are the stumbling blocks obstructing peace with justice. They should remember that God's covenant with Israel was always conditional, and that it was the failure to fulfill their part of the contract that resulted in the Israelites being expelled from the "promised land" on more than one occasion. It is only through God's good grace that they have been given back more of the land than they have occupied at any time since the Kingdoms of David and Solomon.

Repeated efforts to achieve a negotiated settlement between the two parties have failed. It is obvious that a new approach is required. A small commission led by someone of the stature of Jimmy Carter should be established. It must represent all the major players including Iran and Syria. It is only realistic that Hamas and Hezbollah be involved in the negotiations because substantial agreement and compliance by their supporters is key to a genuine peace.

It should be remembered that Jewish terrorists, later respected citizens, were key to the establishment of the state of Israel. Palestinian "terrorists," who perceive themselves as "freedom fighters," are key to the establishment of a state of Palestine. I urge every Jew and every evangelical Christian who only see their side of the situation to read *Blood Brothers*⁵ by Elias Chacour. They are likely to be shocked, as I was, by the extreme treatment meted out by overzealous Zionists.

Negotiations must not be allowed to fail. The U.S. will have to confront its Jewish lobby, and the wrath of fundamentalist evangelicals, and adopt an even-handed approach to the resolution of the dispute. Canada, too. If it is impossible for the two sides to reach agreement on all points, a solution that is considered just by the majority of players on both sides will have to be imposed. Failure is not an option.

At a Bar Mitzvah that I had the pleasure of attending in January 2009 the Rabbi asked the congregation to pray for Israel. I took him at his word and have been doing just that, though perhaps not in the words he intended. I have been praying that Israel change its strategy; that it give up occupation of its neighbors' land after more than forty years and allow a viable Palestinian state to be born — a state where the two nations can live side by side in peace and cooperation, with neither physical nor psychological walls between them.

I don't think the Israelis have any real conception of the amount of hate they have generated by such heavy reliance on their military superiority. Nor do they comprehend the extent of healing that will be necessary to convince both their neighbors and the world at large that their intentions are honorable, and worthy of respect and support.

Their extreme right-wing elements should, in this context, abandon their fantasies of a new Jewish Temple on Temple Mount.

Destroying either the Dome on the Rock and/or the Al-Aqsa Mosque would bring on World War III for sure. The Mosque is a House of the God of Israel and, with the kind of peace that must be pursued, the day might come when Jews and Christians would be invited by its owners to share its use as a place of worship being "People of the Book" as the Qur'an describes those of us who worship the God of Abraham, Isaac, Ishmael, Jacob and Esau. Isn't that too far-fetched to be taken seriously, you ask? Nothing is impossible with God working through men and women of goodwill who worship Him.

The moderate Muslims we met in the Middle East are willing to listen. They might prefer a state where Jews and Arabs enjoy a common citizenship, but they have accepted the existing reality. The state of Israel is here to stay and God, with the help of the United States and its allies, will not let anyone drive the Jews into the sea. Now it is time for the Palestinians to have a state of their own.

It is Israel's turn to meet them half way. The Palestinians will not accept any settlement that is less than just, nor should they. A just settlement, that includes large-scale international financial support to help the Palestinians build a homeland they can be proud of, is the only way to end the Intifada against Israel and its protector, the United States. Osama bin Laden made this very clear in the aftermath of September 11, 2001, but the U.S. administration of the day chose not to listen.

No more time should be lost. The fortress mentality of erecting fences that, in the end, will protect no one, must be abandoned. Hate must be replaced with love and compassion. It is the only hope of a world where both anti-Semitism and anti-Americanism subside and the welcome mat is extended equally to all of God's children. That kind of world is possible if we would all treat others as we, ourselves, would want to be treated.

All Muslims must Cooperate

There are few sights sadder than watching members of the same religion locked in mortal combat over differences of one kind or another. Christians did that for a long time after the Reformation and it is only recently that peace and cooperation has been given a high priority.

Divisions in the Muslim community are much older. The predominant denomination is Sunni with Shias being a distant number two with 10-20% of the total.[6] The historic background of the split between these two groups lies in the schism that occurred when the Islamic prophet Muhammad died in the year 632, leading to a dispute over succession as a caliph of the Islamic community spread across various parts of the world. "The dispute intensified greatly after the Battle of Karbals, in which Hussein abn Ali and his household were killed by the ruling Umayyad Caliph Yazid I, and the outcry for his revenge divided the early Islamic community. Today there are differences in religious practice, traditions and customs, often related to jurisprudence. Although all Muslim groups consider the Quran to be divine, Sunni and Shia have different opinions on hadith.

"Over the years, Sunni-Shia relations have been marked by both cooperation and conflict. Sectarian violence persists to this day from Pakistan to Yemen and is a major element of friction throughout the Middle East. Tensions between communities have intensified during power struggles, such as the Bahraini uprising, the Iraq War, and the Syrian Civil War."[7]

A further escalation of the violence is taking place in Iraq. The Sunni Muslim minority has long accused Prime Minister Nouri al-Maliki's Shiite-led government of discrimination. A group of militants promoting an Islamic state in Iraq and Levant, or ISIL, working in league with the Sunni minority, is creating mayhem in large sections of this strife-torn country. Some experts are concerned that the conflict may extend beyond the borders of Iraq and encompass a wider area in the Middle East.

Watching the carnage, the random and unnecessary killing and perhaps worst of all the pitiful plight of the hundreds of thousands of women and young children is enough to bring tears to the eyes of even the most jaundiced observer. These innocents are the "collateral damage" of an evil conflict.

This may be the place to observe that any conflict between denominations or sects of one religion, or between one religion and another, constitutes an affront to the Creator! They must stop! Every one of them is a breach of the Golden Rule that is allegedly the common belief of all the major religions.

An end to the internecine conflict within the Muslim world would be a huge step toward a peaceful world. Is this possible? Yes, with Allah all things are possible. So leaders of all Muslim sects should get together and call on Him to help them to practice what has been written in the Qur'an and create a long overdue miracle.

* * *

In looking to future relations between Christianity and Islam it is important to understand the different and opposite perspectives of the cross that history has spawned. I was raised in a tradition that enjoyed singing, "Onward Christian soldiers, marching as to war, with the cross of Jesus going on before." Sometimes you could almost imagine the soldiers marching, arms swinging, as they prepared for battle. So for us, the cross is a symbol of sacrifice and victory.

The Muslim perception is just the opposite. According to their understanding rooted deeply in the Crusades, the cross is a symbol of invasion, war, rape, pillage and conquest. The fact that the Crusades were sponsored and supported by the leaders of a centralized Christian Church, allegedly based on the teachings of the prophet Jesus who is widely and favorably quoted in the Qur'an, only underscored their distress.

It should come as no surprise, then, that some of our Muslim friends are willing and anxious to work with us to build a better world in the "Spirit of Jesus," provided the distinction is made between "the Jesus of Christianity," and "the Jesus for the world."

All followers of Jesus of Nazareth should be deeply disappointed that his message of love and compassion became so distorted within a few centuries of his death. It lost all resemblance to its roots. Christianity substituted rules, oppressive wealth and conquest for compassion in the same way that Judaism had, and that Jesus objected to. The wheel had turned full circle to the point where the most profound elements of Jesus' teaching has been lost.

The Doctrine of Exclusivity

"I am the way and the truth and the life. No one comes to the Father except through me."[8] This sentence has probably caused more strife and turmoil than any other sentence in history. The group of scholars known as the Jesus scholars believe that the statement was the creation of the Johannine community, and that Jesus never said it. I agree, because it sounds so unlike the Jesus I know.

But let's assume, just for the sake of argument, that he did say it. What he did not say was that only card-carrying Roman Catholics and "born again" Southern Baptists need apply.

Will Mahatma Gandhi, who set an example to the world as to how to bring about change without the use of violence, spend eternity in Hell? No way!

Will the Dalai Lama who has taught love and compassion between peoples of all faiths be subject to the eternal fire? Positively not!

Will Stephen Lewis, former United Nations Ambassador for AIDS, who did such a magnificent job of alerting the world to the human tragedy that had developed in Africa be destined to Hell? Hell no!

Will the English woman I read about who married an Iraqi and converted to Islam in order to work amongst the poor in Baghdad be eternally damned? Definitely not! Jesus will say "welcome friend" because she, along with the others, will qualify in accord with his own criteria, as follows:

> Then the King will say to those on his right, "Come, you who are blessed by my Father; take your inheritance, the kingdom prepared for you since the creation of the world. For I was hungry and you gave me something to eat, I was thirsty and you gave me something to drink, I was a stranger and you invited me in, I needed clothes and you clothed me, I was sick and you looked after me, I was in prison and you came to visit me."
>
> Then the righteous will answer him, "Lord when did we see you hungry and feed you, or thirsty and give you something to drink? When did we see you a stranger and invite you in, or needed clothes and clothe you? When did we see you sick or in prison and go to visit you?"

The King will reply, "I tell you the truth, whatever you did for one of the least of these brothers of mine, you did for me."

Then he will say to those on his left, "Depart from me, you who are cursed, into the eternal fire prepared for the devil and his angels. For I was hungry and you gave me nothing to eat, I was thirsty and you gave me nothing to drink, I was a stranger and you did not invite me in, I needed clothes and you did not clothe me, I was sick and in prison and you did not look after me."

They also will answer. "Lord, when did we see you hungry or thirsty or a stranger or needing clothes or sick or in prison, and did not help you?"

He will reply, "I tell you the truth, whatever you did not do for one of the least of these, you did not do for me."

Then they will go away to eternal punishment, but the righteous to eternal life."[9]

If one reads that passage literally there may be quite a few complacent born again Christians who will find that their passports have expired.

There are far too many right-wing Christians who spend their time worrying about issues like abortion and homosexuality. It is interesting that Jesus never mentioned either. He spent a lot of time talking about the poor, widows, the sick and marginalized people who seem to have fallen off the radar of organized Christianity.

Furthermore Jesus was a peacemaker who eschewed violence. So how does that square with the policies of the people who have been running the world for the last half-century. It doesn't! The constant search for enemies to justify militarization is one hundred percent opposite to the teachings of Jesus, and Christianity has been getting a very bad name by association. It seems that a thorough heart examination is urgently required.

To start with a clean slate, we will have to seek forgiveness for our sins. It would be difficult to imagine a more heinous sin than complicity in 9/11 followed by false accusations as to who was to blame. The United States should get on its collective knees to ask for forgiveness for making the Arab Muslims the scapegoats and then launching a phony war on terrorism that was the child of U.S. foreign policy.

The Israelis should get on their collective knees to ask forgiveness of the Palestinians for the way they have been treated as second-class souls in the land of their birth. This should be followed by a peace treaty that recognizes the Palestinian right to have a state of their own, and a mutual vow to cooperate in all ways possible to make life more peaceful and prosperous for both.

Then all of us in Western (formerly Christian) society should get on our collective knees for squandering our magnificent birthright. We have engaged in two horrendous world wars in which millions of people died, and many more wounded. We undervalued the crucial role Russia played in the Siege of Stalingrad. Worse, since the Berlin Wall came down, Western vulture capitalists were quick to cherry pick Russian assets, and NATO began to expand its membership eastward toward Moscow. I am certainly not a fan of Vladimir Putin, and I have a basic distrust of anyone who had headed a national intelligence agency. But if I were in his shoes, and saw that I was being provocatively encircled by NATO, and then saw Western politicians visiting Kiev to encourage protesters to overthrow a duly-elected president just because he was favorable to Moscow, and succeed, I would be enraged. How was he expected to react? Was he expected to just keep his calm and do nothing? If Western diplomats spent more time reading the Bible they would be familiar with the axiom, "As you sow, so shall you reap!"

Once Putin responded by annexing Crimea and supporting Russian-speaking insurgents in eastern Ukraine the west found itself in a predicament that is extremely difficult to resolve. Sanctions may not produce the desired results. And if they are too harsh they may only result in reinforcing Putin's determination to expand his empire by one means or another. This at a time when the epoch of empire-building and power-block making must end. NOW! We must begin a new era of cooperation between nations undergirded by compassion. IT IS OUR ONLY HOPE!

The West is God's prodigal child even if we have been unaware of it. We had the knowledge and power to arrest global warming but refused to use it. We had all the resources necessary to eliminate poverty, illiteracy and homelessness on a global scale but we chose instead to spend trillions on arms and armaments and encouraging tribal and sectarian conflicts by making the lethal weapons widely and readily available.

So perhaps we should not only make the technology for "free energy" universally available but also institute a sort of tithe dedicated to balancing the scales of justice planet-wide, with much of it to be used for infrastructure including, and perhaps especially, the conversion of our fossil fuel economy to a clean energy economy before our future deteriorates to the point where it is beyond the point of no return.

That the World is going to hell in a hand basket is self-evident. Just watch the daily news stories of rape, fraud, embezzlement, bribery, murder, mass murder, riots, car-bombings, sectarian violence and civil war, and it is difficult to believe that the carnage will ever end. Yet the popular press only gives us the bad news. The good news isn't news – at least in the world of commerce. One has to dig for the other side of the story.

Positive Signs of Hope

Despite the seeming hopelessness of the situation there are signs of hope everywhere. There are literally thousands of individuals who are showing the way for the rest of us. The following three examples just happen to be stories of people I know personally but there are many others involving dedicated individuals of diverse faiths.

The first relates to Dr. Margaret (Peg) Herbert, a former psychology professor at the University of Ottawa. One of her students was a young nun, Sister Alice, from Lesotho, a small but beautiful inland country completely surrounded by South Africa. In August 2004, when Peg was wondering aloud where she might go for her summer vacation, Sister Alice said, "Why don't you come and visit us, in Lesotho?" Peg accepted the challenge and that was the beginning of a very dramatic and unexpected turn in her life's work.

Peg was so moved by the sense of hopelessness felt by grandmothers whose children had died of Aids, leaving them with the responsibility of raising orphan grandchildren, that she was called to try to do something that would relieve their suffering. She resigned her post at the University of Ottawa and began providing assistance both tangible and psychological through an organization that adopted the name "Help Lesotho."

The obstacles often seemed insurmountable. After a few years Peg began to construct two buildings to provide a myriad of services including dormitory facilities for young girls who qualified for leadership training. As a former builder I must admit that I have never seen two projects that posed more formidable obstacles that would try the patience and persistence of a saint. But she overcame, and the two desperately needed facilities were officially opened by His Majesty King Letsie III in November 2009, amidst rejoicing and dancing so joyful that even we staid old Caucasians got caught up in the spirit.

In 2014, as Peg and her able African staff of co-workers plan the 10th anniversary of this marvelously successful experiment in the transformation of the lives of thousands of young African girls and boys, and the restoration of hope for myriad grandmothers, all eyes were focused on the future. The model works. A dreamer with an action plan, and the fortitude to overcome seemingly unmovable obstacles, can change the world for the better one little area at a time.

Another in my "most unlikely" category of stories that demonstrate God's transforming power involves a former Republican Congressman from Michigan, Mark Siljander. A promising young politician with a strong "conservative" bent, Mark has engaged in a sómersault career that he and his close associates would have considered as pure fantasy.

While still a Congressman, the FBI provided him with a bullet-proof vest because Palestinian President Yasser Arafat had allegedly taken out a contract on his life in revenge for a strong pro-Israeli stance. This Christian was so "right wing" that he walked out of the National Prayer Breakfast in Washington because someone read a few verses from the Qur'an. At that point no one could possibly guess that he would subsequently buy a copy of the Qur'an, and then study Arabic so he could read it in the original which is the only version Muslims accept as being authentic.

Some time later, after his new knowledge transformed his life, Mark was actually asked to host a luncheon for President Arafat and Leah Rabin, widow of the assassinated Yitzhak Rabin, when Arafat was in Washington to address the National Prayer Breakfast in 1999. Mark's reluctance was understandable. But after prayerful consideration he had to walk the talk, as he so ably describes in his remarkable book *A Deadly Misunderstanding*,[10] which I highly recommend.

His ability to speak Arabic, and his new found friends in the Muslim world, enabled him to engage in personal diplomacy. His new style of thinking can turn enemies into friends. A few examples of rewired pathways that he personally witnessed and contributed to have helped resolve conflicts in the Western Sahara, both Congos, Darfur, Sudan; release of Korean missionaries captive in Afghanistan, release of Iranian converts and Pastor Terry James' decision not to burn the Qur'an.

But, unfortunately, important elements of the U.S. government were not interested in peacemaking. They were interested in war-making and empire-building for the benefit of the military-industrial complex, and the business elite. So Mark was harassed and persecuted by the Department of Homeland Security. He had to spend a year in jail before being released to carry on his ministry of love and reconciliation.

Many Rivers, One Ocean

Mary Jo Leddy has been on my honor roll for a long time. She first came to my attention in 1984 when Pope Paul II was visiting in Canada, and Mary Jo, then a Catholic nun, was one of the commentators for the Canadian Broadcasting Corporation television network. She had the quaint habit of telling the truth as she understood it. This did not always endear her to Catholic officials, as I learned from my good friend Father Sean O'Sullivan who was privy to that inside information. But it did earn her high marks from more objective observers.

For many years now, the former nun and her predominantly Catholic staff, have been in charge of Romero House for (mostly Muslim) refugees in Toronto. The veteran *Toronto Star* columnist Rick Salutin wrote about her in one of his articles on religion. "[She] adamantly refuses to allow anyone there to try to convert others. But she also passionately insists 'that each of our religions is like a river going toward a great ocean; we're all going there and you have to get into one of those rivers and swim to get to the ocean. I don't agree with consumerist shopping around. You have to enter one of the rivers.' "[11]

Rick Salutin's article contained considerable wisdom that I am taking the liberty of repeating here.

> Religions won't fade away. But that's not really my point. My point is, we should be grateful that religions like Islam are potentially transformable. If they weren't, then all the hopes for a postsecular society – where multiple religious and other voices treat one another respectfully – would be dashed, and irresoluble religious strife would be not only our past but our future. That's because religions are sturdy organisms that are not eliminated easily. They've outlasted many apparent replacements, like Marxism, humanism and a substitute faith in science.
>
> Why won't religions like Islam simply fade away, removing all those risks they involve? It's partly due to what you could call an innate religious impulse – a drive to seek and find larger meanings. Philosopher Friedrich Schleiermacher located the impulse in feeling. Psychologist William James said it was emotional. Historian Rudolf Otto found it in 'the numinous,' a sense of the inexpressible. A seminary teacher of mine, Abraham Joshua Heschel, wrote about 'God in Search of Man,' a phrase that struck me dumb when I saw it as the title of his book. Poet Francis Thompson said that what he called 'the hound of heaven' had pursued him 'down the nights and down the days' no matter how resolutely he fled. Fred Reed says, 'I was a person without belief.' But over the years, 'that belief in unbelief seemed thinner and thinner to me.'
>
> Even the new atheists don't deny that these impulses exist, but they want to free them from traditional religions, with their trouble-prone baggage. Why not at least hope the old religions die off, making room for people to proceed individually, one at a time, in pursuit of their 'spiritual' needs?

Because most human beings don't seem to want that either. Houses of worship sprout like mushrooms. I know someone in Toronto who built a shul in a former outbuilding in his backyard as a tribute to family members who were murdered in the Holocaust. It lacks regular members or a rabbi, but people find their way to it. A friends' kid had his bar mitzvah there this fall.

Humans are gregarious. They want to bind themselves to others through a tradition that does no harm until it turns into a crusade to control.[12]

I agree with Salutin, that even if religions as we know them are unique to Earth, they have become so ingrained in our culture and heritage that we are not going to give them up. The alternative is to persuade them to use their formidable collective power creatively, in accordance with the will of the Infinite Creator and the mutual benefit of all humanity, when everyone strives to treat others as they themselves would wish to be treated if the roles were reversed.

In family matters, as in matters of state, it is the foundation for dispute resolution. It is difficult to imagine a problem that couldn't be solved with its honest application. So all is not lost. The magic Golden Rule is ours to grasp to help us cope.

So we have to do two things. First, we must put irresistible pressure on our governments to make the changes essential to our survival. Second, each of us personally must try to make right decisions so we can evolve to a higher state of consciousness in accord with the Creator's plan for us.

I hesitate to use the word righteousness because it conjures up an image of an old fuddy-duddy looking down his/her long nose at us ordinary sinners. But Webster's Dictionary defines it as "acting in an upright moral way" which is a laudable goal that we should all strive for.

For example, we are all racists. I have met a few people who claim they are not but scratch the surface a bit and you will find that we are all in the same boat to a greater or lesser degree. So we have to fight the tendency to relegate people who are different than we are to a lower status. It is hard work to say and honestly believe that "there but by the Grace of God go I," and put ourselves in the others persons shoes.

In the battle to favor moral decisions it is good to be aware of that part of our history that indicates we are subject to "external influences" in addition to those that we can see. There are spirits, good and bad, bombarding our consciousness with conflicting advice.

When a voice in our head says it's okay to steal, be aware that it is not right to steal. When a little voice says it's alright to take a bribe "because everyone does it," be aware that the tempter's tale is false. There are some people, influenced by a good spirit, who refuse point blank to enrich themselves unlawfully.

If you are tempted to harass or violate a male or female companion there are always two choices – satisfy your lust at any cost to the victims emotional psyche, or desist because that is the right thing to do. The same test applies to watering the whiskey, including a tainted carcass in with good meat, delivering and using cement that is not up to standard, uttering a bellicose demand that an insurgency be met by the use of massive brute force instead of negotiating a peace, etc.

The bottom line is that we can listen to the voice of our Creator, and His helpers, or we can attune our ears to the Evil One, and his followers. Quite a few Earthlings have chosen the Light, and are making a real difference. They have to be joined by a tsunami of lives willing to follow God's rules instead of our own desires. That includes trying very hard to live according to the Golden Rule which is universally endorsed by all major religions.

The choices we make will determine the history we are writing.

Notes

Introduction

1. U.S. President Abraham Lincoln's letter to Col. William F. Elkins, November 21, 1864. Archer H. Shaw, *The Lincoln Encyclopedia: The Spoken and Written Words of A. Lincoln Arranged for Ready Reference*, (New York, Macmillan, 1950).

2. The Habeas Corpus Act 1679 is an Act of the Parliament of England passed during the reign of King Charles II.

3. Justin Gillis, "Panel's Warning on Climate Risk: Worst is to Come," *New York Times*, March 31, 2014.

4. Bill Moyers, "How Wall Street Occupied America," *JUSTnews*, Vol. 15, No. 2, Winter 2011-2012.

Chapter 1: The New World Order

1. "Joint Intelligence Objectives Agency," National Archives and Records Administration. (http://www.archives.gov/iwg/declassified-records/rg-330-defense-secretary/). Retrieved October 9, 2008.

2. Brian Johnson, *The Secret War*, (London: Methuen Inc., 1978), p. 184.

3. Clarence G. Lasby, *Project Paperclip: German Scientists and the Cold War*, (New York: Scribner, 1975).

4. Paul Forman and José M. Sánchez-Ron (eds.), *National Military Establishments and the Advancement of Science and Technology: Studies in 20th Century History*, (Netherlands: Kluwer Academic Publishers, 1996), p. 308.

5. Steven Dorril, *M16: Inside the Covert World of Her Majesty's Secret Intelligence Service*, (New York: Free Press, 2000), p. 138.

6. James McGovern, *Crossbow and Overcast*, (New York: William Morrow and Company, Inc., 1964), pp. 100, 104, 173, 207, 210, 242.

7. Frederick I. Ordway III and Mitchell R. Sharpe, *The Rocket Team*, (New York: Thomas Y. Crowell Co., 1979), pp. 310, 313, 314, 316, 325, 330, 406.

8. James McGovern, *Crossbow and Overcast*, op. cit.

9. Norman M. Naimark, *The Russians in Germany: A History of the Soviet Zone of Occupation 1945-1949*, (Cambridge: Harvard University Press, 1979), p. 207.

10. Linda Hunt, *Secret Agenda: The United States Government, Nazi Scientists, and Project Paperclip, 1945 to 1990*, (New York: St. Martin's Press, 1991), pp. 6, 21, 31, 176, 204, 259.

11. Norman M. Naimark cites John Gimbel, *Science, Technology, and Reparations: Exploitation and Plunder in Postwar Germany*, (Redwood City: Stanford University Press, 1990). The $10 billion compare to the 1948 U.S. GDP $258 billion and to the total Marshall Plan (1948-52) expenditure of $13 billion, of which Germany received $1.4 billion (partly as loans.)

12. Daniel Estulin, *The True Story of the Bilderberg Group*, (Walterville: TrineDay LLC, 2007), p. 83.

13. *Ibid.*, p. 84.

Chapter 2: The Three Sisters

1. Albert Nolan, *Jesus Today: A Spirituality of Radical Freedom*, (New York: Orbis

2. Daniel Estulin, *The True Story of the Bilderberg Group*, (Walterville: TrineDay LLC, 2007).

3. Memorandum E-A10, 19 October 1940, Council on Foreign Relations, War-Peace Studies, Baldwin Papers, Box 117.

4. Memorandum E-A17, 14 June 1941, CFR, War-Peace Studies, Hoover Library on War, Revolution and Peace.

5. Memorandum T-A25, 20 May 1942, CFR, War-Peace Studies, Hoover Library on War, Revolution and Peace.

6. *Ibid.*

7. Gary Allen, *The Rockefeller File*, ('76 Press, 1976).

8. Daniel Estulin, *The True Story of the Bilderberg Group*, op. cit., p. 81.

9. *Ibid.*, p. 65.

10. J.H. Retinger, The European Continent, London's Hodge, 1946.

11. Daniel Estulin, *The True Story of the Bilderberg Group*, op. cit., pp. 41-43.

12. David Usborne, "Quebec plan to break away stuns Canada," *The Independent*, May 9, 1997.

13. "The Crisis of Democracy: Report on the Governability of Democracies to the Trilateral Commission," New York University Press, 1975.

14. Holly Sklar (ed.), *Trilateralism: The Trilateral Commission and Elite Planning for World Management*, (Boston: South End Press, 1980), pp. 199-209.

15. *Ibid.*

16. Daniel Estulin, *The True Story of the Bilderberg Group*, op.cit., p. 33.

17. John R. MacArthur, *The Selling of "Free Trade": NAFTA, Washington and the Subversion of U.S. Democracy*, (New York: Hill and Wang, 2000).

Chapter 3: Globalization

1. Greg Palast in an interview with *Acres USA*, June 2003.

2. Susan George, "Winning the War of Ideas: Lessons from the Gramscian Right," originally published in *Dissent*, Summer 1997.

3. *Ibid.*

4. Joseph E. Stiglitz, *Globalization and its Discontents*, (New York: Norton Trade, 2003), p. 71.

5. Royal Commission on the Economic Union and Development Prospects for Canada (Macdonald Commission).

6. As reported in the *Toronto Star*, October 22, 1987, in an article "More signs the U.S. believes it beat Canada." Yeutter denied making the statement but *Star* reporter Bob Hepburn added: "However, the U.S. sources, who asked not to be named, are considered impeccable. They were heavily involved in the talks, are extremely close to U.S. Treasury Secretary James Baker and were privy to confidential conversations and documents." I believe Yeutter did, in fact, make the statement because it sounds like him and what he said would have been what any forward-thinking U.S. negotiator would have thought and said privately when they were not expecting to be reported.

7. Based on Michael B. Smith's recollection of the meeting aboard Smith's 34-foot Sabre Sloop, *Wind*, as recorded in *Building a Partnership: The Canada-United States Free Trade Agreement*, Mordechai Kreinin (ed.), (East Lansing: Michigan State University Press, 2001), p. 7.

8. Greg Keenan, "Auto industry's shift away from Canada to gain speed," *Globe and Mail*, October 3, 2013.

9. Thomas Walkom, "Political leaders silent as manufacturing slips," *Toronto Star*, November 16, 2013.

10. *Ibid.*

11. David C. Korten, *When Corporations Rule the World*, (Bloomfield: Kumarian Press, Inc., 2001).

12. Andy Blatchford, "Harper says his EU deal bigger than one with U.S.," *Globe and Mail*, November 16, 2013.

13. Ellen Brown, *The Web of Debt: The Shocking Truth About Our Money System and How We Can Break Free*, (Baton Rouge: Third Millennium Press, 2012).

14. Ellen Brown, "Monsanto, the TPP, and Global Food Dominance," posted on www.MaxKeiser.com, November 27, 2013.

Chapter 4: The Money Mafia

1. Canadian household debt soars to yet another record, as reported in the *Globe and Mail*, March 11, 2016.

2. Susan George is Board President of the Transnational Institute, and author of 16 books, most recently *Whose Crisis, Whose Future?* and *How to Win the Class War*, on her website for electronic download and print on demand, along with six "Susan George Classics."

3. Francis T. Lui, "Cagan's Hypothesis and the First Nationwide Inflation of Paper Money in World History," *Major Inflations in History*, Forrest H. Capie (ed.), (Aldershort: Edward Elgar Publishing Ltd., 1991), pp. 210-212.

4. William Chaffers, *Gilda Aurifabrorum: A History of English Goldsmiths and Plateworkers, and Their Marks Stamped on Plate*, (London: Reeves & Turner, [1800], p. 210.

5. *Ibid.*

6. Walter Bagehot, *Lombard Street: A Description of the Money Market*, (London: Henry S. King and Co., 1873).

7. William F. Hixson, *Triumph of the Bankers: Money and Banking in the Eighteenth and Nineteenth Centuries*, (Westport: Praeger Publishers, 1993), p. 46.

8. *Ibid.*, p. 60.

9. Excerpt from an article by Stephen Labaton, "10 Wall St. Firms Settle with U.S. in Analyst Inquiry," *New York Times*, April 29, 2003.

10. Excerpt from an article by Brian Miller, "There's little repentance on Wall Street these days," *Globe and Mail*, April 28, 2003.

11. David Henry and David Ingram, "Settlement talks heat up at JP Morgan," *Globe and Mail*, September 27, 2013.

12. Bill Black, "Documents in JP Morgan settlement reveal how every large bank in U.S. has committed mortgage fraud," TheRealNews.com, November 29, 2013.

13. Tanya Talaga, "Swiss bankers helped hide billions from U.S. taxes, senators say," *Toronto Star*, February 27, 2014.

14. Nicholas Shaxson, *Treasure Islands: Uncovering the Damage of Offshore Banking and Tax Havens*, (New York: Palgrave Macmillan, 2011).

15. Ellen Brown, "The Leveraged Buyout of America," *Web of Debt Blog*, August 26, 2013.

16. Ellen Brown, "The Global Banking Game Is Rigged, and the FDIC Is Suing," *Web of Debt Blog*, April 13, 2014.

17. Carroll Quigley, *Tragedy and Hope: A History of the World in Our Time*, (Angriff Press, 1975).

Chapter 5: Bank for International Settlements

1. From *Tower of Basel* by Adam Lebor, copyright © 2013. Reprinted by permission of PublicAffairs, a member of The Perseus Books Group, p. 197.

2. http://www.treaties.un.org/Pages/showDetails.aspx?ojid=0800000280167c31

3. http://www.bis.org/about/index.htm?1=2

4. BIS History: http://bis.org/about/history.htm

5. Adam Lebor, *Tower of Basel*, op. cit., p. xviii.

6. Harold Callender, "The Iron-Willed Pilot of Nazi Finance, *New York Times*, March 4, 1934.

7. Adam Lebor, *Tower of Basel*, op. cit., p. xix.

8. See R. Billstein, *Working for the Enemy: Ford, General Motors and Forced Labor in Germany During the Second World War*, (New York: Berghahn Books, 2000). In the late 1990s Ford opened its archives and commissioned archivists and historians to scrutinize its wartime record. Their findings are compiled in a 208-page report, published in 2001. "Research Findings About Ford-Werke Under the Nazi Regime," is available at http://media.ford.com/article _ display.cfm?article_id=10379. The report also notes that Ford and its subsidiaries in Allied countries made a crucial contribution to the Allied war effort, producing vast amounts of aircraft, military vehicles, engines, generators, tanks, and military ordinance.

9. Adam Lebor, *Tower of Basel*, op. cit., p. 104.

10. Henry Morgenthau diaries, Book 755, Bretton Woods, July 16-18, 1944, pp. 9, 21.

11. *Ibid.*

12. John Easton, Economic Warfare Division, to Secretary of State, London, November 27, 1944. NARA. Author's [Adam Lebor] collection.

13. Adam Lebor, *Tower of Basel*, op. cit., pp. 156-157.

14. Dulles Cable, March 27, 1945, NARA. RG22, Entry 134, Box 162.

15. Morgenthau diaries, FDRML. Book 755, Reel 216, p. 183.

16. Allen Dulles to Joseph Dodge, September 20, 1945. NARA. OMGUS-FINAD. RG260, Box 237. File: Johannes Tuengeler. The extracts from the bankers' biographies are taken from this document. The author [Adam Lebor] is grateful to Christopher Simpson for generously supplying copies of this document, which he unearthed in the U.S. National Archives.

17. *Ibid.*

18. Neal H. Petersen (ed.), *From Hitler's Doorstep: The Wartime Intelligence Reports of Allen Dulles 1942-1945*, (Penn State University Press, 1996), pp. 426-427.

19. *Ibid.*, p. 628.

20. Adam Lebor, *Tower of Basel*, op. cit., p. 187.

Chapter 6: The IMF: It's Time For It to Go!

1. Steven Soloman, *The Confidence Game: How Unelected Central Bankers Are Governing the Changed Global Economy*, (New York: Simon & Schuster, 1995).

2. Merril Stevenson, "A Game of Skill as Well: Survey of International Banking," *The Economist*, March 21, 1987, p. 18.

3. Steven Soloman, *The Confidence Game*, op. cit.

4. Michel Chossudovsky, *The Globalisation of Poverty: Impacts of IMF and World Bank Reforms*, (Penang: Third World Network, 1997).

5. Kevin Danaher (ed.), *50 Years is Enough: The Case Against the World Bank and the International Monetary Fund*, (Boston: South End Press, 1994).

6. Michel Chossudovsky, *The Globalisation of Poverty*, op. cit, pp. 58-59.

7. As reported in the *Toronto Star*, March 10, 1998.

8. As reported in the *Financial Post*, May 6, 1998.

9. *Ibid.*

10. As reported in the *Globe and Mail*, January 13, 1998.

11. J. Richard Finlay, "Inner workings of IMF remain a mystery," in *The Financial Post*, January 31, 1998, p. 25.

12. As reported in the *Globe and Mail*, May 6, 1998.

13. As reported in the *Wall Street Journal*, October 13, 1998.

14. *Ibid.*

15. Mark Landler, "Scandal Hinders I.M.F.'s Role in Global Lending, *New York Times*, October 22, 2008.

16. Kevin Carmichael, "Mideast Called on to Shore up IMF," *Globe and Mail*, November 3, 2008.

17. Les Whittington, "No G20 cash for euro rescue," *Toronto Star*, November 5, 2011.

18. Joseph E. Stiglitz, *Globalization and Its Discontents*, (New York: W.W. Norton & Company, Inc., 2002), pp. 106-107.

Chapter 7: The Biggest Heist in History

1. G. Edward Griffin, *The Creature from Jekyll Island: A Second Look at the Federal Reserve*, (Westlake Village: American Media, 2002), p. 24.

2. Jack Metcalf, *The Two Hundred Year Debate: Who Shall Issue the Nation's Money*, (Olympia: An Honest Money for America Publication, 1986), p. 91.

3. *Ibid.*, p. 92.

4. "J.P. Morgan Interests Buy 25 of America;s Leading Newspapers and Insert Editors." U.S. Congressional Record, February 9, 1917, p. 2947.

5. Ferdinand Pecora, *Wall Street Under Oath: The Story of Our Modern Money Changers*, (A.M. Kelley, 1970).

6. Milton Friedman and Anna Jacobson Schwartz, *A Monetary History of the United States 1867-1960*, (Princeton: Princeton University Press, 1963).

7. *Ibid.*, pp. 327-328.

8. Milton Friedman and Rose D. Friedman, *Free to Choose: A Personal Statement*, (New York: Harcourt Brace Jovanovich, Inc., 1981), p. 11.

9. Sidney Weintraub, *Capitalism's Inflation and Unemployment Crisis: Beyond Monetarism and Keynesiasm*, (New York: Addison-Wesley Publishing Company, 1978), p. 104.

10. Milton Friedman and Rose D. Friedman, *Free to Choose: A Personal Statement*, op. cit., p. 251.

11. Josey Wales, "First Audit Results In The Federal Reserve's Nearly 100 Year History Were Posted Today, They are Startling!" *Before It's News*, September 1, 2012.

12. Andy Kessler, "The Fed Squeezes the Shadow Banking System," *Wall Street Journal*, May 22, 2013.

13. "Quantitative Easing," www.wikipedia.org.

Chapter 8: Government-Created Money

1. Garrick Hileman, "Why Bitcoin's Price Has Leapt 65% Since April," Coin Desk, May 28, 2014.

2. Gerald K. Bouey, speech to the 46th Annual Meeting of the Chamber of Co merce, Saskatoon, September 22, 1975.

3. Milton Friedman, letter to Paul Hellyer dated October 15, 1998.

4. E. James Ferguson, *The Power of the Purse: A History of American Public Finance, 1776-1790*, (Chapel Hill: University of North Carolina Press, 1961), p. 16.

5. William F. Hixson, *Triumph of the Bankers: Money and Banking in the Eighteenth and Nineteenth Centuries*, (Westport: Praeger Publishers, 1993), p. 46.

6. John G. Nicolay and John Hay (eds.), *Abraham Lincoln: Complete Works*, (New York: The Century Co., 1907, 2), p. 264.

7. Norman Angell, *The Story of Money*, (New York: Frederick A. Stokes Co., 1929), p. 294.

8. Olive Grubiak and Jan Grubiak, *The Guernsey Experiment*, (Hawthorne: Omni Publications, 1988), p. 7.

Chapter 9: Visitors from Starry Realms

1. Len Kasten, *The Secret History of Extraterrestrials: Advanced Technology and the Coming New Race*, (Rochester: Bear & Company, 2010), p. 242. www.InnerTrad-tions.com

2. *Ibid.*, pp. 32-33.

3. *Ibid.*, p. 32

4. Through telephone and e-mail exchange, April 2013.

5. Don Schmidt and Thomas J. Carey, *Witness to Roswell: Unmasking the 60-year cover-up*, (Franklin Lakes: New Page Books, 2007), p. 38.

6. *Ibid.*, p. 39.

7. Col. Philip J. Corso, *The Day After Roswell*, (New York: Pocket Books, 1997).

8. Yann Martel, *The Life of Pi*, (Toronto: Vintage Canada, 2002).

9. Paola Harris, *Connecting the Dots: Making Sense of the UFO Phenomenon*, (Mill Spring: Wild Flower Press, 2003).

10. *Ibid.*, p. 47.

11. Timothy Good, *Need to Know: UFOs, the Military and Intelligence*, (London: Sidgwick & Jackson, 2006), p. 209.

12. Robert Salas, *Faded Giant*, (North Charleston: Booksurge Llc, 2005).

13. *Ibid.*, pp. 167-169.

14. Downgraded to Confidential, September 15, 1969. Hellyer papers, Toronto.

15. Robert Salas, *Faded Giant*, (North Charleston: Booksurge Llc, 2005).

16. Donald E. Keyhoe, *Flying Saucers from Outer Space*, (New York: Henry Holt & Co., 1954).

17. Wilbert B. Smith, "What we are doing in Ottawa," an address to the Vancouver area UFO Club, March 14, 1961.

18. Wilbert B. Smith, "The Philosophy of the Saucers." Hellyer papers, Toronto.

19. Nickolas Evanoff e-mail to Ray Stone, July 13, 2007.

20. "Description and Performance of Unidentified Flying Objects from 1947-1967," as taken from newsstand sources. Compiled by Malcolm McKellar, Vancouver, Canada, 1968. Hellyer papers, Toronto.

21. E-mail from "George," October 17, 2005. Hellyer papers, Toronto.

22. Hellyer diary, May 11, 2006.

23. *Ibid.*, May 18, 2006.

24. From a transcript of the dinner conversation at the Hellyer condo, July 7, 2006.

25. Ryan S. Wood, *Majic Eyes Only: Earth's Encounters with Extraterrestrial Technology*, (Bloomfield: Wood Enterprises, 2005).

26. Richard M. Dolon, *UFO's & the National Security State: Chronology of a Cover-up, 1941-1973*, (Newburyport: Hampton Roads Publishing, 2002).

27. John E. Mack, *Passport to the Cosmos: Human Transformation and Alien Encounters*, (New York: Crown Publishers, 1999).

28. Linda Moulton Howes, *Glimpses of Other Realities, Volume II: High Strangeness*. (Jamison: LMH Productions, 2001).

29. Travis Walton, *Fire in the Sky: The Walton Experience*, (New York: Marlowe & Company, 1997).

30. Jim Sparks, *The Keepers: An Alien Message for the Human Race*, (Columbus: Wild Flower Press, 2006).

31. *Ibid.*, pp. 167-171.

32. Charlie Paz Wells, *Sowers of Life*, (Sao Paulo: Icone Editora, 1993).

Chapter 10: The Military-Industrial Complex (Currently Known as "The Cabal")

1. President Dwight D. Eisenhower's farewell address to the nation, delivered in a television broadcast on January 17, 1961.

2. *Ibid.*

3. Franz Leopold Neumann, *Behemoth: The Structure and Practice of National Socialism 1933-1944*, (Reprint, Cutchogue: Buccaneer Books, 1983).

4. Steven M. Greer, *Disclosure: Military and Government Witnesses Reveal the Greatest Secrets in Modern History*, "Testimony of Brigadier General Stephen Lovekin," (Crozet: Crossing Point Inc., 2001), p. 235.

5. A private discussion with Dr. Carol Rosin, February 2011.

6. Antony Sutton, *Wall Street and the Bolshevik Revolution*, (New York: Arlington House, 1974).

7. Daniel Estulin, *The True Story of the Bilderberg Group*, (Walterville: TrineDay LLC, 2007), pp. 171-172.

8. Michael Lind, "The Weird Men Behind George W. Bush's War," *New Statesman*, April 12, 2003.

9. "American Century," Pentagon Document on Post-Cold-War Strategy, February 18, 1992.

10. As reported in the *New York Times*, May 24, 1992.

11. *Ibid.*

12. "Rebuilding America's Defenses: Strategy, Forces and Resources for a New Century. A Report of the Project for the New American Century, September 2000."

13. From the text of U.S. President George W. Bush's address to a joint meeting of Congress, September 20, 2001.

14. From a translated text of Osama bin Laden's broadcast taken from the *New York Times*, October 8, 2001.

15. Excerpt from an article by Barrie McKenna, "Bush faces furor over knowledge of attack," *Globe and Mail*, May 17, 2002.

16. Excerpt from an article by Michele Lansberg, "Conspiracy crusader doubts official 9/11 version," *Toronto Star*, May 11, 2003.

17. Reprinted by permission of Eric Larsen, November 21, 2013.

18. Barrie Zwicker, *Towers of Deception: The Media Cover-Up of 9/11*, (Gabriola Island: New Society Publishers, 2006).

19. Architects & Engineers for 9/11 Truth, Pete Denney, "A Summary of Evidence: A Call to Action, August 24, 2010.

20. *Ibid.*

21. Major General Albert Stubblebine III, www.veteranstoday.com/.../i-can-prove-that-it-was-not-an-airplane-that-hit-the-pentagon.

22. Judy Wood, *Where Did the Towers Go? Evidence of Directed Free-Energy Technology on 9/11*, (The New Investigation, 2010), pp. 171-172.

23. *Ibid.*, p. 171.

24. Judy Wood, *Where Did the Towers Go? Evidence of Directed Free-Energy Technology on 9/11*, (The New Investigation, 2010).

25. A new phenomenon requires a new word to describe it. This word is defined in the book, *Where Did the Towers Go?*, op. cit. pp. 131-139.

26. *Ibid.*

27. As reported in *World Tribune*, Middle East Newsline, December 20, 2001.

28. Ben Rich, former CEO of Lockheed's Skunk Works, revealed before his death in January 1995.

29. Daniel Estulin, *The True Story of the Bilderberg Group*, op. cit., p. 84.

Chapter 11: Global Warming — A Recipe for Disaster

1. Paul Krugman, "Enemy of the planet," *New York Times*, April 17, 2006.

2. Gillian Wong, "Public misled, Gore says," *Toronto Star*, August 8, 2007.

3. Andrew C. Revkin, "On Climate Issue, Industry Ignored Its Scientists," *New York Times*, April 24, 2009.

4. James Lovelock, "We're all doomed! 40 years from global catastrophe — and there's NOTHING we can do about it, says climate change expert," April 2008. http://www.dailymail.co.uk/pages/live/articles/news/news.html?in article id=541748&in page id=1770.

5. *Ibid.*

6. James Hansen, *Storms of My Grandchildren: The Truth About the Coming Climate Catastrophe and Our Last Chance to Save Humanity*, (New York: Bloomsbury USA, 2009).

7. Bill McKibben, coordinator 350.org and author of *The End of Nature*.

8. Michael Woods, "Skeptical climate scientist warms up into believer," *Toronto Star*, August 8, 2012.

9. Ivan Semeniuk, "The incredible shrinking summer ice cover," *Globe and Mail*, March 16, 2013.

10. Justin Gillis, "Panel's Warning on Climate Risk: Worst Is Yet to Come," *New York Times*, March 31, 2014.

11. "Another week, another report," *The Economist*, April 19, 2014 (from the print edition.)

12. Shawn McCarthy, "Canada won't budge on environment, Peter Kent insists," *Globe and Mail*, November 30, 2012.

13. John Spears, "BP's punishment unlikely to deter drilling," *Toronto Star*, November 16, 2012.

14. Shawn McCarthy and Nathan Vanderklippe, "Feds bow to Alberta on carbon rules," *Globe and Mail*, August 9, 2012.

15. Jeffrey Jones, "Imperial Oil aims for Arctic depths," *Globe and Mail*, September 30, 2013.

16. Jeff Lewis, "N.W.T.: The latest fracking frontier," *Financial Post*, January 5, 2013.

17. Yadullah Hussain, "Canada to emerge as the fourth-fastest growing oil player in the world: IEA," *Financial Post*, November 12, 2013.

18. Shawn McCarthy and Nathan Vanderklippe, "Canada sees risk in U.S. oil boom," *Globe and Mail*, November 13, 2012.

19. Carrie Tait, "Exxon Mobil moves ahead with massive East Coast oil field," *Globe and Mail*, January 5, 2013.

20. Peter Calamai, "Breeding Perfect Storms," *Toronto Star*, June 1, 2006.

21. Lead Editorial, "The sky-high cost of global warming," *Globe and Mail*, October 31, 2006.

22. Jane Taber, "U.S. sounds alarm over melting Arctic," *Globe and Mail*, November 23, 2013.

23. "Chris Stoner Interviews Dr. Michael Wolf – Former NSA Consultant." http://exopolitics.org.uk/ark%11hive/docs/chris-stoner-interviews-dr-michael-wolf-%11-former-nsa-consulant/

24. Len Kasten, *The Secret History of Extraterrestrials: Advanced Technology and the Coming New Race*, (Rochester: Bear & Company, 2010), p. 82. www.InnerTraditions.com

Chapter 12: Full Disclosure

1. Paul Hellyer, in an address at the Exopolitics Toronto Symposium on UFO Disclosure and Planetary Direction, University of Toronto, September 25, 2005.

2. Dr. Michael Wolf, in an interview with Chris Stoner, former U.S. National Security Council's Special Studies (UFO) Group and Jim Sparks in *The Keepers*.

3. Paola Harris, *Exopolitics: Stargate to a New Reality*, (Bloomington: AuthorHouse, 2011).

4. Len Kasten, *The Secret History of Extraterrestrials: Advanced Technology and the Coming New Race*, (Rochester: Bear & Company, 2010), pp. 80-81. www.InnerTraditions.com

5. Michael Wolf, in *Dulce Book*, p. 233. "Branton" is the writer-editor of the *Dulce Book* which contains input from numerous sources. It is a pseudonym, of course, as you might expect when it contains so much sensitive material. So I went to the trouble of finding the real identity of the individual and sought assurance from one of my prime sources that most of the book is authentic. Much of the material is available from other sources but this 343-page compendium saves a lot of time and research. I don't recommend that you try to find and read it, at

least for now until a full disclosure public inquiry has been established and prepared you for the information overload which is almost beyond comprehension.

6. Ryan S. Wood, *Majic Eyes Only: Earth's Encounters with Extraterrestrial Technology*, (Bloomfield: Wood Enterprises, 2005).

7. Dr. Michael Wolf, in an interview with Chris Stoner, *ibid*.

8. Len Kasten, *The Secret History of Extraterrestrials*, op. cit. pp.6-7.

9. *Ibid.*, pp. 7-8.

10. *Ibid.*, p. 8.

11. JoAnn Richards, wife of Captain Mark Richards, in an e-mail titled "Using Thousands of Young Women," posted by Rayelan, July 8, 2009.

12. *Dulce Book*, op.cit., p. 274.

13. *Ibid.*, pp. 275-276.

14. *Ibid.*, p. 277.

15. Phil Schneider lecture "Underground Bases and the New World Order, Post Falls, Idaho, May 8,1995.

16. *Dulce Book*, op. cit., p.279.

17. *Ibid.*, p. 18.

18. *Ibid.*, p. 19.

19. *Ibid.*, p. 20.

20. *Ibid.*, p. 43.

21. Bill van Auken, " 'Urban Warfare Training' and the Militarization of America," *Global Research*, July 26, 2013.

22. Jim Sparks, *The Keepers: An Alien Message for the Human Race*, (Columbus: Wild Flower Press, 2006).

23. Charlie Paz Wells, *Sowers of Life*, (Sao Paulo: Icone Editora, 1993).

24. *Ibid.*

Chapter 13: The Two Americas

1. As quoted by senior White House reporter Sarah McClendon, President Bill Clinton's reply, February 6, 2008.

2. "Senator Daniel Inouye Warned of Shadow Government," *Before It's News*, December 24, 2012.

3. Alexandra Bruce, publisher, Forbidden KnowledgeTV.com

4. Daniel Estulin, *The True Story of the Bilderberg Group*, (Walterville: TrineDay LLC, 2007), p. 92-93.

5. Stephen Bassett, "Ending the Truth Embargo: Disclosure and the State of the Union," *Paradigm Research Group Update*, October 29, 2013.

6. Peter Coy, "Opening Remarks: The case for a $10.10 minimum wage," *Bloomberg Businessweek*, February 17-23, 2014, p. 10.

7. Rick Westhead, "Why sweatshop owners are starting to sweat," *Toronto Star*, October 13, 2013.

8. Raveena Aulakh, "Tannery Boys," *Toronto Star*, October 12, 2013.

9. "In graphics, Eurozone crisis," BBC News Business, April 25, 2013.

10. *Ibid.*

11. Joseph P. Farrell, *Roswell and the Reich: The Nazi Connection*, (Kempton: Adventures Unlimited Press, 2010), p. 352.

12. *Ibid.*, p. 355.

13. Jeremy Scahill, *Dirty Wars: The World is a Battlefield*, (New York: Nation Books, 2013).

14. Frank Bayerl, "U.S. misuse of drones, assassinations, renditions exposed," *Canadian Centre for Policy Alternatives Monitor*, November 2013, p. 5.

15. Scott Shane, "No Morsel Too Small for Spy Agency, *New York Times International Weekly (Toronto Star)*, November 10, 2013.

16. Michael S. Schmidt, "NSA phone surveillance is lawful, judge rules," *Globe and Mail*, December 28, 2013.

17. Claire Cain Miller, "Secret U.S. court put Web firms in a bind," *New York Times*, June 15, 2013.

18. The Associated Press, "Tweeting commuter shares ex-NSA chief's phone chat," *Toronto Star*, October 26, 2013.

19. "Armed Conflicts Report 2013," *Project Ploughshares*.

20. *Ibid.*

21. Todd S. Perdum, "One Nation, Under Arms," *Vanity Fair*, January 2012, p. 74.

22. *Ibid.*, p. 77.

23. Lisa O'Carroll, "Seymour Hersh on Obama, NSA and the 'Pathetic' American Media, *Guardian UK*, September 27, 2013.

24. "URGENT: documents reveal that Trans-Pacific Partnership contains extreme SOPA-like Internet Censorship Plan," Petition, November 18, 2013. www.fightforthefuture.org.tpp

25. David Rockefeller, *Memoirs*, (New York: Random House, 2002), p. 405.

Chapter 14: An Action Plan for the Redemption of America and Humankind

1. Lewis Lapham, "Pax Iconomica," in *Behind the Headlines*, Vol. 54, No. 2, Winter 1996-97, p. 9, in his 'On Politics, Culture and Media' keynote address to the Canadian Institute of International Affairs national foreign policy conference in October, 1996.

2. Fred Burks, "CBS Reports Pentagon Cannot Account for $2.3 Trillion," www.WantToKnow.info, March 6, 2014.

3. Sunil Dasgupta and Stephen P. Cohen, "Arms Sales for India: How Military Trade Could Energize U.S.-Indian Relations," *Foreign Affairs*, (published by the Council on Foreign Relations), March/April 2011.

4. Thomas L. Friedman, "Save the Rainforest," *New York Times*, November 11, 2009.

5. Patricia Adams, *Odious Debts: Loose Lending, Corruption, And the Third World's Environmental Legacy*, (London: Probe International, 1991.)

6. Niall Ferguson, *The Ascent of Money: A Financial History of the World*, (London: Penguin Books, 2008).

7. Adrian Edwards reporting the highlights of the UNHCR report from Geneva, June 20, 2016.

8. Dr. Hans Blix, Weapons of Mass Destruction Commission, "Weapons of Terror," June 1, 2006, p. 94.

Postscript

1. Howard Brown, unpublished manuscript entitled *Humanity: The World Before Religion, War and Inequality*, which is where the Jewish Bible takes over.

2. Holy Bible, The New King James Version, Micah 6:8.

3. Colin Chapman, *Whose Promised Land? Israel or Palestine*, (Oxford: Lion Publishing plc, 1992).

4. E-mail from Gavriel Gefen to author May 21, 2007.

5. Elias Chacour, *Blood Brothers*, (Grand Rapids: Chosen Books, 2003).

6. Wikipedia, "Shia-Sunni Relations."

7. *Ibid.*

8. Holy Bible, The New King James Version, John 14:6.

9. *Ibid.*, Matthew 25:34-46.

10. Mark Siljander, *A Deadly Misunderstanding: A Congressman's Quest to Bridge the Muslim-Christian Divide*, (San Francisco: HarperOne, 2008).

11. Rick Salutin, "Learning to live with Islam helps us survive as a species," *Toronto Star*, January 18, 2014. Reprinted with permission – Torstar Syndication Services.

12. *Ibid.*

ABOUT THE AUTHOR

Paul Hellyer is Canada's Senior Privy Councillor, having been appointed to the cabinet of Prime Minister Louis S. St. Laurent in 1957, just eight years after his first election to the House of Commons in 1949 at the age of 25. He subsequently held senior posts in the governments of Lester B. Pearson and Pierre E. Trudeau, who defeated him for the Liberal Party leadership in 1968. The following year, after achieving the rank of senior minister, which was later designated Deputy Prime Minister, Hellyer resigned from the Trudeau cabinet on a question of principle related to housing.

Although Hellyer is best known for the unification of the Canadian Armed Forces, and for his 1968 chairmanship of the Task Force on Housing and Urban Development, he has maintained a life-long interest in macroeconomics. Through the years, as a journalist and political commentator, he has continued to fight for economic reforms and has written several books on the subject.

A man of many interests, Hellyer's ideas are not classroom abstractions. He was born and raised on a farm and his business experience includes manufacturing, retailing, construction, land development, tourism and publishing. He has also been active in community affairs including the arts, and studied voice at the Royal Conservatory of Music in Toronto. His multi-faceted career, in addition to a near-lifetime in politics, gives Hellyer a rare perspective on what has gone wrong in the critical fields of both world politics and economics.

In recent years he has become interested in the extraterrestrial presence and their superior technology that we have been emulating. In September 2005 he became the first person of cabinet rank in the G8 group of countries to state unequivocally "UFO's are as real as the airplanes flying overhead." He continues to take an interest in these areas and provides a bit of basic information about them in this book.

Defence Minister Hellyer in his role as President and Chancellor of the Royal Military College, Kingston, Ontario, conferring the degree of Honourary Doctor of Law on his first political boss, the Right Honourable Louis S. Laurent, Prime Minister of Canada, 1948-1957, at Fall Convocation, October 3, 1964.

Dr. Edgar Mitchell, Apollo 14 astronaut, arrives at the Hellyer residence for dinner, July 7, 2006, accompanied by his friend, Susan Swing and Susan Boyne (later Bird) wife of Mike Bird who took the picture.

The Hellyers at lunch with international journalist Paola Harris, and Dr. Courtney Brown, Director of The Farsight Institute, at the Society for Exploration Conference, Boulder, Colorado, June 2008.

Paul and Sandra Hellyer having dinner with Marilyn Salas, and Captain Robert Salas, U.S.A.F. (Ret.) at the Extraterrestrial Civilization and World Conference, Kona, Hawaii, June 2006.

Paul swimming with Prime Minister Pierre E. Trudeau and his bodyguard during an official visit to Guyana following the Commonwealth Heads of Government Meeting held in Kingston, Jamaica, 1975.

Paul consulting his extensive library when checking some fine points for one of his books. (Canapress Photo Service)

Defence Minister Hellyer greeting General Lyman Lemnitzer, Supreme Allied Commander, Europe, and Mrs. Lemnitzer, in the presence of Air Chief Marshall Frank Miller, Mrs. Miller, and George Ignatieff, Canada's ambassador to NATO, as the general arrives for an official visit to Ottawa.

Paul greets President Jimmy Carter at the National Prayer Breakfast in Washington.

Paul singing the role of Peter in the opera Hansel and Gretel at the Banff School of Fine Arts during the parliamentary recess, summer 1954.

Defence Minister Hellyer doing a jackstay crossing from the aircraft carrier Bonaventure to the destroyer Restigouche.

Hellyer, in his role as Chairman of the Task Force on Housing and Urban Development, surrounded by the members of the Task Force, presenting Prime Minister Pierre Trudeau (seated) with the first copy of their report in January 1969.

Paul dropping in to say hello to President Gerald Ford at a formal dinner in Toronto.

The Hellyer family celebrating Paul's 90th birthday, August 6, 2013. (Photo by Whitney Heard)

Paul coming in for a landing at Arundel Lodge, Muskoka, Ontario.

Sandra and Paul on the occasion of his 90th birthday, August 6, 2013. (Photo by Whitney Heard)

Index